JOHN LYDON

STORIES OF JOHNNY

John Lydon - Stories Of Johnny
A Compendium Of Thoughts On The Icon Of An Era
Edited by Rob Johnstone

A CHROME DREAMS PUBLICATION
First Edition 2006

Published by Chrome Dreams
PO BOX 230, New Malden , Surrey
KT3 6YY, UK
books@chromedreams.co.uk
WWW.CHROMEDREAMS.CO.UK

ISBN 1 84240 360 5

Editorial Assistant   Jake Kennedy
Cover Design   Sylwia Grzeszczuk
Layout Design   Marek Niedziewicz

A catalogue record for this book is available from the British Library.

Printed and bound in Great Britain by William Clowes Ltd, Beccles, Suffolk

A Compendium Of Thoughts On The Icon Of An Era

With A Foreword by Alan McGee

JOHN LYDON

STORIES OF JOHNNY

He saw himself now as a full grown man for whom the angels wept
Graham Greene: Brighton Rock

Oh I'm in a rage, waiting for these dynamite daze
Kevin Coyne: Dynamite Daze

Acknowledgements

First and foremost my thanks extend to the contributors involved in the writing of this tome. Despite payments exchanged, these were generally less than handsome and, to a man or woman, the call of reward was exceeded.

So without further ado, please say it one time for; Greil Marcus, Judy Nylon, Clinton Heylin, Pat Gilbert, Kris Needs, Alan Clayson, Barb Jungr, Legs McNeill and Nigel Williamson.

The troops at Chrome Dreams deserve more than a mention, most notably; assistant editor Jake Kennedy, graphic designers Sylwia Grzeszczuk and Aneta Fuks, layout and IT director Marek Niedziewicz and Projects Manager Angela Turner. Regrettably, for now, that's all that's on offer.

Special thanks go to Alan McGee for a foreword that quite says it all, and a generosity that, in a different light, does too. In this regard, please also raise a glass for Vanessa B, the classiest PA in the business.

Extra special thanks go to Kris Needs and Judy Nylon for general assistance with the project and endless supplies of good natured responses to all manner of questions.

A Foreword
by Alan McGee

I first cast my eyes on the man around March 1977 in Listen Record Shop, Buchannan St., Glasgow. I was 16. I knew about Punk but had never seen a Punk band in my life, although I had heard a few random plays of the Sex Pistols' debut single, 'Anarchy In The UK', from which I loved the chorus. I had no idea that what I was about to see would change my life forever. Lydon was on some terrible British pop programme singing, or more like screaming, and having an epileptic fit, to 'Anarchy'. It blew away every preconception I ever had about pop music. It had been T.Rex, Slade, David Bowie, then nothing, some awful metal gigs, then punk rock. Punk Rock *was* John Lydon.

I know Malcolm McLaren and I know John and believe me, Lydon is the original, Malcolm learned so much more from Lydon than Lydon ever learned from Malcolm. I love Malcolm, but Lydon was a martyr for his generation. He blew away an era past and entered an era about to come on us all.

The Sex Pistols were brutally iconic, but PiL meant so much more to me. Times change but for my generation Lydon is an icon that will never be repeated; he is a true one-off and a true British hero. The greatest poet and musical visionary of his generation, he will be remembered as a national hero in 200 years. Unfortunately, because we live in England, he will have to die before he is lauded.

Lydon let me be me, he let an entire generation be themselves. Lydon isn't a pop idol, he's a fucking religion. Lydon is our Jesus Christ, the mainstream will understand when he's gone.

Raise one for us all John.

Alan McGee

Introduction
by Rob Johnstone

A Crash Course for The Ravers

You join us on July 4th 1976. In the United States the people of America celebrate 200 years of independence - having seceded from the British Empire on this day in 1776. The number one single in the U.S. is 'Silly Love Songs' by Wings - one of Paul McCartney's weakest compositions to date; in Britain, the top spot is held by The Real Thing, whose 'You To Me Are Everything' is lowest-common-denominator soul, the like of which has been clogging chart positions for the past few years. The weather in the UK is dry and hot and we're 10 days into a run of what will be 17 with temperatures exceeding 30 degrees. Summer 1976 will be decreed the hottest on record using statistics going back 250 years. It's a mixed blessing though, a government minister for drought has been announced, millions of families are forced to use roadside standpipes, and paddling pools across the land lie deflated as the grass they would otherwise flatten dehydrates and turns brown. 'Global Warming' has yet to enter the vernacular but, what with last summer being a scorcher too, scientists are sniffing 'round for a meaning.

The hot weather of course, being Britain, is the principal topic of conversation and in the future will remain the most pertinent circumstance for which the year is remembered. But the British economy is in terrible shape too; interest rates stand at 17% and over a million of the workforce are unemployed for the first time since the great depression. Industrial action is rampant as well and there's little hope new Prime Minister James Callaghan has the capacity to sort out the sorry mess.

So when, early in the next millennium, nostalgia has changed from a mild comfort to a national obsession, television networks reflecting this trend with yet another documentary film, will legitimately use news footage of picket line assemblies and queues of out-of-work claimants emerging from labour exchanges[1] to compliment that of chubby middle aged white folk turning a deadly shade of lobster.

There will be a third subject worthy of significant inclusion in these programs though, one of a musical and cultural nature, and one which will come to share a platform with grainy footage of Elvis Presley, The Beatles touching down at Kennedy airport and 'Flower Children' attaching blooms to the ends of soldiers' rifles. But right now, what has been christened 'punk-rock' in the music press, remains virtually unknown to the general public, and a minor irritation to many readers of the *New Musical Express*, *Melody Maker* and *Sounds*, whose requirements from their weekly journals stretch no further than dates for the new Wishbone Ash tour, a four page spread on Robin Trower, or a bad Genesis review they can take to task on the letters page. It won't be long though until almost everyone in Britain is aware of the 'Punk-Rock Explosion', and they'll all be forced to take sides - little room will exist for impartiality.

With all modern cultural shifts, by the time the cameras come calling the seeds are sown and the harvest fully realised - and anyone who'll conceivably be touched by its emergence is fully aware it exists. And so it will be with punk-rock; but for now the movement is limited to exposure in media that focuses essentially on rock'n'roll (in its wider connotation) - a genre it will attempt to overthrow but ultimately will prove as much part of as Elvis and The Beatles.

The roots of punk will be debated and argued over long and hard for years to come; tidy minded chroniclers will insist that the aforementioned political landscape had provided fertile breeding ground for its birth. Similar types will point to a music scene so devoid of relevance for emerging generations of young people that no other outcome was conceivable. However, despite *some* truth being present in these assumptions, they're far from conclusive. Scratch-the-surface research of this nature fails to consider the importance of individuals, without whom all the political frustration and rubbish records in the world wouldn't result in a youth cult of any significance.

Punk-rock's true protagonists are easy to spot, and in reality there are only two in the UK. One of them is a right chancer called Malcolm McLaren. Malcolm's been fishing for an angle to engage loosely held beliefs and riddled theories with a way to extract as much cash as possible from a system he claims to abhor, since he was knee high to a milk-bottle. For the best part of a decade he hung at any number of art schools, most of which he was expelled from, until in the early 1970s, following a brief stint in filmmaking, he turned his hand to fashion design. With partner Vivienne Westwood he opened a store on London's King's Road from where he continues to flog his wares. Borrowing extensively from the philosophies of the French Situationist movement, rampant during the late 1960s, both Malc and Viv are insatiable trouble makers but, Malcolm especially, had been keeping an eye on the 'big chance', knowing his and her fashion creations alone - most of which sold to London's still active Teddy Boy community, from a shop then called Let It Rock - were unlikely to satisfy his lusts for notoriety and wealth.

Malcolm already had some experience in the music business; in 1974, on a trip to a fashion show on Manhattan, he bumped into glam-trash proto-punks, the New York Dolls - just dropped by their record label after two hugely influential but commercially redundant records, and wondering quite what to do next. McLaren, sensing that the outrageous approach of the Dolls tied to his presumed skills in promoting such bedevilment could be the spark for something big, offered his services - to rapturous acceptance.

But the flaws in his theory soon emerged; McLaren had taken on an act well past its best and, concentrating largely on the group's image, which he fortified with Communist regalia, had misjudged just how conservative American record labels still were. Upon his enforced return to England though, his brief stint as rock impresario and his mixing with the Big Apple's own burgeoning punk scenesters, left him convinced that such a direction was the key to his master-plan. While McLaren's role in all things punk-rock will become fashionably belittled in years to come, it cannot be denied it was he alone who realised that what was going on in New York in the years predating any kind of English scene, would be far more relevant, impacting and downright life changing to British audiences: this was a gig waiting to happen – elsewhere.

By chance, McLaren already had a group he could work with. Prior to his months in America he'd been approached by a casual employee from the store about managing his band. Malcolm had agreed even though he knew they were nothing special: he had faith in his abilities to transform what was essentially a 1960s and 70s covers act into his dream group – although at this stage he was clearer on what that wasn't than what it was. Two things he was sure about though, they'd have to find a new singer and no hippies were allowed.

That said, current vocalist Steve Jones was equally important to the band, then known as The Swankers, as Glen Matlock – bass player and 'Sex' boutique counter hand (fetish gear and the seeds of punk's *haute couture* now filled the racks that had formerly housed drape jackets and 'brothel creepers'). Although Steve yet had little musical ability, his loveable-rogue persona, laddish sex appeal and dominant force of character made him an essential member; without him there was no group at all.

While Malcolm was away, The Swankers - now rechristened the Sex Pistols - had tried out one Nick Kent - then *NME*'s boy wonder - as guest singer and guitarist, but when he attempted to take over, he was shuffled along. On McLaren's return, Jonesy was still shouting the tunes and, despite Malcolm's contrary instruction, the hapless Wally Nightingale remained on guitar. Steve's best mate Paul Cook played reasonable drums but poor old Wally was never going to make it anywhere in this game; Malcolm knew it from day one, and the others soon came to realise too.

With the band now a three-piece, featuring Jones on the guitar he was still learning to play - one bought back from America by McLaren, formerly belonging to Johnny Thunders of the Dolls - and attempting to sing while doing so, the need for a new vocalist became a must. Malcolm was trying to get Richard Hell in: Hell had just left New York art-punk pioneers Television to form the Heartbreakers with Thunders and fellow ex-Doll Jerry Nolan and had a true punk sensibility and style exceeding any other New York wannabe. Hell was interested, but Matlock, Jones and Cook were having none of it, sensibly insisting on an English frontman.

Heeeeeeere's Johnny

John Lydon is an Arsenal fan from Finsbury Park. From an Irish-Catholic pedigree, he turned 20 in January; while he's often quiet as a mouse, when he is moved to speak he can slay 'em dead with a casual remark. Lydon doesn't suffer anyone gladly, fool or sage; in fact 'suffer' would be an inappropriate choice of words in this regard. He will rejoice in vitriolic spasm whenever an opinion countering his own is aired. While such tendencies could be seen as mean spirited in others, Lydon has a knack of making them appear a dictum of his honesty in which good manners are a symptom of culture and conditioning – a starring role in the dance of the bourgeoisie. Everyone's natural tendency, if riled, is to deliver a well placed 'Fuck off you cunt', augmented by a half grin or a mean scowl depending on levels of irritation or folly - but most folk resist. In John Lydon's world that's dishonesty.

Lydon normally leaves the talking to his mates though, all of whom seem to be called John too. He wandered into Sex a few times last year wearing a Pink Floyd T-Shirt. Upon closer inspection he'd scrawled in felt tip 'I HATE' across the top; his ginger hair was dyed bright green. Steve had spotted him and pointed him out to Malcolm, who immediately told him about the band and suggested he come to the pub after closing. John was asked to audition as vocalist and came back to the shop to sing along to the jukebox. He did nothing of the sort though, instead he shouted and mumbled, and moved like a hunchback possessed of Hell's hardest cases, while Alice Cooper's 'I'm Eighteen' played behind. Using every scintilla of emotion available to him in a performance that no one present could imagine infused into the then rather pedestrian Sex Pistols, John Lydon was bewildering. Malcolm decided straight away he was the man for the job, and while the others had initial reservations, Malc's unwavering confidence was persuasion enough: Lydon was in.

He was an awkward bugger, moaning about anything and everything. Steve wanted to knock him out to start, but just made him the butt of constant jokes. One of these revolved around Lydon's awful teeth, which Jonesy told him were 'Fucking rotten'. Johnny Rotten was born.

Things changed in the band once Rotten came in; despite, to begin with, little input outside of rehearsals, his presence spurred the group, most notably Matlock, and with the line-up complete it was finally time to find some gigs. A set list was required first; a number of covers by the likes of The Who, The Small Faces, The Creation[2] and others were still in place, but now came the start of a songwriting partnership the impact of which will resonate long into the future. Matlock had a good ear for a melody and a riff, and with Rotten as the group's first proper lyricist, self-penned songs emerged fast, the likes of which had never been heard. Malcolm, whose instincts about Johnny were proving correct, moved up a gear too, sending new charge Nils Stevenson 'round town looking for places for the band to perform.

The first show the Sex Pistols played however was put in place by Glen, who got them into the college he'd just left - St. Martin's on Charing Cross Road - on a support slot for pub-rock art-comedians, Bazooka Joe[3]. In parenthesis, significance will be accorded the St. Martin's College show for reasons other than it being the Pistols' debut. This, because a certain Stuart Goddard played bass for the headliners that night. But despite future claims that the Bazookas were an early incarnation of Adam & The Ants - on a not too distant horizon Stuart will be chief show-off in that gathering - nothing could be further from the truth. Bazooka Joe were strictly old wave, had been on the circuit since 1972 and Goddard was one of more than 25 members who came and went throughout their release free career. However, like so many of his contemporaries, Stuart Goddard witnessing the Sex Pistols, at this very event, prompted the formation of his own outfit, The B-sides - later to become the aforementioned Ants.

The Pistols played further student gigs through the closing months of 1975, the most significant of these a Ravensbourne College date in Chislehurst - close to Bromley - where many of punk's future players first got wind of what was going down. By early '76 the band were often turning up at colleges, equipment in tow, either pleading with social secretaries to let them play or insisting they were the warm-up act of prior arrangement. Proper public shows started in February with a support slot at Soho's Marquee Club. It was also to be the last night they'd play *there* though, as an incident involving throwing chairs and trashing monitors prompted a venue decision to ban them, the likes of which will haunt the Pistols until their demise. They moved on to playing strip joints, then the 100 Club, the Nashville, the Lyceum ballroom, the ICA and the Screen On The Green, amongst other unlikely venues, often still as support to the most dubious of no-hopers.

For all the speculation and debate, in late 1975 and early 1976 the Sex Pistols were the only British punk-rock band in existence, despite the term not yet being used to describe what was still more a twitch than a movement. The Pistols were first labelled 'Punk-Rock' in an *NME* piece by deputy editor Neil Spencer. Caroline Coon used the phrase in *Melody Maker* a little later to describe the entire scene and, she states, with the sanction of the Pistols and The Clash, both of whom she was by then on good terms with. There *were* groups playing the live circuit in London who'd later be included in punk's looser confines, most notably The Stranglers – or The Guildford Stranglers as they still were – and The Hammersmith Gorillas – later to drop their geographical tag too - but until the handover, still more than half a year away, these groups remained 'pub-rock' acts.

Since 1972, pub-rock has been used in the music weeklies as a catch-all for any British bands (albeit mostly from London or its home counties), made up of white males, that weren't 'Prog', 'Heavy', 'Glam' or 'Jazz-Rock', or from the elite class of 1960s ex-mod and beat groups now taking the American stadium circuit for every last dollar. They often played storming shows at smaller venues or the back rooms of licensed premises, but rarely featured on the chart. By the middle of the decade the term extended to the white soul smoothness of hitmakers Ace, the country meanderings of Flip City - featuring the artist soon to be known as Elvis

Costello - or Shakin' Stevens & The Sunsets[4], revivalist rockers beloved of one Johnny Rotten.

The early pub-rock scene will be summed up best by Brinsley Schwarz's Nick Lowe whose 'the regrouping of a bunch of middle-class ex-mods who had been through the hippie underground scene and realised it wasn't their cup of tea' touches the pulse nicely, and he should know; the Brinsleys were a fine example of the style, and Lowe himself became one of punk's early backroom boys. But the second wave of pub-rock had come to fruition by mid-75, and the main players now, unlike their predecessors, managed to capture the essence of the live scene on vinyl: the future looked, well, palpable at least.

This new breed of tight, sweaty, raw r'n'b types, exemplified by Graham Parker & The Rumour, Eddie & The Hot Rods and, most importantly, Dr. Feelgood - whose Wilko Johnson will prove a major influence on many artists coming through over the next five years - has recently become medium sized news in the music press and on late night radio. From San Francisco, The Flamin' Groovies, having found themselves without a contract at home, were playing London too, and could be seen as the godfathers of pub-rock's newer, meaner acts. The Pistols had added their anti drugs anthem 'Slow Death' to the set at some of the college shows, but the 'Groovies were much more 'garage' than 'pub', having been born of the same impulse that created The Count Five[3], The Standells and US chart-toppers, ? & The Mysterians – unsophisticated but often explosive 1960s guitar acts from America's backwaters (collectively termed Garage-Rock because of the locations in which they'd often rehearse). These bands were the bedrock that lay beneath much of American punk's topsoil; indeed The Mysterians were termed '*Punk*' by US critic Dave Marsh in the anti-hippy *Creem* magazine, as far back as 1971. Lenny Kaye, guitarist in Patti Smith's group, himself part of the original garage scene, used the term the following year as an all encompassing fit for the above named and plenty more besides, when he brought together the best of 1960s garage on the *Nuggets* compilation. The term 'Punk' has been bandied around the New York scene since, extending it's cover from MC5 and The Stooges to this season's new Bob Dylan, Bruce Springsteen; San Francisco's Tubes (who encourage the tag with their 1975 tune 'White Punks On Dope') and beat poetess Patti Smith. But just recently punk has become a tighter-fit for any bands playing CBGBs - now that city's most radical music venue - when a magazine called *Punk* emerged, with Lou Reed's cartoon image gracing the 1st cover, Patti Smith's the 2nd and Joey Ramone's the 3rd. A year ahead, issue 8 will feature cartoon Sex Pistols. It's an irreverent, hand-written comic-like reaction against what its creators - John Holmstrom and Legs McNeil – consider a drab and self-satisfied American rock press – a category in which they include the formerly hip and afore-mentioned *Creem*. But in the tiny area of America where *a style of* punk, from a similar impetus as that about to explode in the UK, has taken hold, the revolution was velvet: it would not be televised. It's high time the whole shebang cranked up a gear; for that it needs to move to the home town of the man it will come to be associated with first, foremost, and forever.

The Ramones, for whom Joey is singer, will prove most influential of the CBGBs bands for Brit-punks, and will be the first New York group to play in the UK since the pre-McLaren New York Dolls: their record came out here in April, John Peel played it start to end in one sitting, they're touring Europe this month and are in the UK right now. Tonight they play the Roundhouse in London's Chalk Farm, their first show outside of New York, on a bill with The Stranglers and The Flamin' Groovies. Confusion will emerge when it's claimed all the Sex Pistols and all The Clash - now second in punk's pecking order but themselves pub-rockers to a man 'til they saw the Pistols play (ironically as support to frontman Joe Strummer's own band at the time, The 101ers) - were in the audience. This, because The Clash play their debut gig tonight - supporting the Sex Pistols in Sheffield, 100 miles north of the capital. Strummer himself will be the source of this inaccuracy, claiming to camera he and his entourage climbed through the lavatory window of the Roundhouse to avoid payment. He meant Dingwalls, back into Camden half a mile, and a hop, skip and jump from Clash central - new rehearsal space just by the lock - as The Ramones will be hastily shuffled onto the same bill there tomorrow. For the record, the night after that, 6th July, The Damned, now third in terms of punk credibility, will play their 1st show, at the 100 Club; also as support to the Sex Pistols.

It would be foolish to claim that the British punk-rock movement proper will begin tonight; such exactitude should be left to those lottery-ticket journos who need an orderly chronology. But, should it be required, a better example of its D.O.B. is difficult to pinpoint. Some will nod in the direction of a two day punk festival, organised by Malcolm McLaren and coming up in August at the 100 Club; the less well informed to a hilarious television appearance by the Sex Pistols towards the end of the year, just a few days after the release of their first single, which will give the newspapers - tabloid and broadsheet alike - front page material the following morning. But these will just be early developments in the scene, albeit ones which will provide welcome press opportunities, giving the public at large a chance to realise quite what they've been missing. Today there are a handful of punk bands in Britain that barely anyone knows about. Only the Sex Pistols have played a gig so far[5], but the shows mentioned above will change all that for good.

To recap, a year ago a bunch of 'back-to-basics' groups, unconvinced by rock-music's often alienating modern trends, were on the live circuit, and new ones were coming through each month. Many of these were average at best but some provided as good a night out in a music setting as any available in the UK so far this decade. In addition to the aforementioned Hot Rods, Feelgoods, Groovies and Rumour, were The Count Bishops with wild American frontman Mike Spencer, whose frantic stage presence equals that of The Stooges' Iggy Pop at his feral best. Kilburn & The High Roads, featuring perilous Ian Dury up-front and moulding the music hall tradition to a 'yakety sax' infused dirty rhythm, makes for a style of barely paralleled originality, and Mickey Jupp's Legend, often tarred with a prog-rock brush due to releases coming out on that genre's favourite label, Vertigo, are exponents of self composed r'n'b that even the mighty Feelgood choose to cover. On a vaguely different plane, Doctors Of Madness, fronted by Velvet Underground fanatic Richard 'Kid' Strange, his hair dyed bright blue, were certainly something different and will be touted as precursors of punk, but they don't quite make the grade; The 101ers, ready, willing and able to challenge the mainstream but waiting for the blueprint to appear, and long haired post-glam rockers London SS, formed by future Clash co-host Mick Jones and soon to be Generation X's Tony James, were spending their time auditioning punk's future elite but never playing a gig under the name. This whole bunch, and others of similar sway, were aware that changes in approach, style and music were on the horizon and each wanted to be first on board, but didn't yet have much idea what that entailed. A *fin de siècle* mood was overwhelming the likes of Strange, Strummer, Jones and James, but nothing was coming naturally.

'As soon as I saw (the Sex Pistols) I just knew. It was something you knew without bothering to think about.' Joe Strummer

In Manchester, soon to become punk's second city, science students Howard Trafford and Peter McNeish, Stooges fans tired of most else on offer, were scratching around and talking about starting a group, but were frustrated by an incapacity to nail it down – 'it just had to be different'. These future Buzzcocks are the best examples to flag, but hundreds of their ilk around the country, just as frustrated and moaning about 'boredom', 'the establishment' and other benchmarks of life's imperfections, were hanging out in bedrooms, pubs, schools and colleges, waiting, consciously or not, until they see, hear – or hear about – the Sex Pistols.

'My life changed the moment I saw the Sex Pistols. I immediately got caught up trying to make things happen. Suddenly there was a direction, something I passionately wanted to be involved in. We thought they were fantastic; it was "we will go and do something like this in Manchester"' Howard Devoto (né Trafford)

But the Sex Pistols in early summer 1975 were themselves not even in the same league as future Buzzcocks, Clash, Damned, Generation X, or others from the early dawn. McLaren's big ideas were taken on board to some degree, mostly by best educated Glen Matlock, but the pre-Rotten ensemble were fans of The Faces, Bowie, Roxy, *et al*, with a liking too for Mod-era 60s bands, and they, essentially, wanted to be like them. Their main impetus for forming a band was, well, to be in a band, with the associated good impression this would doubtless leave on the fairer sex. It was the impossible dream, but hopefully they could end up as rich as Rod Stewart.

Whether the Pistols too were disillusioned with music trends as they were and frustrated by the social structure of Britain, is hard to know; Glen Matlock will claim so in his autobiography[6], but what is sure, once Johnny shows up it doesn't take the boys long to realise they're onto a winner at last. Their own fortunes take a quantum leap in August 1975.

John Lydon is from a different place than any other player in Britain's first wave of punk, not least because, prior to his audition for the Pistols, he'd had no desire to join a group, be a star, tour the world – or particularly 'change it' in general terms. His instincts had always told him to challenge, but to challenge everything; he'd never accept the world as it is. But they also told him to search out alternatives, find his own truth, and mistrust anything and anyone he felt uncomfortable with. He had used this dictum to garner an eclectic taste in music, far wider than any of the others now gaining ground. He cared for a few early Bowie sides but saw him as a fake; a man whose talents and vision far outweighed his passion and honesty. Few on the scene even know who Peter Hammill or Kevin Coyne are, and are only vaguely aware of Captain Beefheart and his lofty imagination. If into Reggae, they'd go little further than what was recommended, often the 'Get Up, Stand Up' militant sloganeering variety, in opposition to the spacious dub landscapes that Lydon prefers. Johnny will seek out what is available, listen to as much as he can and decide himself what's worthy. His outlook is so different to that of his contemporaries that comparisons remain futile. While this is no derision of others from the early punk movement, particularly those whose contributions will make for the most colourful and exciting period of rock music certainly since the mid to late 60s - if not the dawn of the genre itself - without Johnny Rotten, the outsider, firing the starting pistol, bringing a certain something that no one can quite put a finger on to an otherwise barely happening party, it wouldn't be overstating the case to suggest there'll be no punk movement of any significance in Britain whatsoever.

John Lydon is the other protagonist of punk-rock; his early association with Malcolm McLaren appears to have been built on a joint respect and the parallels in their outlooks are many - not least their mutual hatred of hippies and all they stand for. But he's much, much more than that. Whether he's just the angriest of young men with more spunk than the rest of the new breed put together, or the one chosen to light the flames of fury destined to burn the old guard's complacency – spark-meister of the '5 Star Rock 'n' Roll Petrol' if you will[7] – is a confection to enjoy elsewhere. But whatever Johnny has, he has it in droves; he is vital and urgent and if his involvement in all that occurs this summer and beyond is pure chance or has been destined for millennia, without it punk could, in say, 30 years time, mean a bunch of forgotten 1960s outfits, a magazine from New York that ran to a half dozen issues or a band called The Ramones who played in Britain a couple of times to half interested crowds, most of whom can barely remember attending. It might even remain the term of abuse so often hurled by police detectives in black and white movies at low level criminals, essentially accusing them of welcoming the advances of higher ranking but sexually desperate jailbirds - in exchange for 'privileges'.

The Devil In The Detail

'I didn't plan on a future.' John Lydon

Having read so far, you'd be forgiven for believing this volume to be another retelling of the British punk scene in the mid to late 1970s or, at best, the part John Lydon played in it. Perhaps even the sub-title of the book suggests so. It isn't.

What has been written above may be familiar to many readers, but it would be arrogant and presumptuous to assume it superfluous. Curiosity in this book's contents shall hopefully come from a range of impulses; to think interest should be forthcoming only from those well-versed in its subject's involvement with punk-rock, would be badly informed and, from a commercial viewpoint, rather stupid. John Lydon has been involved in numerous projects since the Sex Pistols' split in early 1978, indeed many would say that at this juncture he'd yet to reach his creative peak. Recent television appearances afford him a household name today (keep up at the back, it's 2006 now) equally familiar as when those inane headlines first appeared. And when producers of a BBC exercise requested potential viewers to vote for their 'favourite Briton' a couple of years back, was it really just those who'd pogoed at the Roxy or read the manifesto who put him in at a healthy (but not comfy) 87, one below Bono but above Richard Burton, J.R.R. Tolkein, Sir Walter Raleigh and Tony Benn?

The period covered so far brings the story of John Lydon to the point at which notoriety was assured, when more than just the inner sanctum knew his face and when, essentially, his career was about to begin.

So read on and discover that *Stories Of Johnny - A Compen-dium Of Thoughts On The Icon Of An Era* is everything it claims to be: the era referred to is of course that of punk, but such an ac-colade surely doesn't carry limitations for other areas of achieve-ment - even though many would be more than satisfied with this reach alone. But John Lydon, like most true artists, is never satis-fied, and despite punk ultimately being what his name will remain associated with first, when it ended for him (by his own hand), he was ready for his second coming. Each stage in his extraordinary life and career, including his pivotal role in punk-rock, are dis-cussed, debated, dissected, and reported in the pages that follow. But through it all he remained the epitome of punk, whether the music he was making - if indeed he was making any - shared much with the accepted view of what that was.

What this isn't, is a biography of John Lydon. For that go first and last and always to Lydon's own book , *Rotten: No Irish, No Blacks, No Dogs* (Plexus, 1994). However, that tome goes no fur-ther than his split from the other Pistols' in 1978, leaving a canny open window for a much anticipated second volume. While we wait, dots are joined by Ben Myers in his *Lydon: The Sex Pistols, PiL and Anti-Celebrity* (IMP, Publishing 2004) which takes the story, in its currently available edition, to 2004. For the best history of British punk and the Sex Pistols, head straight for Jon Savage's *England's Dreaming* (Faber & Faber, 1991). For what came next, it's *Rip It Up And Start Again: Post Punk 1978 – 1984* by Simon Reynolds (Faber and Faber 2005) or nothing.

With a remit that only required those involved to say what they wanted about a man they were all keen to write about - whatever their position (it goes without saying that the views expressed herein are those of the individual contributors) - the chapters were bound to repeat splinters of information and history, but only as introduction or linkage for central themes. Each section here should be seen as a stand alone essay; one author's take on whichever angle they choose to view John Lydon from. If the results reveal something to the reader outside their existing awareness or, when sown together, the complete work provides a image of a man, so often misjudged and poorly represented, at odds with general preconceptions - or even reveals a little more about the human condition as represented by John Lydon, then the project has been a worthy one.

Notes:

1. Precursor of the Job Centre.
2. London art-Mods, introduced to the Pistols by Malcolm McLaren, who knew them from art school days. Pete Townsend was a huge fan. John Lydon would claim them as his own discovery and play them on a desert island discs type program in 1977.
3. Despite claims to the contrary, The Swankers - or possibly The Strand, the group's former name – did perform live on one occasion in 1974, at Salter's Café, just down the King's Road from Sex.

4. Stevens will become a **bona fide** *pop success after punk's glory days are long passed, with a sanitised, chart-friendly version of his 1970s routine.*

5. The Clash were almost beaten to second place, gig-wise, by Buzzcocks, who'd planned to play their debut by opening for the Pistols' at their first Manchester Lesser Free Trade Hall gig on 4th June, organised by Pete and Howard. But when co-members bottled it, brought in as replacement were the never-to-be-heard-of-again, Mandala Band. If Manchester's Slaughter & The Dogs count, they did play live before The Clash, but that bunch claimed they'd been playing their boot-boy-punk live in Manchester before the Pistols had played their version in London: most scoff.

This first Manchester show by the Pistols became the Ravensbourne College gig of the North, as all Joy Division's future members; Manchester's very own Malcolm McLaren, Tony Wilson, and a young Stephen Morrissey were in attendance. Mick Hucknall, later of Simply Red, was there too. Buzzcocks' debut performance however was supporting the Sex Pistols (and, ironically, Slaughter & The Dogs) on their return visit, July 20th

6. I Was A Teenage Sex Pistol *by Glen Matlock* (Virgin Books, *1996*).

7. The title of the B-side to The 101ers' single 'Keys To Your Heart'.

Rob Johnstone

Rob Johnstone is Senior Editor and Managing Director of Chrome Dreams. He lives in Surrey.

Lydon at the "Anglomania" party

The Ballroom Blitz:
From New York To Baghdad
by Greil Marcus

*My name is Charles Giteau/ My name I'll never deny, from the folk song
'Charles Giteau', attributed to Charles Guiteau, assassin of James A.
Garfield, 20th president of the United States, who supposedly sang the
song while awaiting execution.*

*'Sex Pistols' meant to me the idea of a pistol, a pinup, a young thing. A
better looking assassin." Malcolm McLaren, 1988*

*At least I got my name. No one can take my name off me. My name
does mean something. It stands for something. It stands for something
true. No one can take that away from me.
Johnny Rotten, 2003*

What The World Knows, The World Forgets

As the world knows, Johnny Rotten, born John Lydon in 1956,
first came to public attention as a member of the Sex Pistols, a band
that emerged out of the milieu that had grown up around Sex, a London boutique run by the designers Malcolm McLaren, the band's
manager, and Vivienne Westwood. First conceived as a walking
poster for the shop, the so-called punk group made its first appearances in late 1975. In a series of incendiary singles released over
the next two years, from 'Anarchy In The UK' to 'God Save The
Queen' to 'Holidays in the Sun', the band, with Rotten at the front
and McLaren in the wings, took on the whole of the social order:
pop music and the Royal Family, God and the state, the imperial past
and the impoverished future. Rotten left the band after its last show
on its sole American tour, in January 1978; while legally enjoined
from the use of his chosen name he reverted to his given name for
the formation later that year of Public Image Ltd., or PiL, which he
insisted was 'a company, not a band'. With its line up of musicians

29

shifting, PiL performed and recorded into the 1990s. In 1996 and 2003 the Sex Pistols reformed for reunion tours. Seemingly desperate to remain in the public eye even if no longer able to catch the public ear, from 1999 through 2005 Rotten made forays into Internet radio (*Rotten Radio*), television (*Rotten TV*, *John Lydon Goes Ape*, *John Lydon's Shark Attack*), the nature travelogue (*John Lydon's Megabugs*), *What Makes Britain Great* – a series made with the Belgian historian Marc Reynebeau – and the reality show *I'm A Celebrity – Get Me Out of Here!*. In 2006, as if from the alley running behind the temple of culture, Rotten recorded a podcast for 'AngloMania: Tradition and Transgression in British Fashion,' an exhibition at the Metropolitan Museum of Art in New York that celebrated the work of Vivenne Westwood, who since her days at Sex had become the most celebrated English designer of her time.

At The Party

At the party to mark the opening of 'AngloMania', as the *New York Times* gleefully reported, the likes of Charlize Theron, Charlotte Gainsbourg, Tom Ford, Drew Barrymore, Gemma Ward, Sarah Jessica Parker, Minuccia Prada, Julian Schnabel, Ralph Fiennes, Sienna Miller, John Galliano, Jonathan Rhys Meyers, Lily Cole, Alexander McQueen and Lindsay Lohan, not to mention *Vogue* editor Anna Wintour, the Duke of Devonshire and Vivenne Westwood herself, had no need to notice Johnny Rotten, even if everyone did. 'When John Lydon, the former Sex Pistol known as Johnny Rotten, found his seat – the last at a long table and arguably the least desirable in the highly orchestrated seating plan – he was visibly upset,' Cathy Horyn reported. 'Which was funny' (by which Horyn clearly meant, 'amusing'): 'You wouldn't expect a punk to attend a society dinner, much less be aggrieved by his placement. Mr. Rotten stormed out twice, cursing museum workers. Eventually he took his seat.' 'I'm Johnny Rotten,' Eric Wilson quoted him saying, 'and nobody here knows me.' As it should be, Wilson was saying, for an 'oafish,' 50-year-old man 'who wobbled around the edges of the party,' 'responding to anyone who ventured an introduction with unpleasantness that bordered on the wrong side of rude.' 'Ta-ta,' Wilson said.

It was really too perfect. For Horyn and Wilson, it may have been a mere flick of the NOKD wrist, but the business of fashion writers is telling their readers what they want to hear, and what their readers want to hear is that just as they are blissfully inferior to certain orders of humanity, they are just as certainly superior to others. It's pure pleasure to be reminded of the compromises and failures of those whom you might have once admired, or feared, especially when the compromises and failures of others – with the has-been stripped naked in the public square, or the museum ballroom that stands in for it – are so much more spectacularly degraded than one's own.

Out The Door

It's unclear what compromises Johnny Rotten has made, under whatever name, at any time or place. In press conferences and one-to-one interviews, on stage and on record, before the camera or behind the microphone, from 1976 to the present day he has been intransigent, mocking, cruel, unforgiving, and unwilling to concede an inch. 'They can't get rid of us. And there's a reason for that. It's truth. You can't hide truth. You can't manipulate it. You can slag us down, but you'd be wrong. I've not put a word out wrong, not ever,' Rotten said in 2003, when the *Billboard* interviewer Scott Martens challenged him on the legitimacy of one more Sex Pistols trip around the block.

People who refuse to admit mistakes – and in a philosophical sense, not out of a sense of privilege, protection, and entitlement – can be very scary. They don't speak ordinary language. You can't tell if what they're offering you is argument or noise, a challenge or a shield: simple meanness, the reflexes of a bully, and the terror of being exposed for nothing more, or the mental agility of someone who was out the door before you walked into the room.

31

In 1979

In 1979 PiL released its second album, *Metal Box*. Like so much of its a-company-not-a-band rhetoric – the band was, then, Lydon, the guitarist Keith Levene, the bassist Jah Wobble, and drummers – the object seemed more concept than anything else: three 12" 45s (for the depth of sound only a 45 could provide, one was told) packed in a film canister. (Today, as a single CD in a tin can, the packaging is if even more conceptual: a pill box.) The late music critic Robert Palmer wrote of seeing the thing in the window of a record store, stopping, staring, 'wondering what it was' – and what, he didn't have to say, such a thing could sound like, if only to live up to the unlikeliness of what it looked like.

Today, more than a quarter century later, it sounds like music – or an argument about music, or about how to walk down the street – that no one has even tried to catch up to, PiL included, save for stray tracks over the years and the 1980 live album *Paris au Printemps*, credited to Image Publique S.A., which took the signal *Metal Box* numbers 'Chant' and 'Poptones' to places they'd never been before. Not long ago I walked into Amoeba Records in Berkeley – a huge,

independent store with new and used CDs and vinyl, DVDs and videos – and caught the *Metal Box* opener 'Albatross' in the air. It cut through the somewhat depressed atmosphere of the place – the oppression of too many products. It still didn't fit. It came from somewhere else – not that you'd necessarily want to go there.

This was drone music. You could imagine that for all the hate the Sex Pistols threw The Beatles' way it all came out of that last, long chord at the end of 'A Day In The Life'. If you listened long enough, hard enough, or casually enough to *Metal Box* – not listening at all, ignoring the record when it was on, until a scratch of melody or a vocal inflection or a word or a phrase that seemed to come out of nowhere but fit perfectly ('Still the spirit of '68') snuck up behind you – you began to hear themes, cries, distortions, chords, choruses, words, and sound effects that made you wonder if they were less present in the grooves than suggested by what was. It was a miasma of doubt, refusal, arrogance, and utter vulnerability, with Lydon chanting, not singing, stretching out his vowels until his voice lost any ordinary character, appearing in the sound as himself a distortion, someone who sang from something other than an ordinary body. If the music was about walking down the street, if you saw the man inside of it coming, would you turn around and walk the other way, cross the street, or pass by under his gaze, sneaking just a glance to see if his eyes were as bottomless as his voice implied they had to be?

As Robert Palmer said once he'd gone into the record store, bought the set, taken it home, shaken the discs out of their can (they were packed so tightly you couldn't prize them out, you had to turn the canister upside down and shake it, with the result that the discs fell onto each other, scratching themselves), and put them on, it was perhaps the most extreme version of 'art for art's sake' pop music had ever produced. The music could sound that way because, to someone used to pop, it seemed so formal, so relentlessly focused on its own shape, on the generation of its own rules. And yet the last thing the music did was turn its back on the world. It was a version of it: one that said, finally, that nothing you wanted would come to you as you wished. The slow, dragged out pace of the songs and the beaten, punished sound of the singer said there was nothing new under the sun, but inside the music, the idea itself felt new, and liberating.

Bad Conscience

The man singing inside the songs on *Metal Box* is a man with a bad conscience. He's filled with guilt, disgust, self-loathing. The sight of other people fills him with revulsion; the sight of himself in a store window as he passes by is even worse. But what on *Metal Box* is a kind of art statement, or a dramatic role, is really the role Johnny Rotten, or John Lydon, has played from the beginning, and is playing now.

In Colin B. Morton and Chuck Death's comic strip 'Great Pop Things', the *leitmotif* of which involves the pop dream of changing the world (Eric Clapton: 'Tried to Change the World by Being God'; Abba: 'Tried to Change the World by Snogging Other People Behind Each Other's Backs in Public'), Johnny Rotten appears in many forms, most effectively as a compost pile, if a compost pile could be made of corroding safety pins, a rotting t-shirt, filthy spiked hair, and bleeding sores. In 'The Adam Ant Story', as Adam ('He Tried to Change the World by Dressing Up as an Ant') muses over band names, Rotten looms over him like the Elephant Man, screaming: "GO AWAY I DON'T LIKE ANY OF YOU, MAAAN!" A 'Where Are They Now?' feature from the 1977 Liverpool punk fanzine *The Assassin* reaches into the great no-future to catch up with the erstwhile Antichrist: 'It all went horribly wrong,' he says. 'I burned up all my hate.' But that never happened – or, if it did, John Lydon never admitted it.

As time went on, he insisted with greater and greater vehemence on his place in history – or, to put it more precisely, on what he'd done, and why the world had never been the same since. Time and again, as he ran through the litany, it came off not as the pathetic boast of a bum on the street but a maddened, patient argument less with people than with life: an argument against the fact that people will do almost anything to deny that the world can change.

Changing The World

The pop critic Neva Chonin was reviewing a 2003 Sex Pistols show; the headline in the *San Francisco Chronicle* read 'Sex Pistols' Lydon tries, but can't revive rage on reunion tour at Warfield.' 'What can you say,' Chonin said, 'about a 25-year-old legend that died? That it changed your life, changed music history, and hated The Beatles?'

As a bad conscience, as someone who would never say yes, Johnny Rotten inspired millions and influenced only Richard Butler. Colin B. Morton and Chuck Death, for their strip celebrating the Sex Pistols 1996 reunion tour ('They Tried to Change the World Again 20 Years After They Had First Changed the World'), brought Princess Di into the band, and it made perfect sense: why wouldn't she have a Johnny Rotten poster on her bedroom wall, as a talisman that she too could say no, just as Daniel Day Lewis's Gerry Conlon has a Johnny Rotten poster in his prison cell in *In the Name Of The Father?* To one person the picture promises that she too can say no; to another, a man whose own voice is imprisoned, it says that there is someone who speaks for him. Princess Di is having the time of her life in her 'Never Trust a Hippie' t-shirt, spewing her lines about the hippie she married: 'What is a man what has he got two great big ears and he talks to pot plantsaah!' Gerry Conlon was out by 1996, forty-one when John Lydon was 'fat, forty, and back': didn't he belong in the band, too? Or was he already in it?

Sinéad O'Connor always was, and never more so than on 3 October 1992, for her famous appearance on *Saturday Night Live*. There she was, in a long formal gown, with a Star of David necklace and a nose stud, her head shaved, chanting her rewrite of Bob

Marley's 'War' unaccompanied, her face shifting by imperceptible degrees from saint to thug, rat to Hedy Lamarr. Then for the last line she produced a picture of Pope John Paul II, ripped it to pieces, and shouted: 'Fight the real enemy!' It was her version of 'Anarchy In The UK', her acting out of the challenge John Lydon had issued to whoever might have the strength to take it up. Like 'Anarchy In The UK' – with the names of terrorist organizations reeling off the radio as if the newsreader were announcing his membership in each group – it was a classic media shock. And it was more. When someone acts as a bad conscience, that means he or she acts as yours. Even if you were with O'Connor all the way – after the fact, after that strange, suggestive tearing sound of *switch, switch, switch* came over the air, live on the East Coast, uncensored as the signal passed through the Midwest to the mountain states to the West Coast – you had to realise that someone in this intransigent would, like Johnny Rotten, sooner or later put you on the other side. And it was more than that. If what O'Connor did seems like a cheap stunt, self-aggrandising, a set-up, ask yourself this: given the chance to say what I want to the whole country, would I have the nerve? That was the question Johnny Rot-

Sinead O'Connor

ten asked from the first moment his voice was heard in public.

God Save The Queen

On his 2006 podcast for 'AngloMania', Johnny Rotten read out the lyrics of 'God Save The Queen' as a manifesto, or an illegal broadcast: 'Common sense from a common man.' He was too modest: common sense, maybe, but from an uncommon man. No one else would have written what he wrote, or said what he said in the words that he found. 'God save history/ God save your mad parade,' with the *r*'s in parade clattering like a stick run across a picket fence? He read with evident satisfaction; you could hear him shuffling the pages. 'I come from a time,' he said, 'when it was treason, to discuss the monarchy, in any other way, other than complete and total idolatry. I changed that. The Sex Pistols changed that. We changed that. Now you change that.' He still knew how to do it, he had told Todd Martens in 2003. He'd been trumpeting how the Sex Pistols were still on their own, still scorned, touring without a label or corporate support, 'chipping away at the system bit by bit in as many ways as possible.' 'Aside from touring without a label,' Martens said, 'what else are you doing to chip away at the system?' 'I'm going to Baghdad,' Rotten said. 'The Sex Pistols will play Baghdad. You're offering them democracy; well, let's give it to them in the ultimate extreme.' Martens was not impressed. 'Wanting to play Baghdad certainly makes for a good soundbite,' he said, "but how

serious are you to see it through?' 'I'm deadly serious,' Rotten said. 'The show will be free of charge. It would be mean-spirited to be charging them US dollars. I will do it. I see no reason not to. They could use a good bleeding view of how the world is.' 'With all the chaos in Baghdad, aren't they getting that view now? How would a Sex Pistols concert show them the truth about democracy?'

And that, you can imagine as you read this exchange, that was the opening John Lydon had been waiting for. 'How can you even ask that to the man who wrote 'Anarchy In The UK'?'

The Story Untold

You can laugh; as anyone who cares knows, the Sex Pistols did not play Baghdad. Or you can listen, to the way Johnny Rotten has chosen his words over these many years, and know what he would say next: *Not yet. That war isn't going away any time soon. Nor am I.*

© *Greil Marcus 2006*

Greil Marcus

American musicologist and scholar Greil Marcus is the author of 1992's *In The Fascist Bathroom* (Harvard University Press, 1993), a compendium of his essays on Punk. He has written about music since the start of his career in the late 1960s, when he joined the team of the newly created *Rolling Stone* magazine. Through the 1970s he continued there, while also contributing to the seminal *Creem* and *Village Voice* journals. In 1989 he authored *Lipstick Traces: A Secret History Of The 20th Century* (Harvard University Press, 1990 / Faber & Faber, 1992) in which he forged a link between the Sex Pistols and the Dadaist art movement.

He is also the brains behind 1991's *Dead Elvis* (Doubleday) a collection of writings on cultural obsession. His most acclaimed work however remains *Mystery Train* (Penguin, 1991 / Faber & Faber, 2005) his stunning study of American music and culture.

Glorious Rage:
The Look And The Sound Of The Voice
by Barb Jungr

When the great British public were first exposed to 'punk' on that now infamous Bill Grundy *Tonight* programme, for me two things leapt out of the television. One was the unforgettable and iconic painted face of Siouxsie Sioux, the other was the sneering, razor sharp, ice thin, blood-drawing voice which we later learnt had come out of the mouth of the Sex Pistols' front-man and singer, John Lydon – or as he was then, Johnny Rotten.

The timbre, the sound of each person's voice is unique, an aural fingerprint which helps distinguish Frank Sinatra from Johnny Mathis, Madonna from Morrissey. The sound of the voice can take many forms, from the jazz purring of Peggy Lee to the angry roar of NWA.

In pop, voices rely on the microphone which provides the ability for them to tower over a band, so even someone speaking can be heard above loudly played drums, bass and guitars. The timbre, the style in which the singer uses the voice, their mannerisms, 'vocal tics' and ornamentations, all create the 'sound', the sonic footprint that once stamped on our ears reminds us always of them, and only them.

Punk had plenty of defining vocalists – Rotten, Strummer, Weller, Siouxsie. Delightful voices flew out of the window in the company of the music that punk rose up to defy, and in their place came a forceful, declamatory, take-no-prisoners style. The singer, the frontperson, had to be charismatic both visually and vocally, and these early trendsetters created the sonic breach through which all their followers would subsequently pass. And Johnny was there, up-front, leading the new breed, marking the ground, pacing the spaces, like a caged cat. Michael Flatley may care to think of himself as a 'Celtic Tiger', but he's a Celtic pussycat beside Johnny Rotten.

But what is it that makes a voice memorable? Why, heard once, are some voices unforgettable? The French philosopher Roland Barthes attempted to understand this phenomenon in his now legendary essay on what he called 'the grain' of the voice. Essentially, he identified something that might be thought of as the quality that sits outside the words being sung and beyond the pitches and rhythms the voice is making, coming rather from the tongue, the throat, the body of the voice. In recent years researchers, philosophers and those who critique our popular culture have sought to understand the significance of 'texts' such as records, videos and films, and these often can only be understood by seeking for and identifying such elusive qualities as Barthes vocal 'grain'. Robin Markowitz explains this as the distinction between 'meaningful singing and singing that makes meaning.'[1] In this respect, Johnny Rotten's voice is hugely significant.

Sociologist Simon Frith suggested that: 'In listening to the lyrics of pop songs we actually hear three things at once: words, which appear to give songs an independent source of semantic meaning; rhetoric, words being used in a special, musical way, a way which draws attention to features and problems of speech; and voices, words being spoken or sung in human tones which are themselves "meaningful", signs of persons and personality.'[2]

Rotten's voice and his lyrics are inextricably bound together. The anger of punk, the energy-in-attack on the musical and political establishment in the words are there in every part of the voice. And through this there's a consonance that amplifies; a sense of authenticity. In addition, Rotten was very clearly singing as an Englishman. There was no fake American accent in his delivery (perish the thought!). His vowels, his diction, placed him squarely in, and of, London. Punk in Britain was not going to be confused with its American counterpart. It was English; or Irish. Scottish or Welsh. You were exactly who you sounded like. This was for real, there was no covering up. No techniques or accents to hide behind. Nothing *faux*. No fanciness. No beauty to distance the listener from the message. Fuck that, the singer spat in every way.

When the Pistols performed, and the music kicked in, Rotten let rip, full pelt, nothing held back, his voice sounded as though every fibre of his body was taking part in his delivery. When he screamed 'we mean it maaaan…,' not everyone liked it, but they couldn't doubt the sentiment.

Often singers' speaking and singing voices are very different. The early Sex Pistols recordings however reveal that Lydon talking and Lydon singing was a close match; he even displayed similar vocal tics in both realms. The inflections, tonal changes, and mannered use of the voice was present in all of its public displays. Here in speech as well as song were the slides over notes; the 'glissandi'. The held sneering of 'Li...aaaaar' is there in the speaking voice too. But the vocal machine-gun attack he would employ whenever a simple sneer seemed insufficient was something else: that inspired rolled 'R' of 'moron' in 'God Save The Queen', insulting all classes of British society about to celebrate without question the continuation of the monarchy, as well as the traditions of classical singing, was nothing short of brilliant.

If Simon Frith is right in his assumption that, as listeners, 'we can hear someone's life in their voice'[3], then everything we knew about the Sex Pistols was given to us in Rotten's performances. As soon as he tore into a song it was abundantly clear he was mad as hell and wasn't going to take it anymore. There was both attack and distance, rage (but not unconditional fury). He knew who the enemy was. 'No future for you' seemed to come from the spleen of someone utterly dispossessed.

Musically, Lydon's timing is spot on. His pitch remains consistent and his control is realised if somewhat unorthodox. In the early days however, Malcolm McClaren directed his new charge – the proposed voice of a social and musical revolution dismissive of pop's traditions and accepted doctrines – to the customary vocal coach, with the intention of teaching this untutored shouter to 'sing properly'. McClaren's choice of instructor for this mammoth task was the well known coach, Tona De Brett.

I spoke to Tona recently regarding Lydon's approach to learning and her approach to teaching him, asking her first what was there in his voice when they first met;

Tona De Brett: 'Nothing was naturally there. And in fact when he came to see me, he did not want to learn to sing, he just wanted to make a big noise and become famous, notorious perhaps. Certainly the actual business of singing was not foremost in his mind. It was

McClaren's idea and when John first came he sat in the corner of the room and didn't utter a single word, as I talked about what a good idea it was to know about breath control and about quality and all these things.

'I was rather embarrassed by his lack of any reaction (I was much younger and less experienced then). And this young man was sitting in the corner of the room with his head in his hands. So I said to him, "Look, if you're not even going to talk to me you might as well go". Whereupon he lifted his head and said, "I can't do. I've been sent". That was not an obvious start. However, it made us both roar with laughter, which broke the ice. Then he said "I don't see what good singing lessons are going to do because I just shout", so I said, "OK, if that's what you are going to do then you can probably cope quite well on your own."

'We did try to pitch a note but there was no way I could get him to actually vocalise any sort of tune. I tried all the ways I knew, I played something on the piano, he sang or made a noise somewhere quite different. I sang it at him at his pitch. No. No way. I got a guitar out (which I don't really play), and strummed a bit. Nothing. So I said, "I know, what you better do is start something and I will find where you are on the piano and then we'll be off". So he started something and I took a moment to find it and by that time it was lost. So you see, I didn't have anything to work with really.'

I asked Tona if he actually sang anything in front of her; her face said all I needed to know. 'But doesn't he have a hugely developed rhythmic sense?' I enquired.

'Of course, that was no problem' Tona replied.

And the speech-singing on records is sort of in tune.

'Oh good, that's quite interesting' Tona laughed, 'but it's certainly nothing to do with me.

'I would say he came three times, and each occasion we'd have long discussions about music and things he listened to; he said he liked The Doors, who I liked as well, particularly 'People Are

Strange'. He said he really loved that. But as for singing it, there was no way. Not in my music book.

'I dare say with the surrounding stuff going on, guitars and drums, he kind of tuned in over time, but he certainly wasn't a natural. I have instructed a lot of singers how to preserve their voices, but I am quite amazed that a lot of the punk people managed not to damage their voices, the way they shouted and misused things.'

Tona went on to talk about instructing Ari Up from The Slits who she sent to a voice specialist. 'Some of them still damage their voices beyond any possibility of recovery... but Johnny somehow didn't. Keith Flint from the Prodigy reminded me of Johnny, because there again, his ear was practically non-existent, he's not the main singer, but he also gets by with a great sense of rhythm; he was a dancer,

Tona De Brett

45

a performer, just like Johnny was. I mean, the dressing up was the most important aspect.'

Whether Lydon benefited much from his singing lessons or took away with him anything of lasting value remains vague.

'Maybe he did, I don't think at the time that I had exercises on tape or on disc but he might have, because I think he was very new to the whole scene, the band, and he might well then have concentrated on listening to other people a bit more. This may have helped, but from my point of view I wasn't very helpful because there wasn't much voice there and I couldn't, over the few lessons that we had, really produce anything. So there you have it. If I had been wiser at the time I might have got more out of him, but the band's time was limited because they wanted to get into studios and do things and then the last thing you fit in is singing lessons.'

On the early Sex Pistols' recordings Lydon's performances are very tightly controlled. As Tona La Brett pointed out, listening is a vital ingredient necessary for singing and in the studio and at gigs he certainly had the opportunity to develop his ear, whether that was conscious or not. It's possible that the input of various producers was significant in restraining and focussing this extraordinary front man, and, in the very first instance at least, Chris Spedding certainly had the right approach to channel Lydon's innate abilities, but whichever way you cut it, Rotten/Lydon wasn't simply 'shouting'. Maybe Tona's suggestions took time to gel in him, maybe he listened further to Jim Morrison or one of his reggae influences and something rubbed off, but there's a definite musicality in what he does, wherever that came from.

On those early records, Rotten was using everything he had, and to great effect. And as he developed he began to use elements of his vocals to very specific effect. The rolled 'r's become more frequent and a signifier of his performance. The vocal glissandi (slides) from, to, and between notes, the drawl, the use of the vowel almost as a weapon, pushing the lyrics along, the growls; these distinctive ornaments suddenly appear in his peers' vocal performances. Without the Pistols, without Rotten, the singing style of the British punk movement might well have been very different.

Descriptively, Lydon's voice has a pronounced nasality. He operates high in the male range, which gives a thin sound, but provides a commensurate facility to 'cut' through and across the other recorded or performed sounds around him. It has some relation to the high rock tenor voice, and his edginess reinforces his suppressed anger. There's a metallic quality to his voice, suggesting a feeling of strength. That high nasality references the witches and wizards from childhood. There's angry command and comment and he enjoys delivering sound as though the words, the rhetoric, carry him along on their tide of emotion, both the emotion he's feeling and the emotion he wants the listener to feel. There's no sex there though – not surprising really, coming from the man who pronounced that sex was 'two and a half minutes of squelching noises'.

This is a voice of ideas; thoughts, commands, refusals and rebuttals. It isn't a voice of seduction, and in that respect it again arises from outside the arena of popular music, where 'lovey-dovey' became the *lingua franca* of pop. 'The popsters did their thing, and now its time for us, we have more important messages to deliver'. Somehow, all of this is in the sound of that voice, alongside a massive quota of personality.

Moving to PiL, Lydon was freed from the constraints of the tight song structure formats of the Sex Pistols. Suddenly, his voice is alone, out there in the mix. The lure of free expression sometimes exposes his vocal, and the sincerity of before is sacrificed. The route the musicians take is less easily available to Lydon, who seems more at home with tight attack and fast pace. The tuning now sounds more renegade and almost wilfully 'out' at times. But there's also an attempt to be more lyrical vocally. But still, on tracks like 'Public Image', when the bass drives and that staccato attack can be focussed around something solid, he's still very much 'there'.

Sometimes however, the sense of him being a man alone is so much a part of the vocal sound it is almost unbearable; 'Run away, run away, sewing the seeds of discontent' he intones mournfully. In PiL's music there's something slightly amiss and it's noticeable in the way that the voice swings from the tonal qualities of the Pistols' records to something Lydon seems to be trying to find; timbral changes and a varying sense of style suggest he is moving forward but is vocally in a state of transition. The anger has sometimes been mollified by the sweet, acrid smell of success and its trappings, but painfully, they fail to disguise reality. The rhetoric isn't much different but the alienation in the vocal performances still feels real.

Lydon's recent television appearances and rising public persona have acted as reminders of the quality of play and intelligence he always brought to his work. The sense that his performances were both based in reality and also distanced from whoever John Lydon is, have been back in evidence. In speech, Lydon's voice has deepened, and become 'manly' where it once was boyish. He has established himself, as his website declares, as an 'army of one'. To return to the younger man, and his singing, its interesting to visit the history of the semi-spoken, accented voice in British culture, because Lydon's style, however unique, has some curious and interesting precedents.

In the history of singing there are many landmarks. The Bel Canto and operatic style of vocalising, popular in Europe and America (and still in use today in western musical theatre and classical music) was challenged by the crooning voices of vocal jazz, and the popular singing style was born. That style has remained and is still the most popular form today. But the semi-spoken/sung style of delivery can be found in a variety of differing genres; blues, jazz 'scat' singing, reggae (most notably in the performances of the rapper's predecessor, the 'toaster' or MC), punk, rap, certain styles of pop and in some traditional music. It was significant also in the Brechtian song style (or Sprechgesang – which is also present in some contemporary classical compositions) and in many comedy songs from various ages. In Britain, it was an essential component in the traditional music hall style, and remains as such in its enormous (but often unappreciated or overlooked) legacy. Music Hall performers used the British working class accent and its conversational elements to signify to the audience that they were all equals and could laugh at and lampoon together the folly of the establishment.

There's a fascinating although not surprising parallel between the vocalising of many music hall performers and Johnny Rotten. His is a direct descendent of this vocal style; cheeky, knowing, aware and often shrewdly political and class critical, allying audience and performer against the outside world. Many British performers drew on this same source, notably Anthony Newley in the early 1960s (whose style was borrowed from by David Bowie in his 'Laughing Gnome' era) and later in the decade by Steve Marriot with The Small Faces, Ray Davies with The Kinks and, occasionally, Roger Daltrey with the Who. Both John Lennon and Paul McCartney were also hugely influenced by the British music hall, and although this was seldom blatant on The Beatles' hit singles (unless we include the dreaded 'Yellow Submarine'), on album cuts such as 'Martha My Dear' and 'When I'm 64' the style is unmistakable. Lennon's comedy dialogue at the beginning of the *Let It Be* album is also pure music hall knockabout.

In the early 1970s this style had become largely forgotten as rock music became 'serious' (in that, what it was that had made pop music fun had become virtually anathema to the new breed of musicians) and English vocalists often adopted pseudo America west-coast twangs. But perhaps England's foremost contemporary music hall interpreter was keeping the flame alight, if not burning high, with his pub-rock band Kilburn & The High Roads. It was the onslaught of punk that rightfully put Ian Dury high in the charts and made him one of Britain's best-loved performers, appealing to the punks and the grandmother's alike (at least those not party to tracks

Max Wall   *Ian Dury*

like Plaistow Patricia). Dury even composed the little known classic, 'England's Glory', for music hall legend Max Wall.

Chas and Dave went on to bastardise the style to its lowest common denominator, but the Sex Pistols are rarely given credit for having a comedic, music hall approach, largely emanating from Steve Jones' slapstick humour and Johnny's strong British working class background (one seemingly untainted by his actual Irish-catholic pedigree). It was most obvious after Lydon left on tracks like 'Friggin' In The Riggin', sung by Steve Jones, but the original line-up were certainly the most humorous of the first wave bands. Viewed today, the 'shocking' Bill Grundy interview is little more than four working class blokes making fun of a 'right old toff'.

The musicologist John Potter rejects the relevance of elements of vocalising in punk, saying; 'The determinedly working-class enunciation of punk singers in the 1970s was more to do with image and the perception of audiences, than with the class factors which seemed to be implied by the accents used.

'Although many punk singers were from working-class backgrounds, the basic punk concept was dreamt up by Vivienne West-

wood and Malcolm McClaren as a set of fashion icons which happened to draw on working-class symbolism (and other, in fashion terms, 'deviant sources').'[4]

This view however is far too simplistic and dismisses the essential and myriad circumstances that led to 'punk' (as both a style of music and a social upheaval) taking hold. Although the input of McLaren and Westwood is often now dismissed out of hand, not least because of Lydon's own retelling of the circumstances, there can be no doubt they had a significant impact on both the commercial and visual aspects of the era. But to credit these characters with much more than that, and to propose, as Potter does, that punk characteristics as removed from their remit as vocal styles were somehow part of Malc and Viv's master-plan, verges on the ridiculous.

What cannot be denied is Lydon's central roll in much of punk's development. As Mary Harron wrote at the time, he was in 'the middle of that spinning disc'. And he fitted the punk stereotype like no one else around. He was working-class, he was raw, and angry, and poor. He was also ambitious. Interestingly, he has been spoken about in a similar vein to the young Dylan, as a man 'hungry' for ideas, soaking up everything and anything he could. Taking whatever he needed from wherever he could find it.

Whether the vocal style he created for himself was the result of a conscious decision making process is doubtful, but his initial impulses when first asked to vocalise came from somewhere. Taking from his own speech patterns (with help perhaps from a half-remembered refrain by Captain Beefheart or Iggy Pop), stylising these, finding a way of expressing them alongside the musical accompaniment, this was his and his alone. Malcolm McClaren did not create 'John Lydon – Singer' anymore than he created 'John Lydon – Thinker' – or even 'John Lydon – Sex Pistol'. To be fair however, while he has often been known to take credit for much he had little influence on, I'm not aware even *he* had the front to claim victory for John Lydon being voted amongst the 'top 30 vocalists in pop' by the writers of *Mojo*.

Moments of creation cannot be separated from individuals; the times and places of their origin all play their part. London in the heat-waves of the early 70s, Britain politically and socially at that time, Lydon's own sickly childhood and need to be recognised, honoured, seen and heard, all have played their part in the makeup of his performances.

Paul Cook spoke of John's 'audition' for the Pistols at McClaren's King's Road boutique, *Sex*.

'...he came round the shop the next day. Malcolm had the jukebox there and we said, "What can you do?". We put on Alice Cooper's 'Eighteen' and said, "Go on, sing." he just went into an act in front of the jukebox, going into spasms. This was late at night, about one in the morning. He wailed and screamed. I was in stitches. I thought, yeah, he's great. We said, "Come down. We'll try it out". That's basically how it happened. That's how we met him. Malcolm didn't really know what to make of Johnny's act, but we knew we needed a front-man.'[5]

Tona De Brett told me she often found herself, when discussing prospective vocal tuition for a new band's singer with a record company, enquiring whether it was just the sound of the voice that was important or if the entire image or 'package' was the real objective. On some occasions, the company would take 'a long time replying'.

John Lydon came to be a vocalist by having the visual, physical and emotional charge to be chosen as front man for The Sex Pistols. He developed the sound to go with that, quickly and, if not efficiently by traditional confines, then certainly by punk standards, drawing from every possible inspiration.

And out of that came, surely, the most significant, creative and, in retrospect, iconic vocalising that that genre and period had to offer. It's certainly legitimate to criticise much subsequent punk vocalising as impotent rage and callowness. But Lydon is innocent in this regard by means of his character and his honesty. While this style was aped to death, it was rarely, if ever, replicated.

Pop music opened the door for people, driven by the need to communicate, who would never have been regarded as great singers but who had great voices; punk re-established that field of opportunity. John Lydon's voice communicates in spades. If in doubt, go back and listen again to those records. Listen to him jump out of the speakers like a ravening animal; eccentric, intelligent and above all, alive.

1. Markwowitz, Robin, 1998, 'The Grain Of The Voice' essay posted on Rants 'N' Raves Bulletin Board, Cultural Studies Central Bulletin Board, http://www.culturalstudies.net
2. Frith, Simon, 1996, Performing Rites. On The Value of Popular Music, *Oxford University Press, pp159.*
3. ibid, pp186
4. Potter, John, 1998, Vocal Authority, Singing Style & Ideology, *Cambridge University Press, pp 153*
5. Paul Cook quoted in Colgrave, Stephen and Sullivan, Chris, 2001 Punk, *Cassell Illustrated, pp98*

My thanks to Tona De Brett for her contribution to this essay, Tona is a highly respected vocal tutor and writer and can be contacted at www.tonadebrett.co.uk

Barb Jungr

Barb Jungr is a vocalist, performer and recording artist. She also writes, broadcasts and lectures extensively on the subjects of vocal technique and singing. She is the co-author of the highly respected *Woman: The Incredible Life Of Yoko Ono* (Chrome Dreams, 2004). Barb is best known for her work in the vocal medium of Chanson – the classical, lyric-driven French form of song. The creator and performer of countless stage productions, she tours furiously and is a member of the female revue *Girl's Talk* with Mari Wilson and Claire Martin. Barb has also released several solo albums, three of which concentrate on covering the music of Bob Dylan, Jacques Brel and 1960s Pop respectively.
More information / tour and record dates www.barbjungr.co.uk

Idiot Dancing:
30 Years Out On The Floor
by Kris Needs

'At least we're not picking spots any more. That's progress for you!'
John Lydon

'I am not a walking history book and should just be judged by what I do, as I do it.' That was John Lydon refusing to retrace the past again when I interviewed him in 1993. Not that I'd asked. Having followed John's actions since he first tossed a mic-stand with the Sex Pistols, that unpredictable, even contradictory approach to life has emerged as his most fascinating personality trait.

In that time, he's gone from persecuted Jubilee disruptor to jungle-loving national treasure, dropping some of the most innovative and challenging music known to man on the way. Always out on his own and often causing a stink, Lydon has become a bottomless well of entertaining moments. As his music has receded, his irrepressible personality, founded on brutal honesty, razor-sharp wit and a knack for uproar, has burst forth on everything from chat shows to bug documentaries. Apart from encountering John on a social basis, I've interviewed him during various stages of his career. From the Sex Pistols at the peak of their notoriety, through PiL albums and onto his colossal excursions in dance music with Afrika Bambaataa and Leftfield. The last time was in 2002 for punk's so-called Silver Jubilee. Or, as John put it, 'My Silver Jubilee'. During these many hours of conversation, much time was spent either feeling frustrated at the world and its injustices or simply laughing my arse off.

It's widely assumed that John Lydon hates the press. Thirty years on, many people still think he hates everybody. The truth is, John has only ever despised fakes and those who've tried to earn a fast buck off his back. He doesn't suffer fools gladly and isn't afraid to speak his mind.

This is not intended to be a detailed account of John Lydon's career or analytical review of his work. Just six encounters at strategic moments where the tape recorder was turned on (for some of it), plus an unexpected footnote.

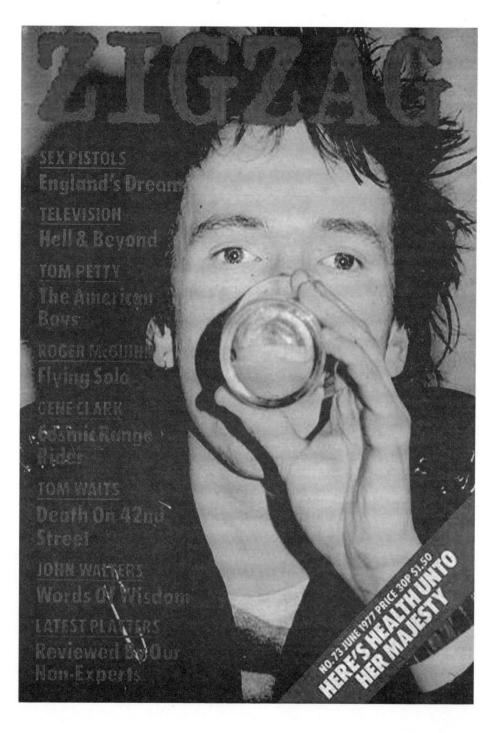

ZIGZAG

SEX PISTOLS
England's Dream

TELEVISION
Hell & Beyond

TOM PETTY
The American
Boys

ROGER McGUINN
Flying Solo

GENE CLARK
Cosmic Range
Rider

TOM WAITS
Death On 42nd
Street

JOHN WALTERS
Words Of Wisdom

LATEST PLATTERS
Reviewed By Our
Non-Experts

NO. 73 JUNE 1977 PRICE 30P $1.50
**HERE'S HEALTH UNTO
HER MAJESTY**

1. Jubilee week, 1977: God Save The Queen

I inevitably ran into John during the rise of punk rock in 1976. We were often at the same gigs, drinking at the same bar. Sometimes his own band was playing. Of course, he was always surrounded by acolytes and hangers-on, but also a gaggle of close mates from Finsbury Park kept his feet on the ground as the Sex Pistols rose to become public enemy number one.

That seemed to happen overnight. When I saw the Sex Pistols at Dunstable's 2,000 capacity Queensway Hall in October '76, there were about 80 people there to apathetically undergo a boomy run-through of their emerging classics. It couldn't take away the impact of John's robotic entrance during 'Anarchy In The UK'. A few weeks later, the Pistols couldn't get a gig at all after the Bill Grundy palaver. Their notoriety went on, stoked by sensationalising tabloids and music papers gripped by the fever of a new movement they still couldn't quite understand.

In 1977, I was editing a magazine called *ZigZag*. It's widely acknowledged as the original fanzine, having been launched by Pete Frame in 1969 with the idea of covering artists who usually got overlooked in the mainstream press. *ZigZag*'s printer-publishers offered to print Malcolm McLaren's one-off *No Future* broadsheet free of charge in return for an exclusive interview with the Sex Pistols. This was at the height of the 'God Save The Queen' controversy and the Queen's Silver Jubilee. Since the Anarchy tour interviews had been few and far between.

You could say I was nervous about interviewing the infamous Johnny Rotten. I was in the same camp, having endured much blinkered abuse for coming in at Frame's invitation and steering *ZigZag* into reporting the new punk movement. But John's reputation preceded him. Would I get the psychotic stare and curt, barbed dismissal reported by other hacks? Or would he be the bloke I'd seen at the bar in Dingwalls or the Roundhouse, guffawing and taking the piss. Obviously I hoped for the latter.

It wasn't a promising start when John stalked into Malcolm McLaren's Glitterbest office, off Oxford Street. 'I'm ill', he croaked, and talked about visiting the doctor. Sid was otherwise engaged, but

Steve and Paul arrived soon after and we set off up Oxford Street. To my relief, John started chatting – about the ban on the single and the whole Pistols' controversy. He was easy to talk to, with no hint of wind-ups or aggression. I just did what I always did in my 'job' as a journalist, which was forget that I was a journalist and concentrate on having the best time possible. That way I'm not nervous and the interviewee can, hopefully, relax. From that moment on, although I never lost sight of what John had achieved and stood for, I regarded him more as a mate and, hopefully, he didn't lumber me with the journalist tag. Since then, I've interviewed him at least six times, so it must have gone okay.

After settling in a booth in the Oxford Street Wimpy Bar, which used to stand on the corner of Hanway Street, John starts in Rotten mode as we talk about how the single crashed into the charts with no help from the BBC, who obviously banned it. They will soon find out that the record was actually kept off the top spot due to the gross embarrassment it would cause in Jubilee week.

'We've proved the BBC don't rule everything,' says Paul Cook.

'Fuckin' good 'n' all,' grunts John. 'They've been doing too much for too long, the fucking BBC. Fucking bullshit. They're just cunts. The single is nothing personal against the Queen. It's what she stands for... a symbol.'

At the time, the Pistols were banned by about every local council in the country after the Bill Grundy show furore poleaxed the Anarchy tour. Regardless of that, the Pistols were always so different to what else was going on at the time – chaotic, threatening, painfully real – that promoters winced anyway.

'It's worse now,' says John. 'It's much harder for us to get a gig now. It's like insurance, health risks, obscenity charges... it's up the wall. In London the only ones we can play now are all-nighters. You have to keep totally underground. You can't publicise them... you

just get raided and God knows what. It's taking off. All those other bands are coming through. As soon as they hear our name they're gonna try and stop us again.'

The Pistols had already had their relationship with EMI scuppered before a short stint with A&M, who got as far as pressing up 'God Save The Queen' before mysteriously dropping them like a hot potato. Ostensibly, this was because of band misbehaviour, but John thought it ran a lot deeper. Why do you think A&M did an about-face so quickly?

'Absolutely no idea. A lot of internal bullshit. Someone was definitely putting the boot in up top for us. They still are.... Christ, they all complained! I thought, "You snobs". (Fellow A&M recording artist and prog-bore) Rick Wakeman sent a telegram about us. How pompous! I mean, there's the most important reason in the world to survive. The fact that an arsehole like him has got the nerve to criticise another form of music. Maybe it's not to his taste, but tough shit. We enjoy doing it and people are listening to it, and surely that's all that counts.'

The furore around the song could only suggest that the Pistols were being used as an example, a scapegoat, by their opposition, presumably in the hope that others wouldn't try and follow.

'Definitely, but we're winning. Whereas in the past any band that has stuck its neck out has always backed down, we haven't. Never will. That's the difference. And just as soon as it gets fucking boring is when I'm going to fucking stop.'

This interview gave rise to the rumour that Glen Matlock was kicked out of the Pistols to be replaced by John's old mate, Sid Vicious, because Matlock liked The Beatles. It wasn't as cut and dried as that, as John explained. 'It just got a bit too much in the end. He hated our guts with a passion, really hated us. I can carry on working with someone who hates me as long as there's some kind of respect for musical ideas. He hated everything we had ever done, thought it was too strong. Heavy, like. He wanted it to be watered down, like The Beatles. When "Anarchy" came out, he hated it. We can't carry on with an arsehole like that.' He added, that Sid was fitting in, 'very well... You see, he ain't so bloody serious about it. Music's meant to be fun, not like some crass music machine. That's what Glen wanted.'

I wondered what John wanted to change the most.

'The way it's all business manipulated like the way a record company literally buys a band and then tells them what to do and the silly arseholes do it and the public don't even bother to question it. That's factory fodder.'

You want people to question things?

'Yeah. When we started everybody questioned us. They thought we were a big hype. There was one rumour going around we were already signed to EMI before we started. That was great. At least we've got people questioning things. That's what counts. Whether they come to the wrong conclusion or not is their business. I don't really care, cos I know what's either right or wrong. My point of view. But at least you should try. You don't need a music degree

VIBES 2

BURY'S MUSIC MAGAZINE

FAST BREEDER

FANZINES

MOTORHEAD

SeX PISTOLS competition win an EMI copy of 'ANARCHY'!!

GONG

THE NOSEBLEEDS

10P.

or 20 A levels or a far-out musical university. That's not what it's about at all.

'Everyone seems to think it's inevitable we'll end up with Rolls Royces and mansions in the country, but if you look back on your (puts on academic voice) "rock history", only one generation has done that (the mid to late 60s superstars). They managed to live quite successfully before, even though half of them killed themselves one way or another. But, I mean, so what? They had some fun.

'It's nowhere near us, the 60s. We're nothing to do with them. They had it easy. They were brought up to think that was what it was all about. In that respect, we've learnt a hell of a lot off of those bands. How not to be, how not to do it. It's not about that at all. Yeah, we've gone around in a limousine once or twice, but I couldn't tell you the difference between that and a Mini Cooper. I just don't like those big cars at all. I think they're dreadful... like houses.'

What about the people who say they're too old to appreciate what you play?

'I think it's ridiculous. What kind of attitude is that? That's a cop-out. It's not how old you are anyway. It really means they've given up thinking, which is absolutely obscene.'

Even then, John was seeing beyond punk and it's own burgeoning book of rules and regulations. 'We get just about everybody at our gigs. All different kinds, which is how it should be. That's why we started. We've had Hells Angels turning up at our gigs and all they do is dance at the back.'

Unrest was already simmering within the ranks of the punks themselves. Punk was supposed to be about disruption, to think for yourself and make changes in a positive direction. Once present and correct in leather-and-spikes uniform, newcomers seemed to possess just as much narrow-minded intolerance as those who put punks down. This usually came from the more sheep-like factions who had probably picked it up as a trend from the latest tabloid report. If the truth be known, there was often more prejudice from punks against people who weren't into it than the other way round.

'Yeah!' agrees John. 'They're probably worse. They're more con-descending in their attitude, which is what pisses me off. They think you have to turn up in certain gear. They don't realise how stupid and juvenile they are. It's not about what you wear, it's what you are that counts.'

That last line was hoisted out of the feature and used as a headline by a music paper reporting on the state of punk and its image. John had just put his cards on the table. Punk meant you could do anything and attitude counted much more than Kings Road threads. He would reinforce that philosophy time and time again.

'Fucking hell, the other week I decided to go around as a teddy boy, and did. The amount of people who were shocked that I'd sold out. Pathetic. It's ridiculous. The idea would be like for all sections to just join up in one big huge mob, and understand it as music and not just as a gang warfare weapon... the great separation technique.'

John was also not amused by punk's trendiness factor, which saw last year's Bryan Ferry imitators leaping on the bandwagon. This not only applied to the image but – particularly – the music.

'Sure, now it's us, which is ridiculous. The whole idea of our band was not to have 30,000 imitators but 30,000 different attitudes in music. I'm surprised that we even had to begin for people to re-alise what was happening to them. Half the new bands are no better than the old bands, really, in their attitude. Nothing's really changed that much, which is bad.'

John never much rated the Class of '76, especially the ones who sang about, 'how terrible it is to be on the dole'.

'It's complete crap. Nonsense. It's not terrible to be on the dole. It's jolly good fun being paid for doing nothing.' That day, John ad-mitted that he found The Clash's attitude 'confusing', but added, 'A lot of people have fun going to see them. That's what it's all about.' He dismissed The Damned as being like, 'a very dirty version of the Bay City Rollers', and confessed to liking The Slits, The Adverts and Buzzcocks.

John's large, eclectic record collection would later become re-nowned. 'I have thousands of records. It's my... uh... hobby. I've just about everything. I love all music, full stop. Shakin' Stevens & The Sunsets – I saw them the other night. They were great. Fuckin' good singer. That was a teddy boys' night but no one touched me.' The first the world got to know about John's eclectic musical adolescence was the legendary Capital Radio appearance where he played his favourite records by artists like Can, Peter Hammill, Tim Buckley and Captain Beefheart, along with much reggae.

Every interview I've done with John Lydon has devoted some time on the subject of the press who, it has to be said, seem to have had it in for him ever since he set foot on a stage in late 1975. At this time, the Pistols had only been gigging for just over six months and had already received a barrage of slag-offs, apart from the few who knew that they were changing the course of music. Minor incidents were exaggerated and private lives poked and sensationalised to entertain the masses whose breakfast reading, or indeed lives, needed livening up. The Sex Pistols were a godsend for the tabloids who, in the process of their concerned warning reports, succeeded in making them a household name. That day, John's eyes sharpened into black lasers as he condemned both press and believing public with cold, hissing contempt.

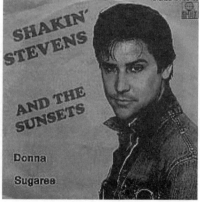

'I have never believed the national press and I'm surprised a lot of people did. The gullibility of the British public is excessive. They're just ridiculous. They make me sick. I can't believe people are so naive.'

The music press didn't fare any better. 'I think they're worse parasites than the nationals! They're scandal seekers. They love to build people up and then destroy them. They take out all their paranoia on groups. It's ridiculous.

'Ever since we first started, there's always been a cynical bastard in the press going, "No, no, it can never take off, you need the press, blah, blah". We've proved them all wrong. They didn't wanna change. They liked it easy. Their free LPs and tickets to New York to see some band. We're not gonna do all that.

'We never plan our future. Never. That really is a negative thing to do ten years in advance. The songs we write change all the time. Like attitudes change. Not permanently. I mean, I might completely change my mind tomorrow, hate everything or like everything. That's the way you should live.'

True to his words, everything would change for John, probably more than he could have imagined that day in the Wimpy Bar. Early 1978 would see the Pistols disintegrate at the end of their kamikaze first US tour. The whole experience with the Sex Pistols changed Lydon, sending him into an extreme form of counteraction. He wouldn't play rock 'n' roll for years, or kowtow to its accompanying rituals ever again unless it suited him. Two years in the Pistols supernova hardened him for life.

2. 1979: *Metal Box*

Barely pausing to lick his wounds after the Pistols played their final gig at San Francisco's Winterland in January '78, John roped in old mates Jah Wobble and Keith Levene, who Lydon had met when Levene's old band The Clash supported the Pistols in '76. By the end of the year, Public Image Limited had released their first album.

I loved that album, especially the churning, slow-motion rage of 'Theme', stinging bile of 'Religion' and motorik disco revels of 'Fodderstompf'. But it befuddled and enraged many, especially those looking for regurgitated Pistols. Especially the press. John had all but abandoned his familiar sneer and was now intent on bending his voice from tortured highs to menacing lows and most points in between. Levene disgorged a spectacular sheet metal wall of guitar psychosis, while Wobble's dubwise earthquake remains the most bowel-movingly compelling bass sound in music history. Somehow, Canadian drummer Jim Walker managed to underpin all this with a deft funk attack somewhat reminiscent of Can's Jaki Liebeziht. I wrote in *ZigZag*, 'PiL have already got their own sound and this album has moments as biting as any Pistols song. No resting on laurels. No waste.'

ZigZag itself underwent a temporary setback when its publishers went bust in mid-1979. The comeback issue planned for that Christmas was already laid out with a world exclusive preview of The Clash's new *London Calling* album. Then came a call from the Public Image Ltd camp. They had finished their second album but didn't want to be stitched up. They trusted *ZigZag* after a lengthy interview by Robin Banks, which had accompanied the first PiL album, plus my album review had been just about the only positive one they got. In May, I'd been granted an early press copy of 'Death Disco', the jaw-dropping first single off the next album. That had moved into a different gear altogether, especially when one of your other favourite groups is Chic. John's mum had died and his screaming over Keith's adaptation of 'Swan Lake' and Wobble's nuclear fever funk was amazingly gripping. They'd followed this with the acrobatic mixing desk shenanigans of 'Memories'. PiL were gaining a frightening head of steam but also coming in for lots of flak. I wasn't having any of that. There was nobody operating anywhere remotely near them, except the New York band Suicide.

So it was I found myself on a Friday night in Chelsea, looking for an address in Gunter Grove off the Kings Road. As I located the relevant steel-plated door, it swung open and down the steps bowled a familiar figure clad in big, furry red coat. 'Hello, coming down the

offo'? I'm going to get my supplies,' is John Lydon's opening greet-
ing. I wouldn't emerge for another 18 hours.

'I do like talking, it gives me something to do,' declares John as
we settle on a mattress in his room to watch TV. The conversation
flows like the lager and, before long, we're heading downstairs to
hear the new album. The historical nature of this night wouldn't hit
home until years later when *Metal Box* started being hailed as one
of the most influential albums of all time. That night in Chelsea, I
just thought the music which John, Keith Levene and Jeanette Lee
were blasting at me from the monolithic front room speakers was
some of the most startlingly innovative I'd ever heard in my life.
Seismic, provocative and out there, the album showed that humour,
dancing, menace and serious sonic experimentation could all pulse
together. Gloriously.

Right now, John Lydon was on top of his game. What he was up
to with PiL was genuinely groundbreaking and indeed truer to the
original punk ethic than any of the groups hell bent on still copy-
ing his old band. PiL was trying to find new, interesting ways of
doing things, whether it be packaging, the music, gig presentation,
even press interviews. John has never been less than totally honest
– again, about how he feels at that particular time. In late '79, he

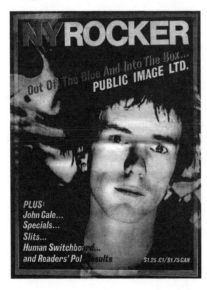

was still smarting from the way the Pistols had imploded and was pissed off with standard music biz procedure. He hated the imitators and wanted to get as far away from conventional rock 'n' roll as possible.

That night, John was excited. 'We started immediately after the last album, and recorded it on and off. Lots has been thrown out. We don't just go into the studio to record a track. We go there to learn stuff to fucking progress, know what's happening, generally mess about with sound and anything else... If we weren't given a release date on *Metal Box* we'd still be making it. It'd come out eventually like a fuckin' encyclopaedia! Would have been a laugh but that is going too far'.

Metal Box first strikingly appeared as three twelve-inch singles packaged in an embossed metal tin. This had been expensive for the group, who had to put up £35,000 of their own advance to pay for it (Each tin cost 75p to make and Virgin would only do 50,000). 'It's simple. Twelve-inches have a better sound quality. You can go mad, and get it all on plastic without distortion and racket. It's just sense. You put it out in the way you think it will sound best.. It's not an album anyway. It's a tin of material. If we're gonna be extra-technical, *à la* Virgin, it could be counted as a double album. It's definitely the length of a double album.

'It was being bored with the way albums are continually thrown out. The same fucking shape and format forever and a day. You go back 25 years. They're still the same. Nothing's changed and it has to.'

After the bold opening statement of the first album and unorthodox PiL approach to gigs and TV shows, John was painfully aware that there was always a bunch of cynical snipers in the undergrowth waiting to shoot him down.

'Fine. Anyway you look at it I'm entertaining them then. Look, if we're so god damn fucking awful and have no place in society as we know it today, etcetera, why can't these bastards not keep mentioning us? There always has to be a dig.'

What's causing the fuss at the moment – the tin?

'Well look, we're not making fuss over it. We're not throwing it in your face and going, "Oh look, what a glorious product!" Fuck all that shit. Look at your average music journalist, right? Ninety-nine per cent of them are pissheads. Spoilt brats. They get free gifts almost continuously. "We know it all, we've seen it all". They get very cynical. Ultimately, they're dictated to by their editors, who're ultimately dictated to by their publisher or whatever. If they don't do whatever record companies want them to then they won't have their adverts, and adverts dictate, do they not?'

PiL's disdain for the press manifested itself when they insisted the press pay for review copies (although I was quite happy to receive mine in the post one day with a PiL sticker on the package). 'You gotta fight those bastards,' glowered John. 'Us in the band see no one else doing the same. No one's standing up for their rights. They're all wankers trying to be pop stars or whatever. It ain't on, is it?

'See, it's not like the Pistols or any of that because we're just going above the media. It's a way away from how things have been done for God knows how many years. We're not looking for slavish idolisation. Did I not tell the world right from the start that I didn't wanna be a star? Have I not followed my beliefs? Where have I changed?'

When *Metal Box* appeared, Virgin were also releasing Pistols barrel-scrapers, like hits collections and live albums. Despite PiL's future visions, the past still seemed to colour everything John did.

'Yeah, the past they weren't involved in. I'm afraid I don't live in history books. We're trying to write the next chapter not 'look back' pages. That's the way the whole music business has been manoeuvred. You have to have an image, ready packaged. You have to have your promotion ready, your gigs, your interviews, etcetera. Now why can't a band just say, "Bollocks, fuck all that, we'll do something else for once", not what it has been, not follow the format. That's why they have to live in the past. It's easier that way.'

You've been called self-indulgent.

'More like self-respect. Look, the fact that you walk on(to) a stage is self-indulgence because you must feel yourself to be important to be there. And what's wrong with that anyway? What's wrong with being proud about yourself? Is it not worse to have your pictures plastered all over the place in nice poses? Is that not a worse scheme of things?

'It's always been that toerags like us could never do what we're doing. It's always been for the university boys. You know what I mean? They don't like the yobbos to take over. They don't like that at all.'

The interview with John and Keith went on all night. John would disappear every so often to reappear in a different jacket, intersperse blasts of the new album with chest-caving dub and keep up a running line of banter, one-liners and the occasional anecdote. It seemed perfectly natural to sit cackling through berserk Saturday morning kids' show *Tiswas* for two hours after all this.

3. 1981: The Flowers Of Romance

The third PiL album was *Flowers Of Romance*. I remembered the name as a loose band which Keith, Sid Vicious, occasional journalist Steve Walsh and Viv Albertine (later of The Slits) toyed with in late '76/early '77. Recorded in October to November 1980, the album was again like nothing PiL had done before and certainly not like anybody else. Over a year had elapsed since *Metal Box*. In mid-1980, Wobble had moved on to a solo career, taking some old backing tracks with him. He later formed an improvisational group with Jim Walker called The Human Condition (who I tour-managed in '81, resulting in a fractured skull after a 5am fall down a

ZigZag

April 81 No 112 0p/ $2.00

Dancing Did they did didn't they
Red Rhino inhabit the ?
Adam in colour
ANOTHER Pretty Face
Lyn Seymour, Maggie
Be Smart and Glam
Slymer K ALIENATION
P.I.L Blossom
readers poll, your bonce
Sector 27 & a message
SCREAMING lord sutch
VARDIS
Fleshtones from USA
STRANGLERS not just in black
Misty BLACK & BLUE
Martian Dance; ANT

& MORE

Dutch staircase). Unfortunately, there was some acrimony between the two camps which lasted for years.

Keith had all but packed away his guitar. Instead, using Martin Atkins as stand-in drummer, carrying out experiments with 'found' sounds on odd instruments like violins and even a broken banjo, adding subtle synthesiser embellishments and... not much else except the drums. Ah yes, the drums! Pared down but pumped up to their most primitive and powerful, whether tribal-flavoured, metronomic or simply like having a door slammed in your face.

If PiL were stretching the standard voice-bass-guitar-drums format outside and beyond its rock 'n' roll framework before, this album saw them discard that format completely and dive into a new sound which was mainly acoustic source-wise but massively heavy in reproduction. Skeletal, experimental and spaced-out. Around this time, tribal rhythms had sprang to prominence with the Bow Wow Wow/Adam Ant crew. But next to this mighty surge they sounded like grannies knitting along to Gary Glitter. Lydon, Levine and Jeanette Lee, who was now a high-profile member of the group, spent much time creating a drum sound which was boomy and crunching, down to resonance and harmonic overload. My notes at the time said PiL's drums sound like they're ten foot wide and hit with sledgehamers. A gut reaction to limp syndrum popping of the time?

It was strong and uncluttered, leaving John to further experiment with a unique vocal delivery which ranged from wailing from a Mosque in 'Four Enclosed Walls' to dryly taking the piss out of sex on 'Track 8'. John's voice is set back on most of the album, sometimes sounding like a cheeky gnat with a loud-hailer. He bows the bass on the album's title track, which also came out as a single, resulting in a memorable *Top Of The Pops* appearance where John sported a vicar's dog-collar. In the pantomime age of the New Romantics, where synthed-up Alvin Stardusts bellowed like drowning hippos, PiL had come up with another far-reaching, visionary – and natural sounding – racket. It was about the furthest out they'd go. Predictably, it went over most people's heads.

The interview took place in March in the boardroom of Virgin's Portobello Road HQ. It's the same trio as before – John, Keith and

Jeanette. Red Stripe makes a return appearance too. The mood is slightly different as we're gathered on enemy territory – i.e. the record company. PiL are now well and truly going where few have gone before (although there were now PiL imitators too. That could be pretty dire but up in Glasgow Bobby Gillespie was trying to start a group with himself banging on the *Metal Box* tin for drums).

'It's a very cut-and-dried album,' explained Keith. 'It's like, "This is PiL now". Boomf. We're never gonna sound like this again.'

'One thing I'm pleased about with this album is that we used instruments – not because they're instruments but because they have effects on ya,' added John. 'Sounds that make you feel certain things, like they were perfectly in tune with the song. That I like.

'We didn't wanna make another *Metal Box*. We've done that sound to death. Now it's up to the imitators to continue it, as they are doing. Reaping the praise for their efforts!'

Apart from the ridiculous cavortings of the New Romantics, there was another movement, sparked off the back of PiL's endeavours, which pushed another Year Zero 'new music' kind of ethic. Much of it was highly pretentious. One term used was 'futurism'.

'We're the only band that deserves that title,' snorted John. 'All the rest are electric teapots. Spandau Ballet! Have you heard their album? Ah, they're great! Worse than the Bay City Rollers could ever hope to be! Amateur hour! Stuff like jamming at rehearsals which you'd chuck out and wouldn't consider putting on to plastic. To them that's a *tour de force*! That's fine if people want sub-standard crap.'

Adam & The Ants' brand of tribal teenybop also got short shrift from Lydon.

'They're misusing the word tribal. I dunno what they're up to, but if Adam & The Ants think they've got a tribal feel and they use two drummers for that feeble tin can noise, which is impossible to dance to, then I'm sorry, that's just not good enough. It might be for some but it isn't for me.'

In this interview, John and – especially – Keith spent a lot of time talking about how they constructed the music on *Flowers Of Romance*, especially those drums. They were obviously very into it. This made the constant sniping at the group's approach all the more frustrating. Many still thought that John was still playing an extended, self-indulgent joke with PiL. To which he replied: 'If we are a bunch of pranksters, it's a very expensive joke we're running here... Trouble is with this kind of stuff, it's very boring for your average reader. They don't want to know. It's not a glorious world of having your picture taken, fantastic interviews and alcohol binges around the universe. It's not like that at all.'

At this point, PiL expressed a desire to move into films, but cash was not forthcoming, especially from the record company. Richard Branson was only willing to open his wallet for a Pistols reunion. 'I want some money but I'm not prepared to join the fucking professionals to make it,' says John, referring to Jones and Cook's current outfit. 'Begging me to join Steve and Paul! Fucking true.'

'Then we're talking about a different project – money, cars, Las Vegas, everything we want,' adds Keith.

'And boredom,' continues John. 'Two steps backwards. I want my fortune on my own terms, thank you very much.'

The original PiL did have lofty ambitions, but it could never work due to a combination of lack of financial backing, public apathy, drug abuse and, most crucially, the collective falling apart leaving John to go it alone with a succession of collaborators. Every group has its classic line-up, and PiL's was actually Lydon, Levene and Wobble. John wouldn't work in such a strong group structure again, but another purple patch was coming up.

4. 1986: World Destruction & Rise

Nearly five years had elapsed when we met again in an interview capacity. In that time, PiL had started a riot at New York's Ritz and what finally emerged as the *This Is What You Want, This Is What You Get* album had precipitated Keith Levene's departure. The final breakdown of the original PiL collective was a confused affair involving a bootleg version of the original tracks with Levene. This now left John in complete control. Twice bitten, thrice shy, he had collared Martin Atkins to bring the released version home. The end result was a confused but compulsive album which

Afrika Bambaataa

yielded the anthemesque 'This Is Not A Love Song' and brilliantly tense 'Bad Life'. In '83, John had led a cabaret pick-up band for a while, and starred with Harvey Keitel in a taut psycho-thriller called *Order Of Death*.

His most impressive venture of this time was a collaboration called 'World Destruction', which saw him trading vehemently-ominous nuclear warnings with godfather of hip-hop, Afrika Bambaataa, founder of the Zulu Nation. This was produced by NY avant-funk innovator Bill Laswell and released on his Celluloid label under the name Timezone in December '84. Laswell remains one of the great musical boundary detonators who, in the first half of the 80s, managed to leap between the proto-hip-hop of New York's Last Poets, future-shock electro of Herbie Hancock and African artists like Manu Dubango. 'World Destruction', with its massive guitar-lurch beatbox slam, reinforced the already existing theory that Lydon didn't make his first inroads into dance music with 'Open Up'. One of the most effective collisions of rock and black music to date, it predated the gestating Run DMC/Beastie Boys rock-rap interface and could be heard howling out of NY's black radio stations.

'Bambaataa wanted to make a record with me,' explained John. 'He did one with James Brown – you know, people that he likes in the business for their energies I suppose. He got Laswell to produce it and we got on alright in the studio. He only works on what he wants to work on. Bill has no social life at all, other than his work. I do like these obsessive characters. They're very healthy.'

Lydon's estimation of Laswell was further boosted by the fact that 'he drinks like I've never seen anybody drink! Just never stops and it never knocks spots off him ever. He's relentless! He made me feel like a rank amateur and I'm pretty lethal on the stuff, but God Almighty! He's got more than one hollow leg, that's for sure. He'll drink anything! In the studio, because you're so tense and nervous, I suppose you don't get all that drunk because your adrenalin is so high. The alcohol doesn't kick in at all.'

The Laswell connection resulted in *Album*, a heavyweight immersion in raging guitars, indeed 'rock', with John at his most direct and insurgent. Seemingly out of nowhere, he started his second decade in music with a blazing, lapel-shaking statement. It was as if he was strategically taking a metaphysical dump on those of little imagination who chose to 'celebrate' punk rock's tenth birthday by putting him down as some rich loafer resting on his laurels. This became John's re-entry into the mainstream music biz with the artier PiL ideals out of the window.

Writing in *ZigZag*, I commented that, 'Once again, John Lydon has proved, rather effortlessly, that he's still out on his own, still "has it" and nothing has dulled his spark into a page in the history books. This would be a much greyer place without his periodical forays.' As he'd said back in '79, he was indeed writing the next chapter. It still made intriguing reading. We needed *Album* in 1986. It reared up, 'like a malevolent lobster and crunched our testicles in rampant iron claws,' wrote yours truly for some reason. Rampant power, Eastern modes, hypnotic mantras and wildly accessible songs, delivered with John's singeing whine cutting through the dense bombast; proud, prodding and protesting.

Lydon seemed to realise that the only person he could trust was himself, and he was now in a position to go where he pleased as new generations discovered the Pistols and early PiL. He delighted in calling the shots and kicking against the pricks. In mid-'84, he relocated to a beach house in Malibu, California, where he would happily relax with wife Nora and watch his 50 TV channels.

The interview took place at John's then-management office on Notting Hill Gate. He was sporting dreadlocks held aloft by hair-

grips and a natty, baggy suit completed by old school tie. Again fuelled by a carrier bag of Red Stripe, we seemed to pick up where we left off last time. Since then, I'd encountered Lydon several times, including a bizarre small-world encounter at Newark Airport where I'd missed a plane to LA and he was en route to Boston.

I realised that this was the first time I'd ever interviewed him on his own. He's on fine form, with his humour veering more in the direction of the toilet than usual, even if I had seen him the night before on the sesh at a Big Audio Dynamite gig. John's always had a thing about spots and starts playing with a zit. 'God, I'm squeezing the spots out! I was so hungry last night when I got home, the only thing in the fridge was a tin of double-whipped cream and spring onion! Ha ha! So the farts and the spots and the belches and the stink is running right rancid today!' he declares proudly, before letting fly with the manic giggle which would become more familiar as the years went by. Not to mention a few well-placed farts and belches.

In January 1987, John and the other Pistols collected a settlement of around a million pounds from Malcolm McLaren, as well as the right to use the Sex Pistols name if they so desired. John savoured the court hearing. 'I enjoyed myself. I really, really wanted to get into that box. I'd been worrying about it for months and months and the moment had come... and Malcolm settled! Boo hoo hoo!' Mock-burying his head in his hands, he then declares, 'Because it would have been his turn after me. Then the fun would begin. I mean, what you gonna say against me? I haven't told a single lie. He turned up in knickerbockers and a barrister's blue long-flowing mac-type thing. He looked just stupid – and there'll be wallies in a few months wearing exactly that!'

John had turned 30 the previous January. Now he was as old, rich and famous as the rock stars he set out to dynamite from their pedestals ten years earlier. But his targets had changed to a whole new bloated herd, poncing about on yachts and producing spineless, crashing synth durges for expensive videos. A new breed equally as deserving of the withering stare and venomous oration as the old targets. If not more. The UK was in the grip of a post-New Romantic pop vacuum with A-Ha riding high, along with Nana Mouskouri. Like the dull calm before punk, this was the lull before acid house, due to arrive shortly from Chicago.

Originally, 'Rise' was to be called 'Single' because, like *Album*, that's what it was. The marketing plan was stating the obvious so as to give no clues to content or foster any preconceptions. This so confused dealers that a hasty 'proper name' had to be tacked on at the last minute.

'I hate that,' glowers John. 'Why should I give it a name? That's what it is. A single, but it confused too many people.' But 'Rise' made it on to radio and subsequently rose up the charts.

'Stunning stuff! I'd love to sit here and lie and say, "Yes, it's all part of my devious campaign to manipulate the world", but it hasn't been that way. It's not as if we need Virgin this time around to do anything at all. The record was liked by the radio before it was even released.' Probably all the more satisfying because the lyrics were based on a South African interrogation manual.

'I have to go to the toilet. I'm dying!' John disappears for a while then returns complaining that someone left the window open. Cue further lavatory banter. 'We talked about this before. I remember. I've given up meat. I found it made me sick a lot. I think I'm actually allergic to it. Red meat anyway. It works against you. I haven't looked back to a toilet since. I remember those meaty shits! God, sitting there for hours trying to squeeze it out. Oh ho ho! No thanks! Bye bye! Who needs the past?'

Yes, the toilet section of the interview. 'It's much more interesting. I'm sure there's chaps there who wonder why they've got all kinds of weird illnesses. Diet, boys and girls. Honest! B-U-R-P!'

It's more fun to talk about shit.

'We have done so far – the music business, journalism, It's a natural progression!'

We start talking about the one thing which John feels journalists always put last on the list: music. Particularly Captain Beefheart, then recently retired from music, is one of the few artists who John would label a genius.

'It definitely applies,' he says, getting serious for a moment. 'When you think of things like *Trout Mask Replica* – absolutely superb! When I first got that I laughed all the way through. I thought it was hysterical. The nerve of the man! It's really very bloody brilliant – one of my relentless pursuits of pleasure. That and *Fun House* by Iggy stand the test of time, without a doubt. It looks like Beefheart's given up completely. He's made his own world and he's quite happy in it.'

Captain Beefheart never followed any formula on any two albums, like other Lydon favourite Tim Buckley. Neither did PiL. There was always an element of surprise in what Johnny did next.

'But I don't do it deliberately that way. It just tends to be like that. I've never made any two records that sound even similar. That's the way it should be, I think. I don't run out of ideas. I enjoy myself. (*Dramatic voice*) "They were all waiting for the surprise. They all thought they knew what it would be". I don't do things just to shock them. I don't care. I do it to entertain myself and then if Joe Public likes it, fine. Takes me a long time to make an album too. I want it to be completely correct.

'We were working on this one for about two years, me and the live band, but I couldn't really use them in the studio because they're too young and it would have put the cost up a lot, a hell of a lot. So, if you're going to use session people then go for the absolute best. Go to the extreme.' Japanese composer Ryuichi Sakomoto, former Zappa guitar cohort Steve Vai, Shankar on violin with Laswell playing bass. The big surprise was the presence on drums of the mighty Ginger Baker, the polyrhythmic powerhouse who drove the Graham Bond Organisation, Cream, Blind Faith and Airforce.

'My April Fool joke finally backfired on me!' said John, refer- ring to a snippet he placed in *NME* claiming that Baker had joined PiL. 'No, he was fine. I was dreading it a little, everybody was, but we sat down and thought about it and what a good hoot it would be. He just goes in and does it. No pretentious nonsense.'

And he's a maniac, which helps.

'Yes, he is completely bonkers.'

Mention of the potshots about Baker being part of the old guard prodded Lydon into another anti-press tirade. Most didn't know that he had worked to further the cause of African music for years.

'Yes, he has, and not a lot of people in the music business realise that, particularly some of those silly journalists who don't know nothing about it and have condemned him outright without consid- ering anything. He introduced African music to the Western world. Without a doubt he is the man responsible. We're talking 15 years back! Do you remember that video he did? In a landrover with his drumkit. He'd literally drive from village to village, set up and play! That's a fantastic piece of braveness! Africa's pretty backward but 15 years ago it was a hell of a lot worse. He's just a really nice Cockney chap.'

Steve Vai   *Ginger Baker*

Lydon's scathing about the new pop hierarchy. 'It's foolish. Stupid. It wouldn't be half as bad if that wasn't all there was, but because that is all there is, it's quite nasty. There's no alternative, so fuck it...

'There's no energy left in anything. It's all become really bland. I've missed that ferocious guitar energy in music now for some time. The emphasis these days seems to be on wimped-out keyboards where nail varnish is more important than talent. To hell with that!

'I do view myself as an ongoing force. I'm sorry, I'm not going to do a Spandau Ballet and take the record company to court because the thing didn't sell. "It's your fault!" Is that basically what the situation was with them?'

They said they hadn't been promoted properly. In other words, they weren't as successful as they thought they should be. I knew he'd like this one.

'Well, that's really tragic! That's treating the human race as sheep. If they don't baaah and bleat to your whistle... Well, they're not very good, are they? Let's be honest, it was shocking!'

They should've just played the record in court.

'Your honour, just hear the damn thing! I rest my case. Heh heh heh!'

This particular meeting with John was more of a comedy session, peppered with the odd point. Maybe it was a gut reaction against the recent bunch of austere interrogations performed by over-illustrious hacks trying to conjure the ghost of Rotten by pretentious provocation, raking up an over-documented past or telling him he'd sold out. The overall impression was that John was a happy man, now firmly on the path that has taken him to his current position of larger-than-life personality and a complete natural. The manic giggle follows most statements, but bile still rises like he's a human thermometer at any mention of the press.

'They're wallies. "What kind of car do you have now, John?" "Well, cufflinks are in!" Heh heh heh!...The standard of journalism is really low. There's no qualifications required. All these people set themselves up as geniuses and don't actually do anything except write about other people's work. It's evil and wrong and lazy of them. Parasites. If they're gonna complain, please offer an alternative. That's their stance. Then they condemn that to death too, so nothing stands the vaguest hope. You can never do it right, according to them. No matter what. Always zero out of ten.'

They always have and always will ask what happened in 1976. (And I was making this observation in 1986!)

'Yeah, without understanding it too. That's the shame and the tragedy of it. It's important to explain to people because they can look at it without a prejudicial point of view and they're totally willing to believe that I'm totally sold out because they've read all this bad literature about "those days" and taken it all as fact. Them as journalists should realise that the written word is a lie! (To quote from 'Rise'). It's the business you're in, Kris! Your colleagues out there are of dubious character, most of them. I've made no beefs about my disgust with them, have I?'

No, in fact they print it (Paul Morley – 'he's in twouble!' – had actually just ran a vociferous putdown of himself by Lydon in the stitch-up he attempted in *NME*).

'I know, I know! It's taken me ten years to get them to finally print that kind of stuff when I've been telling them all the time.'

That year, a record company boss talked me into the bright idea of making some of my interviews available to the public on vinyl. First one was this chat with John. The only problem was that the batteries had run down on my recorder resulting in Lydon's voice speeding up near the end. Luckily, John saw the funny side next time I saw him: 'You cunt! I sound like Donald Duck!'

5. 1993: Open Up

I knew something was afoot when I (literally) bumped into John Lydon at Brixton Academy during an all-nighter with ambient funsters The Orb in June '92. The whole place was beaming up on a planet of its own. Hallucinogenic bedlam-au-go-go. Suddenly, a familiar figure sporting a shellsuit lurched into my field of vision and started babbling away. Familiar eyes bored into my face from a distance of about four inches, then he planted a big, beery smacker square on my lips. Ten minutes later, Lydon was being escorted from the building, bottle aloft and football song on his lips.

During the 90s, before it got inevitably commercialised and watered down, dance music was the new punk. It still is in more underground quarters, but that's where it's staying as the cheesy anthems

Leftfield

continue to hog the charts and give the music a bad name. During the early '90s, producers like Andrew Weatherall, Alex Paterson and Youth would always give Lydon a tip of the hat, as would more innovative groups like Primal Scream. The main thing they all had in common was not giving a shit about musical boundaries. Also, dance music echoed punk's DIY spirit, with kids making tracks in their bedrooms – on computers instead of guitars – and starting their own labels to put them out. Away from the corporations and out on the streets – for a short while.

Leftfield's Neil Barnes and Paul Daley were among the frontrunners of dance music's post-rave creative surge after busting out in 1990 with 'Not Forgotten', followed by a string of dancefloor-elevators including 'Release The Pressure' and 'Song Of Life', which they released on their own Hard Hands label. In '93, I had a project called Delta Lady with an American singer called Wonder, which I whipped up after Neil and Paul heard a track I'd done for Andrew Weatherall's Sabres Of Paradise label. They asked if we'd like to do one with them, so we teamed up to produce a song called 'Anything You Want', which appeared on Hard Hands and became a club hit.

Working at close quarters with Leftfield was an eye-opener, a creative volcano with many mutual reference points. While this activity was going on, I became aware of a top secret project which Neil and Paul were also working on. They knew I knew Lydon and eventually let the cat out of the bag – under oath. They had recorded a song called 'Open Up', an incendiary monster-groove which, topped with John's fiery vocals, was obviously the biggest, most audacious dance track of the year. It had to be kept secret for four months while legal aspects were sorted out. When it was first aired at the Ministry of Sound, DJ Billy Nasty only had the Lydon-less dub to play. The music was enough, let alone John's towering performance, which climaxed with him howling 'Burn Hollywood burn!'.

John knew Neil from growing up in the same neighbourhood. A crucial figure in this story – indeed Lydon's whole life – is his school friend John Gray. The pair used to frequent the London gig circuit in the early 70s, catching groups like Can or intergalactic jazz-funk nutters Magma, while nurturing each other's wide-ranging musical obsessions. John Gray had been involved with PiL in a backroom capacity and was always in touch with both Lydon and Barnes. A cross-fertilisation of ideas was inevitable. 'Just the way things work,' said Lydon. 'Not through any deliberate management manipulation. It was just by meeting.'

Lydon had slagged off dance music on American TV as 'musical McDonalds', 'just machines' or '70s disco recycled', but maintained a soft spot for Leftfield. As soon as news of the collaboration appeared, the press hauled out these comments in another bid to undermine his integrity. They seemed to forget John's wholesale immersion in reggae, frequenting of disco clubs like Ilford's Lacey Lady in the '70s, the proto-techno of 'Megamix', mutant disco of 'This Is Not A Love Song', collaboration with Bambaataa and pre-Balearic anthem 'Rise'. PiL was dub, funk and noise you could dance to. The influence of PiL itself on dance music can never be underestimated. That only seems to increase as time goes on. John himself would also say, 'Dance music is closer to the punk ethic than anything else out there.'

'He hadn't shown much interest at all in what we were doing before then, but that's typical John,' laughed Neil Barnes.

First thing Leftfield did with Lydon when they met up in May '93 was have a sesh. Some light refreshments were partaken while Paul, a successful DJ, spun choice items from his record box. It became obvious that the dance music which John had been previously exposed to was of the cheesy variety. Paul played him the real, underground tackle by the likes of Hardfloor and Underworld.

Shortly afterwards, recording took place, although the single wouldn't come out for over six months as the buzz intensified on the promo network. When the song was finally ready to go, Lydon, Barnes and Daley refused to do any press. I had already expressed a fervent desire to talk to them for *NME*, who I was writing for at the time so, going through the back door, John relented. It would be my first and only *NME* cover story.

John was in town that November to shoot the video, so I met them at North London's Rollover Studios, where Leftfield usually worked. Unfortunately, John's hectic schedule – which included hanging out with the Arsenal squad and clubbing with Neil and Paul

GUNS N' ROSES' PUNK HEROES ★ JOHN WOO ★ EAT STATIC
SCRAWL ★ CMJ REPORT ★ PAUL WELLER ★ GALLON DRUNK

NME

the cover returns!
JACK
DUCKWORTH
and all
that jazz

You're
fired!

FLAMING GROOVY!

AYTON and LEFTFIELD burn down the house

– had seen him imbibe enough beer to prompt an oath of absti-
nence. He had the mother of all hangovers and was in no mood to
do press, even more than usual. When the tape machine was off he
was clowning around, catching up with the few years since I'd last
seen him. But, when the red light went on, he became quite terse,
obviously finding it a bit of a pain to talk about a project which had
only started as a laugh and snowballed. Conversation was restricted
to the record.

The trio were concerned that *NME* would home in on a Sex-Pis-
tol-Goes-Dance angle and focus on him. A casual enquiry about his
autobiography meets with 'I'm not going to say a thing about it'.
His past does get a reference with that curt, 'I'm am not a walking
history book and I should just be judged by what I do, as I do it.'
Mention of *Metal Box* gets, 'Yes, if you want a reference point that
would be the one.' I got the feeling if I asked about the possibilities
of a Pistols reunion – not that I planned to – I would be submitted
to some kind of torture.

So, the single?

'It wasn't about using John,' explained Neil. 'It was about using
John's voice. He's always had a voice that's very exciting. We just
thought he was the most suitable singer for what we were trying to
do. Obviously, we had to send John the track to see if he liked it.
It was like, "Let's do it for the track". We thought we had written
something that John would like.'

'They didn't ask me in because they wanted a pop star floating
around on top like a fluffy, little cloud,' said John, paraphrasing an
Orb biggie. Neil would later say how much effort John had put into
the recording. 'The best time we had was when we were in the studio making the record.'

'It just went off really, so to speak,' added Paul. 'We didn't know
what he was going to do.'

'I didn't know myself!' laughs John.

'You did!' argues Neil. 'I don't believe it! Two days before, when you came down and we were playing records, we played you the backing track and you were singing the fucking chorus then! It was all written down.'

John knows he's been rumbled. 'OK, I'm lying. You know darn well I spend a lot of time doing everything. I'm one of those horrible perfectionists with a gross sense of insecurity.'

Later Neil confides, 'I really think he is a great singer. He's got an original, soulful voice. I knew he would come out with something special because he was really nervous. Put John on the spot. That's the best way. We treated him like we treat anybody else. We weren't starstruck. We made him work and he liked that. He did have everything worked out. He's a professional. He plays that down in himself but he really works at it.'

John continues, 'There's such a sorry lack of vocals in music at the moment. It's extremely sad. It's naff. It drives me crazy. As I prove on this song, it's not an impossible thing to go out and bloody sing. To anything. The problem is sheer laziness.'

About the team-up, John says, 'I'm simply into anyone who puts a lot of effort into being themselves, rather than following formats. That's all I'm interested in. I don't categorise my record collection. I couldn't even begin to. It's that diverse and that's what it must be about. If you live any other lifestyle you're just a copyist and a trendy and therefore a temporary figure.'

Of course, Lydon couldn't pull off a project based on playing down his controversial past without some kind of chaos erupting. It was highly unfortunate that 'Open Up' was released the same week that raging forest fires swept through southern California. There was outcry and the video got pulled from top TV programme *The Chart Show*. John had unwittingly planted himself into the eye of another media hurricane. This might have been tiresome and familiar for him but also saw a valuable promotional opportunity go out the window for Hard Hands, a small independent staking a lot in putting out the record. MTV baulked at what it called the 'insensitive' lyrics.

'Who are they to be purveyors of good taste?' asked John in the voice he would usually call up when confronted with blind ignorance. 'There are governing bodies to decide what should or shouldn't be played. They've overstepped their mark. I find that bloody offensive. That's what is offensive in this country. Not a song like this which in no way bears any relation to the catastrophe in California. It's nothing to do with that, so I see it as a bit of victimisation going on. We worked hard putting this video together. There's not a lot of money about here. We cared about the product. It's damn upsetting to see things like that going on. I don't like to be anybody's victim.

'Year in, year out, it just gets more and more restrictive and people just seem to put up with it. How dare they dictate what is good or bad taste? They're supposedly *The Chart Show*. Well, we're in the damn charts and where are we on the show? Nowhere.

'This track was made quite some time back. To accuse us of being insensitive is where the piss off begins. How dare they undermine my work? How fucking dare they? What are we supposed to do, wait until the December floods, which they always have in California, and re-release it then? Would that be sensitive?'

Even in cold print, you can see the steam rising. Deja vu?

'It's not the first time,' he says, dropping to that disgruntled Rotten monotone. 'Probably won't be the last. It's not funny, actually. It's damn annoying. As you know, I've been on the cutting edge of that almost fairly consistently. That costs you sales. That costs you a lot. Let the audience decide.

'I'm very sorry that some English fool (in Malibu) would rather save a pussy cat than himself, but that's not my problem. It should not affect my career... and if the world's not careful I'm gonna go out on a cat murdering spree!'

This last statement is followed by a cackle. John knows that he just lived up to his Rotten public image. I half-expected the next day's tabloids to carry headlines of a PUNK ROTTEN'S CAT-KILLER THREAT nature. John switches his anger to hilarity.

'"Vengeance is mine!" sayeth Johnny. But you know if you quote that in the paper that would be taken as arrogance. But it isn't. It's my natural reaction.

'There's enough people out there who know that in the end, I'm not some shyster. That's all that really counts, regardless of what's said in the press or the banning of videos on TV for absurd reasons that I don't think Dolly Parton would be getting. I could see her singing these lyrics, to be frank. I don't see them as offensive. Jesus, the song to me is about not getting a movie part and burning down the studio in sheer frustration. In a metaphysical sense, of course!'

In 2002, John could look back and laugh about the whole affair. 'Hollywood was burning down at the time, but if I planned that, fucking hell I'm good! That's an awfully extreme length to go to sell a record. The record was done before the fire, but there ya go.'

Having spent much of the 90s immersed in dance culture, I can say in hindsight that 'Open Up' was one of the high points of the last decade. As a DJ, I played it everywhere and the reaction was always pure mania. When the Prodigy hired me as their tour DJ in '96 with almost express instructions to play the Sex Pistols, I would often drop 'Anarchy In The UK' in before they came on but, if anything, 'Open Up' got an even more extreme roar. Like the massive impact of the Prodigy, it was a jolt that this sometimes complacent and formulaic field needed.

There was no strategy behind 'Open Up'. As John said, 'This came along and I just did it. We're mates here. We do these things because we like the world of music. It is important to cross over continually if things are to progress, otherwise they become ghettoised. Ouch – a new idea! We all have that, and then, of course, you get the 20 imitators.'

Neil and Paul reveal that they were asked to remix 'Pretty Vacant' for the dance market. This was greeted by disbelieving guffaws. But

John would love Neil's remix of 'God Save The Queen' nine years later. Phrases like 'punk house' are thrown up amidst the giggles, but suddenly John's tones cut through on a serious note. 'Here, you should lay off the punk references. It's not relevant and a lot of reviews of the record have brought that up, but that's something like 15 or 16 years ago in my past and it is completely disrespectful to what I've been doing in Public Image, which was most definitely not a lazy outfit. Originality always offends. It's been very difficult with that old label and that tag being stuck to me like glue. But it's something that doesn't affect me and it doesn't affect the general public. Unfortunately, they read these rags that you are writing for like they are the Bible and they're not.'

John concludes with a laugh. 'This business is too difficult for a lot of people because they're after quick quid. Risk-takers are very rare and when you run across 'em, grab 'em... and work with 'em!'

6. 2002: God Save The Queen Revisited

The John Lydon of 2002 had not dulled one iota in the 25 years since I'd first encountered him. He was promoting the reactivation of 'God Save The Queen' with its remix by Neil, who had now sadly split from Paul. There was also a boxed set of *Never Mind The Bollocks* padded out with assorted out-takes and B-sides. Punk was celebrating its Silver Jubilee, as the Queen reached her golden.

I interviewed John for a now-defunct dance music publication called *Seven*. At ten o'clock on a dark Sunday evening in London and two in the afternoon in undoubtedly sunny California, John answers the phone at his Malibu beach home. It's soon obvious he hasn't changed a bit. Maybe a bit lighter of tone, sometimes to the point of stand-up comedy, but still scathing when necessary.

'Time goes by and you don't notice it because I don't care. I've always been like that. If I stopped to think I'd realise I'm an old man and I'm not having that. Fuck that. You're only as young as you feel and I've been feeling quite a lot young lately! A lot of people have got to realise it's my Jubilee too! Nye-eur! Thank you. It's my 25th anniversary, or thereabouts. Not wishing to be too historical, but it's close enough. I'll have some of that.'

And 'God Save The Queen' is still as relevant now as it was then?

'Yeah, oddly enough, and that ain't my fault. I wish it wasn't relevant, to be quite frank.'

There's more drug-addled, crime-ridden shithole estates, where the straight dads are fat blokes with shaved heads getting pissed and beating up the missus.

'I know. The whole world's gone Dagenham! The other way is the likes of Billy Bragg, which certainly ain't helping because of that dreary deadpan "Why can't we all be happy in the same little tiny box?" mentality. Apparently – this cracks me up – while I was over there I jokingly said, "Oh yeah, I'm a royalist", and I got taken seriously by him. He apparently stopped during one of his gigs to give a big tirade about how I'd sold out! What an asshole. Think, you humourless idiot. I resent that. That's what happens with that left-wing too extremist point of view. You lose your common sense. You want everything to fit into that student union philosophy. Well, life ain't like that. Nothing's changed.'

John still visits the UK regularly.

'Yeah, and things are changing. Neighbourhoods are getting dismantled. Crime and all that bullshit. Communities used to semi police themselves. It's very hard to be a burglar in a neighbour-hood where everyone's mum knows ya. They're breaking that down and isolating people. Nobody knows their neighbours and it's all unfriendly. You're alone. You are very alone. You will *always* be alone. Be happy your pizza arrived.'

Twenty five years ago you were haranguing the Eltons and Rods and they're still here.

93

'Yeah, same things that I'm saying now. You know what I've got over those cunts? They'll always be older than me! Hahaha! Only they're stupid enough to act their age. I don't understand the word "act" in that. That's a con, innit? Even Pete Townsend said, "Hope I die before I get old". I thought then, "What a stupid thing to say". I hope I die a long time after I'm old. So, the Queen Mum to me is, "Hmm, a nod and a wink, mate!" I want some of that number. It was a bit sad. Y'know, one hundred and one. That pampered lifestyle I would recommend to all of Britain's residents! We should all have that opportunity. So if anything, I'd be all for the Monarchy, but can we all become members?

'At least, she had some sense of dignity. She seemed to mean no harm. The rest are still greedy on the coffers and they show it. That's the disgustingness of it. You can't be having that representing a country – and as for Tony blah blah blah! That mindless cretin. He's the biggest sell-out of the lot. They think he's a joke here. They laugh at him. What kind of Socialism is he preaching really? "Now I'm in power my kids go to posh schools".'

Despite the diversity of John's post-Pistols career, it always seemed to go back to the Pistols, like it's all he ever did.

'Yeah, well it's all part of the same person! How annoying of me, huh? How would I have the wit, and wisdom to calculate it that way? I'd never lift my pen off the paper. I'd still be writing that kind of script. That's expecting too much devious behaviour from a human being. If that kind of anti-folk hero is what you're looking for well you've got one, heh heh. By default, I never thought of Public Image as a three-legged donkey.

'Genuine originality is ignored until it's imitated. After Chuck Berry, rock 'n' roll had to be just in that *clichéd* format. Along came the Stones and everybody had to be like the Stones. Then the Pistols. They all had to be like the Pistols, etc, etc. It's wrong. Rock 'n' roll just got trapped but what the fuck is dance or techno or drum 'n' bass? These are just names. It's all music. As long as it isn't musickening. You get it wrong when you confine yourself to things. We just got on with it. Years later I don't want to be not wanted for making those moves. Those moves made it easier for others.

'Look at the extent of music I listen to. You know, you've been round my house. I have it all, mate. If somebody's gonna put it out on a record, I wanna hear it. I'm sorry but Abba were a damn fine band. Anyone who thinks not is not getting it. It's craftmanship and manipulation, but done properly and there ain't nothing wrong with a thing being done properly.

'God, am I not supposed to listen to mandolin music? What I like at the moment is Bolivian flute music. I love that soppy stuff with the silly pipes and acoustic guitar. It's great! Music from the Andes. I made a little Bolivian pipe for myself from my fax machine, out of cardboard tubes that hold your fax paper. Sticky-back plastic them together *Blue Peter* style, cut some little grooves in 'em and you can honk away a little tune all day long until they get wet and soggy and then you make a new one.'

At this time, the Sex Pistols were plotting a reunion to mark the Jubilee. It would end up being held at a football stadium in the wilds of Crystal Palace. Initially, John had wanted to stage a 24-hour rave but, predictably, 'I can't get the fucking permit. As soon as they know I'm attached to it all the laws go out the window. I find it really intriguing that the concept of a rave with the Sex Pistols really, really spooks.'

Two of the authorities' worst nightmares rolled into one! This time, John isn't averse to some reflection on the punk days.

'I don't mean to wave my own flag but we'd go out and do something so over the top and so ludicrous, but then it would be taken as a classic showbiz move and that's where they got it wrong all the time. If you're basing everything on what somebody else has done that's not progress. That's sterility.

'I'm just a natural born troublemaker. Just can't help it. I'm like that gangly galoot who's always breaking your mum's china. I can't help it. I'm just naturally uncomfortable trying to adapt to other people's rules and regulations. I don't see how they work. There's not enough thought in any of these guidelines as a human being for me to find them efficient.'

With John not adverse to discussing subjects which we'd never laboured in any of the previous interviews, it was interesting to hear his opinions 25 years on. Malcolm McLaren?

'The thing is, he has this weird memory of how things were or weren't. It seems to be that anything that went well, he'll take the credit for and all the bad stuff he ignores, when I think the truth is the other way round! Get off, you know we all rowed together like cats and dogs, and I don't like anyone to take responsibility for any of it. It was teamwork, whether you like it or not.

'I remember Malcolm running after the Bill Grundy show because he was scared of being arrested. He got arrested at the boat trip and managed to get himself out on bail and nobody else. It's the Malcolm we all know and love. A coward, really. Put himself up for Mayor and backed out at the last minute again. He never comes up to meet the match, you know?'

Punk itself?

'The idea of bouncing up and down to Sham 69 turns my stomach. It's like backwardsville. It's like, "Oh, these folks are getting it wrong again."'

Talk to Jah Wobble, who once had a habit of phoning me up at two in the morning pretending to be a debt collector. 'Well, he's still doing it now but on vinyl! I like him dearly for that. That's him. He understands that life shouldn't be taken that deadpan and that serious. Humourless people are the downfall of this planet, with everything clearly explained. Life is a mystery and that's all there is to it. If you're looking for any answers in it you're fucking wasting your time.'

John is still antagonised by the UK press. This time, *The Sun* had declined doing an interview. 'Some things will always be the bumholes of the universe. My response to that is no, but I am British, as opposed to Britney, and it is an English newspaper. The ironies of life never fail to amuse. It just gives me songwriting material. The apathy that's going on in England right now is really disheartening. I've just come back (from the UK). I'm well, well not happy.'

He cheers up discussing the *Rotten TV* venture which saw him on the other end of the microphone as a chat show host.

'I started doing it on VH1, but it got pulled after three shows because they thought it was too risky for the American market, and we're not talking four-letter words here. I'd get politicians on, getting them to open up and be honest. Instead of a load of Bob Geldofs with statistics, I'm talking to them as human beings.'

John had recently shocked many by charming the pants off Richard Madeley and Judy Finnigan on UK teatime TV.

'Yeah, I loved it! It was bizarre. I thought, "Here's a real challenge. Can I out-knife this pair?" It was a giggle, but the giggle was they'd hired extra security because they thought I was gonna riot. What dopes! Why do they believe this? They were most surprised when I gave them an autographed banana – a thing I like to do occasionally. Their own banana but with my signature on it. One for each of them. They were very grateful. He said he was gonna frame it. Maybe she took hers to the shower! I guess I won't be on their show again! (he was wrong, and has since returned).

'Don't make things like Richard and Judy's show your enemy. You go on these things, you talk and you find out that the barrier's not really there or, if they are, at least you know for sure.'

It's more subversive that way.

'Bloody right it is! Parkinson ran like the clappers from me but he's got to eat humble pie now he's seen what a nice guy I really am. Well I am! (*Pauses*) Ha ha! Stick 'em where it hurts. I want *Rotten TV* on proper networked TV. Regular channels, because I'm fucking good enough to take 'em all on.'

One final thought?

'At least we're not picking spots any more. That's progress for you.'

7. 2004: I'm A Celebrity... Get Me Out Of Here (You Fucking Cunts)

Ironically, John garnered his most expansive and positive press coverage ever from a TV appearance of a completely different nature – nature being the operative word as he popped up among the wannabe's, has-beens and z-list 'personalities' on ITV's primetime blockbuster, *I'm A Celebrity... Get Me Out Of Here!*

It was a clever move which probably only Lydon could've pulled off. Here he was, appearing every night on prime time TV, swearing more than he ever did on the Bill Grundy show and being actively encouraged to be outrageous. But John's honesty, sense of humour

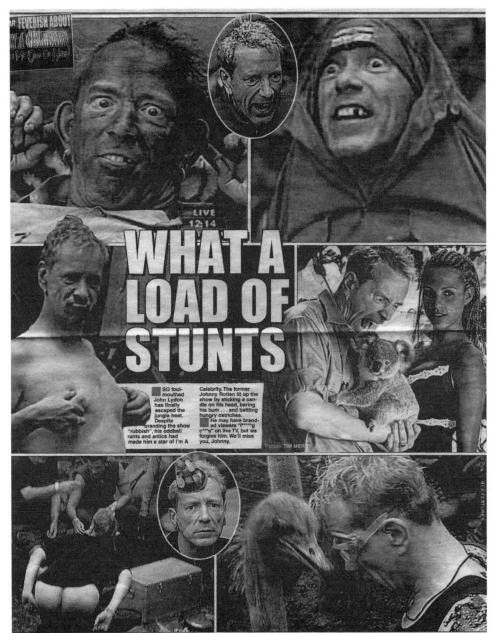

LIVE 12:14

WHAT A LOAD OF STUNTS

SO foul-mouthed John Lydon has finally escaped the jungle heat. Despite branding the show "rubbish", his oddball rants and antics had made him a star of I'm A Celebrity. The former Johnny Rotten lit up the show by sticking a candle on his head, baring his bum . . . and battling hungry ostriches.

He may have branded viewers "f*****g c***s" on live TV, but we forgive him. We'll miss you, Johnny.

Picture: TIM MERRY

Pics: REX FEATURES

ROTTEN: FROM WEEDY KID TO WORLD STAR - Centre Pages

and obvious love of the local wildlife seemed to win the nation's heart. At one point he was favourite.

What did the producers expect from John? They obviously wanted the foul-mouthed punk stereotype who would swear, shout and smash his way into the role of hated outsider. Instead, he used the command of English language he had been perfecting since being bullied at school to cut the realest dash in a show renowned for falseness and scheming.

Then there was the Bushtucker Trial, where viewers voted for John to try and obtain food stars from a bunch of ostriches while doused in syrup and birdseed. To the surprise of many, he rose to the challenge and, despite getting severely pecked, won six stars off the 'giant budgies', as he called them. It can't have been any worse than some of the Pistols' gigs. Far from being crushed, John now boosted his standing in the camp and with the public.

For a few days he couldn't go wrong. When Kerry McFadden was depressed at missing her daughter's first birthday, John stuck a burning candle on his head and sang 'Happy birthday'. 'You know me, I'm an old softie at heart,' he told the press, who were doing a massive u-turn after years of shock horror. Even the tabloids got off their soapboxes, with the *Daily Star* declaring, 'his swearing antics are a winner.' Writing in the *News Of The World* – the same paper who tried to bribe the Pistols into misbehaving during the Anarchy tour – Tara Palmer-Tomkinson declared, 'The hero of the show is John Lydon. I thought the former Sex Pistol was going to cause anarchy. Instead he's been very clever and funny.'

John lasted ten days in the jungle, which he described as, 'Canvey Island with palm trees'. Then he started to get into trouble. John wiped the cheeky chappie grins off hosts Ant and Dec's faces by muttering 'fuckin' cunts' when told he'd escaped eviction. Even if the Bill Grundy profanosaurus is now accepted, the 'c' word remains a feared taboo. John later claimed, 'I was talking about being in the count-ry. I wasn't trying to be one'. Two days later, he came out with 'Oh ff... Jesus... Bollocks.' His offending word on the Bill Grundy show was a lowly 'shit'. There was outrage but, when he went walkabout, the desperate producers talked him into staying. The first time, anyway.

John started to seem like he was losing it, admitting, 'This ego-tistical fucking fiasco is annoying me to the point of distraction'. He charcoaled his face black, dyed his hair black with henna, cut nipple holes in his t-shirt and lit a fire by the edge of camp before dancing about going 'lentil mental'. He cut out previous jungle king Tony Blackburn's tooth from a photo and stuck it on his own, while recalling Jack Nicholson in *The Shining* with a manic cry of 'Here's Johnny'.

John hated Jordan, who would later hitch up with hapless midget warbler Peter Andre for the most grotesque celeb wedding of all time. 'If I hear that honky voice one more time I think I'll strangle it,' he said of the woman he described as, 'a page three blow-up balloon.'

'Naggy old bitch... The woman's fucking talentless... I don't like lazy people... it's a parasite.' John's arsenal of insults was tested to its limits. 'I can't stand her. The sex bomb kitten is as boring as the day is long... It's just boring. It's just pointless. It don't do anything and it don't connect.' This must have been Jordan's worst night-mare: stuck in the jungle with a bloke who not only didn't fancy her, but could rip her apart with one choice putdown. Jordan had obvi-ously thought she could thrust out her horrific beach balls and waltz away Queen of the Jungle with a few swift footballer revelations. She found herself looking fake, foolish and lazy. Kerry McFadden, formerly of Atomic Kitten, got the crown instead. John backed her to win. 'I want her to do it for her two little girls. She's a lovely girl. She's not fake like Jordan.'

Ten days in, John walked. In one paper he said it was because, 'Jordan got on my tits', but elsewhere said he didn't agree with the voting system and preferred to leave when he felt like it. That was prompted by boredom, hunger and Jordan. He also voiced a fear of turning into Des O'Connor. The producers were terrified his depar-ture would lose viewers as over eleven million tuned in to watch his departure. The show became boring without him.

One thing which the show and resultant publicity inevitably achieved was bringing John's (usually very) private life to the fore. Unfortunately, there was no dirt to be dug. Any going had been raked during the Pistols. All the public could know was that, for the past 25 years, John had been very happy with the wonderful Nora, who he met through her daughter Ari-Up, then of The Slits.

After strolling free, John was interviewed as he relaxed with Nora on a cruiser off the coast of Queensland. 'You know my background – I'm working class. I come from Finsbury Park and look where I've ended up!'

Interviewed in *The Sun*, John said he quit because he hated the eviction votes, booting off contestants was 'humiliating' and stressed that he had not been afraid to face the public vote. 'I have no fear. I won this thing in the first day.' The eviction of fellow contestant Neil 'Razor' Ruddock had been the final straw. 'That bloody hurts and I thought, "That's it. Sod that". That's humiliation for no good reason at all. You are rubbishing what is a truly brilliant experience.'

He added, 'I came here for the nature – and the nature of *Opportunity Knocks* or *Celebrity Knockout* is not my game.'

John's career after the jungle was a fascinating balance between being a national treasure and foul-mouthed agitator. He popped up on *Richard & Judy* again but outdid himself on Jonathan Ross' show by gritting his face Steptoe-style and rattling out a barrage of 'fucking cunts'. Receiving his Inspiration Award from *Q* magazine, he dominated the whole event with heckling and an X-rated speech. Liam Gallagher could only sit back and watch the master at work. Conversely, John also furthered the interest in nature he'd nurtured in the jungle by hosting some mega-bug extravaganzas for cable TV in which he came over like a punk David Attenborough.

Who could have seen that one coming? As John walked out of camp having once again placed himself at the forefront of the nation's consciousness, he declared, loud and proud, 'I have changed the world twice and I'm going to do it for a third time. I'm a survivor.'

Even if he doesn't quite change it again, the world would be a much greyer place without John Lydon.

© *Kris Needs 2006*
Kris Needs

Legendary music scribe Kris Needs is journalist as rock-star and has played the field as hard as those he not only interviewed and wrote about but often came to befriend (a list that includes Mott The Hoople, Mick Jones, Joe Strummer, Keith Richards, Debbie Harry, Lemmy, Jeffrey Lee Pierce – and John Lydon). Needs edited the UK music press's most unorthodox bible *Zig Zag* from the dawning of Punk until the journal's demise.

During the 1980s, Kris also became editor of teen glossy *Flexi-Pop*, legitimate competition for *Smash Hits,* while DJing at venues such as notorious goth hangout the Batcave. In the late 1980s he moved into the rave scene and played at Ibiza and techno clubs worldwide and created remixes for the likes of Primal Scream.

He is the author of many books on music, including *Trash: The Complete New York Dolls* (Plexus, 2006) and *Joe Strummer & The Legend Of The Clash* (Plexus, 2004). He is currently working on a greatly expanded version of his autobiography *Needs Must* (Virgin, 1999).

Clockwise from top-left: *The Kinks, P.J.Proby, Dave Berry, The Creation, 'Dave Dee, Dozy, Beaky, Mick And Tich', Chuck Berry, The Monkees.* Centre: *Jonathan Richman*

Build Me Up Buttercup:
Rotten Rubrics & Pistol Prototypes
by Alan Clayson

'We were the last rock 'n' roll band' – Johnny Rotten

Trev, a moth-eaten old Mod in Welwyn Garden City, had a daughter, Rita, at art college who kept talking about some new London group called the Sex Pistols. Intrigued, he merged into the shadows when the group gatecrashed a local support spot to Mr. Big, hirsute, tight-trousered and with their very name taken from an album track by the disbanded Free.

In the still-filling hall, four suede-headed louts sauntered onto the boards. Hitting all their instruments at once with a *staccato* 'Right!', they barged into an onslaught of pulsating bass, dranging guitars, crashing drums and shouted vocals. In between numbers that all sounded the same, they said things like 'fuck', burped into the microphone and made no attempt to 'milk' the audience. Seemingly anti-everything, they tended to either bring out the hostilies in or provide glimpses of unconscious comedy for anyone who bothered to listen.

What had struck Rita about the Sex Pistols had been their dissimilarity to any other pop presentation she'd ever seen. When she'd caught The Sweet at the California Ballroom in Dunstable three years earlier, some of their continuity had been a bit *risque*, but at last October's freshers' ball, the Pistols had been downright uncouth in the way they addressed the crowd, and she'd peeped slyly at the with-it graphics lecturer present. He'd ceased clicking his fingers to stiffen with shocked dignity, stare hard at the stage and endeavour to control his features. It was part of his pose to never appear shocked.

Well, Trev reckoned he'd seen it all before. Not even the Sex Pistols' name was especially original. In the late 1960s, there'd been Hard Meat – who'd 'got it together in the country' *a la* Traffic – and Balls, a short-lived Midlands 'supergroup' containing former personnel from The Moody Blues and The Move. Next up was Brewer's Droop from High Wycombe, whose hilarious filth and foam-rubber phallus had enlivened the early 1970s club circuit.

These Sex Pistols, pondered Trev, weren't so much something different as a – kind of – culmination of strands of pop that he'd either heard about or experienced directly. For a start, there'd been Lenny Bruce, a sort of blue comedian from the States, whose humor (not humour) appealed to people who liked Cheech & Chong, US hippy funnymen who'd wrung dry all they could from drugs and 'balling chicks'. Thinking about it, that wasn't the Pistols' style at all, apart from the swearing and that. What about The Fugs, the New York burlesque-poetry outfit, with their Brewer's Droop-with-university-degrees spoofs? No, the Pistols were more The Stooges, Alice Cooper or, Trev chuckled, maybe the early Who but with Keith Moon installed as permanent lead singer – and yet...

They'd appeared as if from nowhere during one of pop's slow moments when there was nothing particularly hysterical or outrageous. Like the restoration of 'Merry Monarch' Charles II after Cromwell's joyless Protectorate, all the elements were in place for a swing back to the cheap thrills of the in-yer-face shouting and banging of disaffected youth. Glam-rock had run its course, and cheap spirits, Mandrax, headbanging and streaking were among desperate diversions that were catching on as 1975 had loomed. A fairweather music media and a growing proliferation of self-financed 'fanzines' was becoming increasingly long-faced about monied megastars – the Stones, The Who, Pink Floyd, Led Zeppelin, you name 'em – at Wembley, Earl's Court or Birmingham's new National Exhibition Centre, but otherwise forever in America. Their bass guitarist had just thrown a Green Room wobbler in a mid-West venue designed for championship sport, because of a misconstruing of an amenities rider in the contract about *De Kuyper* rather than *Remy* apricot brandy, and was keeping everyone waiting.

Even those in a lower market league, whose public personalities were halfway bearable, weren't immune from almost audible sniggering in the press. A *Sounds* review of a Roy Orbison show at the Bristol Hippodrome concluded that 'There can be few businessmen around building themselves such a large pension fund with such ease.'

As for the music *per se*, no-one expected it to be astounding – though clever arrangements and technological innovations often camouflaged average songs in need of editing. It's rather a sweeping generalisation, but as playing and production improved, standards of composition fell in favour of the blinded-by-science sound at any given interval. Somehow, most of it was a bit too pat, too dove-tailed, too American. No-one on pop's loftiest plateaux seemed able any more to accomplish what the old beat groups of the 1960s, for all their casually-strewn errors, had committed to tape instinctively. Worse, information that a given artist's latest LP was just like the one before was praise indeed for many – and the future seemed to be in danger of being the past all over again.

Now above the tour-album-tour sandwiches incumbent upon poorer stars, at one point in the mid-1970s, not a solitary note would emit from The Who for an entire year. Yet, if they'd abandoned the world, the world hadn't abandoned them, not while their work was being kept before the public. The most vital nod to them – though not appreciated at the time – was a speedy 'Substitute' smashed out during the Pistols' speculative fiascos, and still in the set at the height of their fame. Nevertheless, the Pistols' party-line on The Who was that the TV-sets-out-the-window behaviour could barely erase their compromising position among 'contemporary' rock's nobility, smirking suppliers of elitist music for over-thirties, epito-mised by George Harrison's reworking on a 1974 album track of The Everly Brothers' 'Bye Bye Love' with in-joking lyrical digs at his first wife and 'old Clapper', i.e. Eric Clapton, her new husband. It was, chortled George, 'a piece of self-indulgence like some other of my songs about things that nobody else knows or cares about.' What about the poor sods who bought the record?

While flicking a V-sign at this distancing of the common-or-garden pop idol from his essentially teenage audience, the Pistols had only fractionally more time for pub-rock in the light of Johnny Rotten's contempt for its 'denim and plaid shirts, tatty jeans and long droopy hair.' Such attire was commensurate with the jovial at-mosphere of licenced premises, where the likes of Roogalator, Bees Make Honey, Ducks Deluxe and Dr. Feelgood gave more thought to the paying customer than any stadium supergroup with its unend-ing *diddle-iddle-iddling* on V-shaped guitars, and lyrics that made

Trash

THE STORY OF THE

New York Dolls

you embarrassed to be alive; where Kilburn & The High Roads' thirty-something Ian Dury, crippled and pugnacious, spat out in Oi! Oi! Cockney his perspectives on London low life, and where Rocky Sharpe & The Replays, The Count Bishops, Duke Duke & The Dukes and France's roly-poly Little Bob Story played with wantonly retrogressive verve – twelve-bar chord changes and a four-four backbeat – for the sake of, ostensibly at least, sheer pleasure.

Street level acclaim was also accorded to all manner of reconstituted entities from the Swinging Sixties ranging from The Troggs to Johnny Kidd's surviving Pirates to the also-ran Rockin' Vickers. There was also a place in the pub-rock sun for The Nashville Teens, The Downliners Sect, former members of Van Morrison's Them and The Searchers, who all resumed recording careers. Moreover, as pub-rock fanned out from London, Ace, Dr. Feelgood, The Kursaal Flyers, Ian Dury, Eddie & The Hot Rods and other of its practitioners were to be swept from the nicotine haze of Islington's Hope & Anchor and the Red Cow in Hammersmith into the Top Forty, and Bees Make Honey landed a tour second-billed to glam-rock supremos, T Rex, just as the wind changed.

More palpable Pistol precedents were being forged by the likes of The Ramones, Television and The Shirts in New York's twilight zone, and in provincial wings such as Boston, where Jonathan Richman and his Modern Lovers – whose 'Roadrunner' would be seized by the scuff of the neck by the Pistols – had debuted in 1975. Half–a-world away from London, therefore, there were already groups with spiky hair, ripped clothes, safety pins and three-chord guitars thrashed at speed to machine-gun drumming behind a ranting johnny-one-note. Crucially, the exhilaration of the impromptu was prized above technical accuracy, and originality counted for more than anything as boring as talent.

Regarded by these incoming US musical renegades as admired elder brothers, The Stooges had been keeping the faith in Detroit back in the late 1960s while The New York Dolls, victims of the same passion, had been the toast of the Big Apple's rock *demi-monde* since 1972 with an excitingly slipshod stage act. It was built round 'Personality Crisis', 'Looking For A Kiss' and other compositions that were reflective of a hard-living corporate lifestyle characterised by alcoholism and drug overdoses – and it is, perhaps, significant that, on their last legs, the Dolls had been managed by future Sex Pistols *svengali* Malcolm McLaren. His provocative ploys (such as projecting them as communists) could not, however, stay the decline of these titans of trash.

The Dolls modelled themselves on The Rolling Stones, both in appearance and personal excesses. In reciprocation, various Stones had hazarded excursions to investigate the British branch of what amounted to nascent punk. The Pistols' quasi-fetishist wardrobe was bespoken by a shop called 'Sex' – formerly 'Let It Rock', specializing in Teddy Boy gear – towards the wrong end of King's Road. The story goes that Mick Jagger once peered into this boutique where, pretending not to notice him, the principal carriers of the punk bacillus exchanged knowing titters. We hate your guts, you long-haired, complacent, millionaire git.

The Who

Improved with age, the incident also had Johnny Rotten banging the door in Jagger's consternated face – a measured disrespect that belied a diligence in making private observations when, purportedly, Rotten and his odious friend, Sid Vicious attended a Stones extravaganza at Earl's Court the previous year. Indeed, the Pistols were to turn out to be more like the Stones than they'd ever wanted to imagine – as acknowledged by Keith Richards: 'I loved the media thing that was happening, but, hell, we'd done that. It was a replay of 1963, 1964...'

Though the Pistols gained national notoriety via cursing on an early evening TV magazine and then beer-induced vomiting in an airport's departure lounge, and a drunken invasion of a major record company's offices, the Stones, The Kinks, The Pretty Things, The Who, The Small Faces and so forth had been there and done

The Small Faces

things like that since what was time immemorial by pop standards. There'd been some unpleasantness with a shotgun when the Things had played Swindon in 1965, and a spectacular onstage punch-up resulted in hospital treatment and rumours of The Kinks' disbandment. They were further beset by a lengthy American Federation of Musicians' ban for 'unprofessional conduct'. In 1965 too, three Stones were fined for pissing against a garage wall.

Crucially, there was the thrilling margin of error that had put teeth into the music of these outfits when the world was young – as exemplified by the Stones' jagged and high-velocity 'She Said Yeah' and, just one degree short of chaos, 1965's 'Honey I Need' from the Things: punk or what? In parenthesis, just as Rotten was criticised for his tortuous vocal endowment, so an appalled former classmate of Jagger would recall in 1963 'him telling me he was now singing in a group. I really laughed. 'What do you mean, singing?' I said, 'You haven't got a voice'.'

There was also a *deja vu* about aspects of the Sex Pistols' career trajectory. As far beyond the Stones in outrageousness as the Stones had been beyond Elvis Presley, the Pistols became too hot for London clubland to hold prior to a small Top Thirty beginning with a maiden single, just like the Stones and 'Come On'.

Like Andrew Loog Oldham, Jagger *et al*'s man-of-affairs, had, Malcolm McLaren welcomed headline-hogging boorishness from his charges. Though heard on 'God Save The Queen', Pistols bass player Glen Matlock had been replaced shortly before its 1977 release by the unstable Sid Vicious whose dubious fretboard skills had been less important to the group than his assault on a gentleman of the press who had merited McLaren's displeasure. Vicious was also descending into a heroin hell, and an overdose was to bring about his death while awaiting trial for murder. This took place around the same time as Keith Richards' heroin bust in Toronto – for which, in a worst-case-scenario, he faced seven years in jail. A morning after comment from ex-New York Doll Johnny Thunders emerged in *Rolling Stone*: 'Well, Sid beat Keith for the story of the year.'

As well as Keith's subsequent court hearing, the Stones weathered the punk storm – as did Led Zeppelin after their Robert Plant and Jimmy Page ventured out-of-bounds to the Vortex, London's main punk watering hole where Rotten and his cronies glared with gormless menace as Robert and Jimmy settled at a table with their drinks. Years later, the calculatedly iconoclastic Johnny telephoned Plant to ask for the lyrics of 'Kashmir' – from *Physical Graffiti* – as he was considering reviving it.

At the height of the Pistols' commercial and cultural impact, Rotten's penchant for Led Zeppelin had to be hidden away from the sort of folk who, in August 1977, raised a gleeful cheer when Elvis Presley's fatal heart attack was announced in another dungeon-like hang-out frequented by London punks; 'It's just too bad it couldn't have been Mick Jagger' was McLaren's charitable comment, and, *sur le continent*, the great *chansonnier* Jacques Brel's passing a year later would have a person or persons unknown risking prosecution by spraying a punky BREL IS DEAD. HURRAH! along a railway cutting between Liege and Brussels.

Benignly, many of pop's Grand Old Men refused to bitch back. Roy Orbison – who was to form a fleeting songwriting partnership with Pistols guitarist Steve Jones in the 1980s – saw only 'a bunch of fresh, new people trying to do their thing like we did in 1954. Disgraceful, we were, denegrated because we played that kind of music and everything. So that's exactly what they are, what we were then.' Mick Jagger shared Orbison's opinion at first, and appeared to align himself with punk's self-denigrating nihilism and trash aesthetic as well as assuring *Rolling Stone*, 'My whole life isn't rock 'n' roll. It's an absurd idea that it should be, but it's no more than anyone's whole life should revolve around working in Woolworth's.' That could have been Johnny Rotten talking when he dismissed rave culture as 'enjoyable, but not the be-all, end-all.'

Outlines also dissolved behind closed doors – because reggae, popular and otherwise, was a fixture on both Mick and Johnny's domestic turntables in the late 1970s. According to Gary Glitter, present at a record session *chez* Jagger, the host was 'an expert. He started explaining what was going on inside the rhythms and commenting on little subtleties of the mix.' Rotten, however, was to maintain that 'after the Pistols broke up, Richard Branson wanted to sign up a load of reggae bands, and the only white person he knew in the world who knew about reggae was me.'

Prior to being taken on by Branson as a freelance Virgin Records talent scout, reggae dominated Rotten's erudite choices on a *Desert Island Discs*-like programme on Capitol (a London radio station), in July 1977. Of these, while Ken Boothe and Peter Tosh managed chart entries, whither Augustus Pablo, Fred Locks, Culture, Dr. Alimantado and other names as unsung now as they were then?

Rotten wasn't able to superimpose reggae onto the Pistols' musical grid – apart from visually with a form of skank-hopping, interpreted by one broadsheet critic as 'trying to kick himself in the stomach' – anymore than Matlock was The Beatles. Indeed, Glen's liking for the four dismissed by Rotten as 'scouse gits', was among reasons given for his exit in 1977. Johnny thought too that, as productions, discs from that era sounded 'tinny'. Nonetheless, there had been plenty of kowtowing to the 1960s beat boom and its aftermath during the Pistols' eccentric exploratory stumblings – which contained a majority of – largely unfashionable – such classics and obscurities, some of them acquired through scouring jumble sales, second-hand bazaars and the few vintage record stores around then.

As well as 'Substitute' – which endured until 1977 – they dredged up The Kinks' 'I'm Not Like Everybody Else' – and 'Whatcha Gonna Do About It' and 'Understanding' by The Small Faces, Mods who were more the 'real thing' than the likes of The Who, The Action or The Creation. They also gave vitality to insolence towards important music industry figures who, despite finding them personally objectionable, were obliged to promote The Small Faces' continued chart triumphs in order to cater for a considerable and, in many cases, equally repulsive teenage following. In this respect, the group anticipated by a decade the Sex Pistols, whose overhaul of 'Whatcha Gonna Do About It' was to begin with the couplet 'I want you to know that I *hate* you, baby/I want you to know I *don't* care.'

Likewise, they rehearsed 'Wild Thing', and – perhaps unknowingly – assumed both The Troggs' take-it-or-leave-it attitude and their *one* guitar-bass-drums-lead vocals set-up (patented in Britain by Johnny Kidd & The Pirates in 1959). 'A second guitar seemed to get in the way,' shrugged Troggs mainstay Reg Presley, 'As for punk rock, we fucking invented it!' In acknowledgement, a Troggs season in 1980 at Max's Kansas City, one of the downtown clubs where the New York punk groups had fermented, spawned a bootleg LP with a title that repeated a much-asked question: *Was This The First Punk Rock Band?*

The Troggs' West Country blood-brothers, Dave Dee-Dozy-Beaky-Mick & Tich provisioned the Pistols with self-penned 'He's A Raver' (flip-side of 'Okay'), which, to a disinclined Rotten's relief, was ousted minutes before the group's maiden 100 Club performance, even as he screwed himself up to belt it out in a face-saving manner that – as it was with other numbers in the repertoire – conveyed the impression that he too was aware of his own ludicrousness. Incidentally, Dave Dee, in his capacity as an Atlantic Records recording manager, considered that it wouldn't do any harm to sign the Pistols for a one-shot release – and said as much in his cameo role in *The Great Rock 'N' Roll Swindle*.

If Rotten had gritted 'He's A Raver' under sufferance, it was he who'd championed The Creation's 'Life Is Just Beginning' – which, 'Eleanor Rigby'-esque strings apart, would have resolved easily to the Pistols' *oeuvre* – and 1966's 'Psychotic Reaction' by The Count Five, an Anglophile US garage band that traded in punk by original definition. The single featured a tempo change reminiscent of The Yardbirds, and was to be resurrected by The Cramps, a psychobilly outfit, as untainted by musical polish as the Pistols.

From mid-1960s US pop, too, came the Pistols' go at The Monkees' 'I'm Not Your Stepping Stone', B-side of 'I'm A Believer'. A more powerful British version was a 'turntable hit' on pirate radio. It was by The Flies, whose lead singer concluded their slot at 1967's Fourteen Hour Technicolour Dream, a 'happening' in London's Alexandra Palace, by urinating over the front rows.

Paradoxically, 1967 was also a boom time for schmaltz, with Engelbert Humperdinck's 'Release Me' and 'The Last Waltz', respectively, keeping singles by The Beatles and Traffic from Number One. There followed a 'silver age' of British beat ruled by a grinning triumvirate of Marmalade, The Tremeloes – and Love Affair, whose *piece de resistance*, 1968's 'A Day Without Love' was, with that same year's 'Build Me Up Buttercup' by The Foundations, in the air when Rotten, Matlock, Jones and Cook were young adolescents. At the tender mercies of the Pistols, both items met the same remaindered fate as 'He's A Raver'.

Of those that didn't, the one of greatest antiquity from the 1960s was aggressive 'Don't Gimme No Lip Child' – with 'all that pushin' and shovin'' – on the back of 'The Crying Game' by Sheffield's Dave Berry, who, after waiting, like Mr. Micawber, for something to turn up as the seasons of pop revolved in time-honoured growth, death and rebirth, was to bloom again as one of few Swinging Sixties luminaries to rate in the punk explosion. Matlock was an enthusiast, shown when his post-Pistols group, The Spectres, retrod Berry's 1965 A-side, 'This Strange Effect'. Furthermore, Dave was also special guest of later McLaren clients, Adam & The Ants, at the Strand Lyceum, where his sloth-like stagecraft was as new and disquieting an experience for punk onlookers as it had been for their Mods-and-Rockers forerunners, who first saw it on *Top Of The Pops* in 1964.

Berry had been a 'local rock hero' to Chris Spedding, another chart contender and highly-waged session player over thirty who was palatable to the Pistols. His 'Motorbikin'' – all guitar tremelo, snarling carburettors and a surly leather boy 'too fast to live/too young to die' – had barged to Number Fourteen in 1975. Punks also applauded his reported resentment at having to forgo a ruminerative studio date for a televisual plug for what was to be his only smash. Spedding was to supervise the Pistols' first demos, and dust off 'Motorbikin'' when backed by The Damned at the celebrated Punk Rock Festival in the 100 Club in September 1976, where he was the only old timer allowed on stage.

The Damned had been the makers of 'New Rose', the first British punk 45. Before that, as well as interminable dub-reggae, the deafening dark of Blank Generation discos had been filled with singles by the more esteemed of those artists who'd come to prominence in the earlier 1970s – and who leading punk icons had said were OK – though the line was drawn on Pistols guitarist Steve Jones' heroes, The Faces, the Woodstock Nation's very own Brian Poole & The Tremeloes.

The Pistols had a more acceptable soft spot for glam-rock, especially Cockney Rebel, Roxy Music and David Bowie. The latter had issued 1973's *Pin-Ups*, an affectionate trawl through British beat group favourites, and was among the first to record a translation of 'Comme D'Habitude', a French ballad that, with new English lyrics, would mutate into a cabaret warhorse for every third-rate Sinatra. It would later be the subject of reactivations by entertainers as diverse as Elvis Presley – and, in 1978, the Sex Pistols.

The previous year, Rotten had treated his Mum and Dad to tickets to a Gary Glitter concert. Afterwards, the Rottens wormed their way backstage to chat with proud familiarity to the former glam-rock overlord, then less a pin-up than a favourite if rather screwy uncle. As such, Glitter inhabited an area bordered by further disparate punk founding fathers like Lou Reed and John Cale, former creative pivots of the Velvet Underground, and Nico, featured singer on the first LP; trouser-splitting PJ Proby; Captain Beefheart, creator of *Trout Mask Replica*, which was either mindless rubbish or *Rolling Stone*'s 'most important work of art ever to appear on a record'; Iggy Pop of The Stooges, whose 'No Fun' would be revamped as a Pistols B-side; The Doors (on Rotten's stereo during an *NME* interview); Marc Bolan of T Rex, and Alice Cooper – to whose 'I'm Eighteen' Johnny had mimed by way of audition for the Pistols.

Another blip on the test-card of that drab post-Woodstock period had been the 1972 Rock 'N' Roll Festival at Wembley Stadium – where Malcolm McLaren was sighted at a stall heaving with goods from Let It Rock, soon to exchange the drapes and bootlace ties for bondage accessories, strategically-ripped garb and Vivienne Westwood's avant-garde creations.

Let It Rock's appellation was after an opus by Chuck Berry, whose 'Johnny B Goode' signature tune was mangled briefly by the Pistols. Moreover, Rotten's catholic taste extended to Teddy Boy revivalists like Shakin' Stevens & The Sunsets – so much so that he dared an evening in a pub where the outfit was playing in the teeth of both McLaren's image-conscious ire and the front page TEDS VERSUS PUNKS headline in *Melody Maker*, focussed on a – possibly staged – confrontation in Sloane Square in July 1977, repeated on subsequent Saturday afternoons. However, the dust had settled

Damned ◆ Graham Parker ◆ Beach Boys LP

SOUNDS

MEGA-
PUNK!

Iggy hits Britain,
page 26.

BOWIE
SEAL OF
APPROVAL

by summer 1979 when the Pistols – now minus Rotten – scored two fast Top Ten entries with xeroxes of 'Something Else' and 'C'mon Everybody' from the canon of Eddie Cochran.

The group was also sufficiently free-spirited to disassociate trademark extra-long hair with what Rotten heard as the agreeably 'chaotic-sounding' music of a reformed Pretty Things, who the Pistols had supported in 1976 (and with whom Matlock would perform in the mid-1980s). Lead guitarist Dick Taylor was to remember McLaren as a Things afficianado in 1964, when they were 'the Sex Pistols of their day. It was too much for the general public in the mid-1960s. The Stones just about walked the line; The Pretty Things went way over it. This was a time, remember, when simply getting married could ruin a pop star's career. The man-in-the-street couldn't imagine The Pretty Things ever being married – except to each other.'

Thus spake Screaming Lord Sutch, a sometime Let It Rock customer, and yet another precursor of punk – as demonstrated by The Damned, honoured one night to bear onstage the coffin from which the fabled aristocrat would leap to start his show. 'I was old enough to be some of their audience's grandfather, but The Damned wanted me to go on tour with them, and be introduced to their crowd, the punks. At a few of their gigs, I went on and sang their encores – 'Good Golly Miss Molly' and stuff like that.'

Nearly forty years earlier, the late Sutch had enjoyed instant national notoriety for recitals in which 'I came across as a Wild Man of Borneo, screaming out from the audience when I was announced. I went mad, jumping onto the piano and attacking the crowd. My backing group wasn't restricted. The madder they went, the madder I'd go. Everyone would play harder, and it made a more exciting gig.'

Evenly divided between horror spoofs and rock 'n' roll ravers, Sutch's vinyl legacy included 1963's 'Jack The Ripper' – 'nauseating trash' sneered *Melody Maker* – which brought him closest to the Top Fifty. While the point was frequently lost without the attendant visuals, the commercial progress of most Sutch A-sides was also hindered by restricted airplay and outright bans. In common with the Pistols – and the Stones and Things – too, at venues filled to overflowing, gawpers tuned into what balanced the slickness of a Broadway musical with the cliff-hanging sense that everything could fall to bits at any second.

Sutch was still grinding up and down Britain's motorways in an overloaded van in 1976, but a man who was an antithesis to such omnipresence also elicited respect from the Pistols, although it had been Rotten's habit to parade up and down King's Road with a doctored T-shirt bearing the legend 'I HATE PINK FLOYD'. The departure of Syd Barrett, the *ultima thule* of pop hermits, from *The Pink Floyd* in 1968 was on a par with, say, Mick Jagger, unable to cope with being a Rolling Stone after 'Not Fade Away', scurrying back to Dartford to live quietly with his parents. Nevertheless, the Pistols – without much hope – headhunted him to produce *Never Mind The Bollocks*, but Barrett, cloistered in a Chelsea flat, wouldn't answer their mob-handed knock.

Syd's is now sadly a 'no return' saga, but, absent from the stage for decades, forty-nine-year-old Serge Gainsbourg, forever synonymous with the infamous million-selling 'Je T'Aime... Moi Non Plus', ventured beneath the proscenium after punk slopped over his native France. At an outdoor punk festival in Epernay (from which the Pistols had been barred for 'going too far'), he gave 'em a couple of his not-so-forgotten compositions to accompaniment by Bijou. a 'power trio' in transition from heavy metal. Who'd have thought that the old boy still had it in him?

Concrete proof that you didn't have to be under twenty-five to be cool, Gainsbourg, an acquaintance of McLaren, was still courting controversy with his direction in 1976 of a sample of extreme cinema, also entitled *Je T'Aime... Moi Non Plus*, in which the shrieking female lead suffers unlubricated buggery, and a latest album, *Rock Around The Bunker* – through which you were left no wiser as to whether it was pro or anti-Nazi, just as the withering blast that was 'Bodies' – on *Never Mind The Bollocks* – was either for or against abortion.

Emitting an aura of fashionable depravity, Gainsbourg, like both Oliver Cromwell and Johnny Rotten, forbade the camouflaging of his physical blemishes in portraiture. There was no air-brushing out of a scab on the bridge of his nose in a deadpanned publicity photo.

Other less passive antics were wilder than those of any punk act, almost as wild as John Lennon's with Yoko Ono, the Wallis Simpson of pop, in the late 1960s, typified by *Self-Portrait*, a film short starring the arch-Beatle's member.

Lennon seemed to have gone the way of Syd Barrett, but Gainsbourg would still be winding people up as the 1980s loomed via 'Aux Armes Et Caetera', a *sotto voce* rendering of 'La Marseillaise' with a chopping reggae afterbeat. Catching it on the wireless, indignant senior civil servants, retired admirals and their ilk stung receptionists' ears with words like 'desecration', 'unpatriotic', 'disgrace' and 'repugnant'. What more did Serge need to be the rage of teenage France?

Jacques Brel had invited similar trouble in 1959 after fellow Belgians had been offended by his, 'Les Flamandes', a *chanson* that could be interpreted as representing them as ignorant and servile. The most conspicuous English language precedent of 'Aux Armes Et Caetera' had been Jimi Hendrix's instrumental disembowelling of 'The Star-Spangled Banner' that, screaming from a lone guitar at Woodstock, had been interpreted generally as a vote of no confidence in the Nixon administration. In Britain, there'd been P.J. Proby's little-known arrangement of the National Anthem as a bossa-nova, but, infinitely more harrowingly us-versus-them was the Pistols' 'God Save The Queen', a swipe at the royal family that almost topped the charts at the apogee of the sovereign's Silver Jubilee celebrations. No disc since 'Je T'Aime... Moi Non Plus' had caused so much upset in the kingdom, sparking off as it did widespread media condemnation and an advisedly 'secret' UK tour by a group already prey to eleventh hour nixing of scheduled concerts by municipal burghers.

Masquerading as lions of justice, striking a blow for decent entertainment for decent folk, some roughnecks tried to re-sculpt Johnny Rotten's face with a razor. Back in the 1950s, Nat 'King' Cole had been beaten up by segregationalist fanatics midway through his act in front of a mixed-race audience in North America's so-called 'Bible Belt'. Following media sensationalization of John Lennon 'boasting' that his Beatles were more popular than Christ, the four's tour of the States in August 1966 broke box office records below the Mason-Dixon line, despite – or because of – public bonfires of their records there, picketing of shows by Ku Klux Klansmen and the possibility of an in-concert slaughter of one or all of the group by divine wrath (or someone acting at the Almighty's behest).

On 29 August at San Francisco's Candlestick Park, The Beatles downed tools as a working band – just as the Sex Pistols would at the same city on 14 January 1978. In common with John, Paul, George and Ringo too, John, Paul, Steve and Sid – soon to die anyway – wouldn't be able as solo attractions to soundtrack the years that followed their group's sundering. The parts would never equal the whole.

Of all the post-Pistols efforts, front man Rotten's were, predictably, the most saleable, albeit on a law of diminishing returns. They also brought to the surface musical leanings that, like Shakin' Stevens-type rock 'n' roll, would have been anathema to bigoted punks. As a North London sixth-former, see, the boy feted to be Johnny Rotten looked every inch the long-haired hippy GCE A-level hopeful with 'prog-rock' albums on instant replay on his sock-smelling bedroom's stereo. 'He'd sit up there almost twenty-four hours a day,' gasped his father.

Johnny's essentially scholarly nature dictated finding much to notice, study and compare in sleevenotes, composing credits and so on. Hardly any piece of such information was too insignificant to be less than totally fascinating – certainly more fascinating than the jolly old A-levels apart from English literature, which was reflected musically in his enjoyment of Chaucerian verse set to aptly mediaeval instrumentation. Rotten couldn't help but absorb either the cultural heritage of his Irish ancestors – and an abiding interest in Gaelic and Celtic folk music was, after an insidious fashion, to pervade his output as an ex-Pistol.

Such tangents aside, young Johnny was specifically fond of Can, who, based in Cologne, were the leading lights of 'kraut-rock', which, by the beginning of the 1970s, was exuding a more universal if icily urban appeal, mostly via state-of-the-art musical machinery keeping pace with detached singing in English and lengthy extem-

Van Der Graaf Generator   *Peter Hammill*

porisations that transfixed some and bored others stiff. They accrued an extensive booking schedule on being promoted in a similar manner to Hawkwind, fixtures at the free festivals that pocked the alternative culture's social calendar in post-flower-power England. They too realised musical moods by open-ended improvisation. Although Hawkwind went in for long-winded 'works' rather than tart two-minute singles, 'Silver Machine', something of a Hawkwind anthem, ascended the UK Top Twenty in 1972 – and an arrangement of it was to kick off turn-of-the-century performances by a latter-day Sex Pistols.

In the same bag, Manchester's Van Der Graaf Generator had a doomy Germanic flair that also captivated Rotten – who chose a solo track by Peter Hammill, their singing wordsmith, on that same Capitol Radio show. He span one each too by Neil Young – whose high-pitched quavering seemed oddly familiar – and Kevin Coyne, a northern performer of the same vintage and artistic persuasion as Hammill. He was an acquired taste and infinitely less precious than Young, Nick Drake, Melanie, James Taylor and their sort. Their primarily acoustic albums reached out more to self-doubting adolescent diarists than devotees of heavy metal, jazz-rock and genres that dominated rock, when a back-street lad called Johnny came to identify with one described in press releases as an 'anti-star', and absorbed Coyne's gutteral vocal mannerisms and raw lyrics concerning unsavoury topics.

Nonetheless, along with other of Rotten's more sophisticated boyhood influences, Coyne left less of a mark on the Pistols than Public Image and associated projects that, outside the remit of this discussion, occupied the years that prefaced Johnny, Steve, Paul – and Glen – experiencing different revelations that arrived at the same conclusion: that there was to be no more circling round the issue. They anchored themselves to the notion that they were going to be Sex Pistols once more, and would have to put up with constantly being told that nothing they'd done since 1978 had ever matched the glory of 'Anarchy In The UK', 'God Save The Queen', 'Pretty Vacant' and all the rest of them. As Jones, Cook and Matlock had discovered long before Rotten, it was easier to let go, stop trying to prove themselves. Bereft of the time-and-situation of punk and the – often unlikely – movements that preceded and influenced it, the Sex Pistols apart had always been doomed to be ineffectual.

© *Alan Clayson 2006*

Alan Clayson

Alan Clayson is a writer, musician and performer who has remained on the margins of the rock world for over 30 years. The author of numerous books on music – including an on–going series about the individual members of The Rolling Stones, a similar one about The Beatles, and biographies of Edgar Varese, Keith Moon, Yoko Ono, Roy Orbison and others too numerous to mention, Clayson also contributes to journals as diverse as *The Guardian, Record Collector* and *Mojo.*

Alan is the author of *The Yardbirds* (Backbeat, 2002), the official biography of the band, and has just completed *Led Zeppelin: The Origin Of The Species – How, Why & Where It All Began* (Chrome Dreams, 2006).

More information www.alanclayson.com

Top-left — Daily Mirror

DAILY Mirror

BRITAIN'S BIGGEST DAILY SALE   7p   Tuesday, June 21, 1977

JIMBO'S CENTRE COURT SHOCKER
See Page 3

INJURED AMIN 'FLEES UGANDA'
By NICHOLAS DAVIES, Foreign Editor

GONE TO EARTH: Amin

Survived

PUNK STAR ROTTEN RAZORED

By STUART GREIG

VICTIM: Punk rock star Rotten.

Ambushed

By JILL PALMER and KENNETH HUGHES

END OF THE WORLD!

But it's all a TV hoax

Top-right — Daily Mirror

Daily Mirror

BRITAIN'S BIGGEST DAILY SALE   Thursday, December 2, 1976   No. 22,658

TV's Bill Grundy in rock outrage

?!★!

Judge in 'murder' pardon shocker
By ANDOT McKINLAY

THE GROUP IN THE BIG TV RUMPUS
Johnny Rotten, leader of the Sex PUNK, blurts a lot of foul-language words on TV viewers last night.

When the air turned blue . .

THE FILTH AND THE FURY!

A POP group shocked millions of viewers last night with the filthiest language heard on British television.

Uproar as viewers jam phones

Shocker

WHO ARE THESE PUNKS? PAGE NINE

Bottom-left — Sunday Mirror

Sunday Mirror

PUNK ROCK JUBILEE SHOCKER

THE FACE OF PUNK: A girl fan watching The Stranglers in Manchester

What's burning up the kids?

A disturbing report on the amazing new cult

by COLIN WILLS

PUNK ROCK — the spitting, swearing, savage pop music of rebellious youth — is changing teenage Britain.

VROOM BOOM   Guide to the motorcycle petrol-savers

Bottom-right — Daily Mirror

Daily Mirror

BRITAIN'S BIGGEST DAILY SALE   ★ ★   Thursday, December 2, 1976   No. 22,658

The Punk Rock horror show

OBNOXIOUS! OUTRAGEOUS!
—See Page 21

IT'S THE PUNK

Meehan rages at Waddell judge

FATHER MEEHAN

TV FURY OVER ROCK CULT FILTH

By STUART GREIG

A STRING of obscenities and four-letter words shocked millions of television viewers last night.

'Forcidable'

Phone protests swamp studio

Disgraceful

Encouraged

ANGRY DAD KICKS IN SET

In With the In Crowd:
The View From Under The Floorboards
by Judy Nylon

Icon *n:* an image, a representation, a simile or symbol, a representation of a sacred personage.

Iconoclast *n*: an image breaker, one who seeks to overthrow traditional popular ideas or institutions.

You can become an icon these days by showing your cervix to 10 million people or surviving the ups and downs of the entertainment business for so long they don't know how else to bill you when you won't go away. To be an iconoclast is to be in another kind of lineage, a lineage with an indefinite shelf life. You can't make an iconoclast with new clothes and a bit of second hand philosophy. Fully realized, iconoclasts have no need to re-invent themselves. They need only to never flinch. Clearly, John Lydon is an iconoclast.

The celebration of Pop Modernism that was Bowie, Roxy and Glam Rock had crumbled under power cuts, the three-day week, 14% unemployment, the IRA's strategic decision to take their battlefront to the mainland *et al*. Everyone was so poor that it all just looked tatty. By this time mainstream music was so naff that it was a relief to just ignore it. The first wave of Punk rose up stripped back to basics. Sinead O'Connor summed up part of the mindset later when she said, 'I do not want what I haven't got.' There was finally no shame to 'not having'. That hardness and focused inflexibility was there to enforce a level game field. However, Punk's undertow was the *Fin de siècle* sensibility of what would become the New Romantics, a bounce back to proportionally based beauty, glamour, melody and the tyranny of hairdressers. Elements of both these styles existed at the same time in London, vying for dominance, they always do. To claim invention for such a natural phenomenon is like claiming control of the weather.

I had been in London since 1970. To start with I had lived in the clique around Roxy Music. The first songs I wrote were done in Eno's little closet sized home studio. I recorded 'with lack of

127

craft' with Brian Eno on *The Seven Deadly Finns* and *Taking Tiger Mountain* (that's me in 'Back In Judy's Jungle') and had been in a performance arts group with a few of the crowd that went to Reading College with him. I lived in Chelsea, then North London and worked as a resident stylist for a studio in the old Covent Garden. I sensed that there was no chance of working as a recording artist if I was unwilling to accept the limited female role on offer to girls (before Punk). But I thought for just a minute there was a way around it when John Cale hired me to work on his album *Fear*. While working in the studio, John became a friend whom I still value very highly, but unfortunately, artistically with John, it was still the same dead zone for girls. I don't play tambourine and I'm

not a chick back-up singer. At street level, something new was just rumbling that would be later known as Punk. I defected to this new wide-open DIY band movement, sold all my Roxy style clothes to a second hand shop in Covent Garden, and moved down by the gas works, off the New King's Road. I never looked back. During the day I ran around town with Chrissie Hynde and at night I worked, writing with Patti Palladin, for our group Snatch, splicing together bulk erased 1/4" tape on her Teac and making loops running around glass milk bottles. We learned about studio sound and equipment quality in that room. Patti still has a very basic amp housed in a blue metal box the size of a pack of fags that was bought for a tenner on Denmark Street. It was called an AX AMP. It doesn't even have an off and on switch but you get the dirtiest guitar sound ever jacking into it and it makes an excellent feed back circuit. We recorded everything 'hot' and sang in unison. If our roots were in American 'girl groups', self-production and the home studio was our way to break free. It was what made us unique and included in the first wave of punk.

My dole check was a bit better than most because I had already worked at a reasonable wage. In spite of having a continual cold and never enough money to even pay on the bus, I remember this period as one with a lot of joyful moments. The Snatch single Stanley b/w IRT came out the week before The Damned's first single and hearing it played for the first time over the sound system at the Roxy was one of life's great moments. My memories of the whole Punk period are colored by the fact I'm female. I remember time as a textural field in which the details are more important because they make it real. The 'personal and emotional' tend to chart punk more precisely than the 'timeline' and because the days were far from routine it was hard to know what was important while it was happening. So far, other than Caroline Coon's *1988: The New Wave Punk Rock Explosion* which anticipates the importance of Punk, all of the numerous histories are written by men. Context is everything; cultural events overlap. For instance, I don't remember meeting people usually, but I clearly knew Viv Westwood before her store was the Sex shop because I remember wearing a pair of faux leather Oxford bags from Let It Rock that she had given me when I was directing the building of the indoor beach, holding a megaphone from the mezzanine level of the photo studio. The same trousers showed up on John Cale in the photo on the cover of his *Helen Of Troy* LP. I don't remember the moment I met Johnny Rotten either. It was most likely in the Sex shop at about the same time I met Steve Jones and Marco Pirroni. I do remember that Johnny rated Captain Beefheart and early 70's German stuff. I'd reviewed Magma for *NME* and was surprised that his taste, like mine, went beyond the VU, Iggy and the usual bands mentioned as influences.

Punk is an ongoing guerrilla war for the mass mind, the movement in mid to late 70s Britain was just a particularly colorful chapter. It is a war that can never reach a final peace. There is always part of the mind that loves revolution. My membership of the Roxy club, London's main Punk venue during 1977, expired on the thirty-first of December that year. For me that was the end of the era. For almost 30 years I haven't been able write about it; I couldn't even think about it without a rush of rage that I was unable to express without crying. Not that crying discredits the truth of what you've said, but I didn't want to speak until I had some understanding of why this area of thought was so toxic. In general I'm emotionally contained, but I still feel very strongly about the rights and wrongs in this period of my life. I remain unconvinced that there is any part of the music business that should be salvaged and carried into the 21st century. It's had a sixty-year run yet remains a vehicle for forty-year olds to take advantage of twenty-year olds. The organization seems more civilized than child prostitution in Asia but the intent is not. Even now the industry continues to blame its problems on 'new technology' rather than owning up to 'repellent practices.'

As a kid, whenever I shouted, 'Just leave me alone' my aunt would say, 'Can't a cat look at the queen?' When 'Anarchy In The UK' was followed by 'God Save The Queen', thereby putting the Pistols' music and image into the public domain, imagine how it must have felt for John Lydon when the Queen knew who the cat was. John Cale, who didn't approve of the Pistols' attack on the Royals, said to me, 'The Queen is the living embodiment of the rules by which gentlemen do business'. It was likely a creed he had grown up with, but now it was a conversation stopper. I'm no ardent anti-royalist - I was born in a country where lawyers and the heirs of robber barons run the government into the ground to compound profit at the expense of the social contract - and the notion of a person being trained from birth for 'the job' doesn't particularly offend me, but I do stress the Crown's obligation to the cat. The degree of public allegiance is directly proportional to the royal embodiment of commonly agreed ethics. You get the training and the castles but you also get dragged down and replaced when you become corrupt by association. And the agreed ethics are constantly to be challenged by people who think like John Lydon. That's the deal, whether you need protection dodging the bullet or the ballot - and there are very few 'gentlemen' who you can safely turn to in business.

Stop anyone on the street and say, 'Name a Punk' and they will most likely say 'Johnny Rotten' or possibly 'Sid Vicious'. To look at it all through Lydon is to regard the glass as half full. There was always something hopeful in John's vision; an insistence that wrong might be righted if you don't cave in. As the Pistols' lyricist, he wrote out universal thoughts in a very local language. There was always a pecking order in a *Lord Of The Flies* sort of way to London punk; if you could gather a hundred or so people who lived through it as part of the 'inner circle', they will almost certainly agree that John Lydon stood front and centre because he was the 'flack-catcher' as much as Sid was the 'sacrifice'.

There was a lot going on. We had no time to do anything but live in the present. We all lived so closely that a 'bleed through' of memories was inevitable. There are several good books on the punk era, by people with more feel for research than interpretation. These state just the bare bones of fact; I refer to them too and I was there, but the way the dots of fact connect when you include the memories of more people is something else. Ultimately this is more interesting to me. For instance, I've read quotes from Chrissie Hynde saying she walked with Rotten to his first gig; but I have my own memories of walking him to the very same event. These are synaptic clips of traipsing small, dark, wet street gutters in Soho with Johnny in front of me; in this memory I am sensing his quiet agitation. No one spoke. There was no costume; he went from the gutters to the stage without changing. I don't remember Chrissie being with us, but then she obviously doesn't remember me being there. However, Chrissie Hynde and I were together a lot of the time; maybe we were both there or maybe the boundaries of memory between us have blurred. I can picture Mick Jones in the very small audience even though I didn't know him then. In this memory grab, he has long hair and a long white scarf. The drummer for The Damned, Rat Scabies, has said, 'Mick looked like he was in Mott the Hoople'. His memory supports mine of the white scarf and the style. In the details, all of us are present in that place and hour. There is architecture, a multi-sided truth that can only be assembled with the bits we each recall. Truth may not go forth naked but it is relentlessly buoyant and certainly makes more sense when you think it through.

It is there in a composite of the details that fill in the space between islands of research. Even though I could read what was happening as it was going down, I didn't have time to catch the implications, to string it together; not until now.

Very few of us were known by the names on our birth certificates; it feels endearing to remember someone as 'Rotten' even if I am now to be confronted with a grown man in his 50s. We were tribal but not along bloodlines or back-stories. There was a subtle linkage by being from a particular location like Bromley or Forest Hill and hitting London at that angle, although I'm not familiar enough with these small enclaves to interpret the fine points. On that level, I still belong to the group of four 'Yanks' - Chrissie Hynde; my partner in Snatch, Patti Palladin; photographer Kate Simon and me. I knew Kate from Chelsea in the early 70s. Palladin I met over a long distance phone call when she agreed to bring me some trousers from a New York designer I'd liked since Doll days. Chrissie and I met when she showed up at Brian Eno's to interview him for *NME* in connection with the *Here Come The Warm Jets* album. The number of Yanks in London expanded when the Heartbreakers, Nancy Spungen, and Jayne County arrived. Because the United States is so large - the entire landmass of the United Kingdom fits into the state of Florida - there was a curious crew formed by cobbling us all in together, but we were not sharing any regional sensibility. By virtue of us each being a minimum 5,000 miles away from our places of birth, we were also not as malleable. Any of the Yanks knew how to source whatever they wanted, wherever they were. I had been on my own all over the world since I was 16. We could never become the kind of pets the music business wanted unless we were strung out and sleepwalking. Malcolm McLaren's idea of social revolution didn't fly because all of the Yanks had already pulled time in Paris and had witnessed the difference between French words and French deeds.

Johnny was never ageist and even before he had much mileage himself it was clear that he had no fear of experience. John chose Nora as his partner. He chose, not some punky version of a "dolly bird", but rather a stunning, athletic looking, tall, blonde, European woman who spoke several languages, did not need financial support and was impervious to the petty imbroglios of the punk crowd. It was an unusual, somewhat daring choice for an 18-year-old boy from North London. Nora was older than John, and her daughter Ari is one of his closest friends. Nora placed herself between The Slits and the worst abuses offered by the record business and stood strong with Rotten no matter what. Thirty years later they are still together, though they were never the kind of couple that the press had any idea what to do with. The media likes 'young', 'doomed', and 'clichéd' couples for 'puff pieces'. Nora and Johnny were way more complicated than that. I remember being in Nora's car with John riding shotgun. She was driving fast to get back to John's flat to go to the loo. We got there and John was pretending to have lost the keys. It was a playful torture. Sort of odd to be included as a witness, but I don't think anyone would be dumb enough to be lured

'*Four Yanks*' - clockwise from top left -
Kate Simon, Patti Palladin, Chrissie Hynde, Judy Nylon

into badmouthing either of them. They would certainly turn on a common enemy; that's how the relationship worked.

That present seemed then like a vast expanse of wet grey dead time populated with home done haircuts and faded black rags, jazzed up with a jangle of chains. But we were energized, even in repose. Mostly I remember walking; walking to get somewhere or walking for entertainment; hanging out at record stalls or waffling for hours over a pint in one of three or four boozers - in Chelsea, Soho or Portobello Road. Rotten could hang around doing nothing like nobody else. He was not the life and soul of the party, but he was wide open and he was fun. I have a soft, tender memory of Lydon, John Gray, Patti Palladin and myself dancing on the backbeat, reggae booming in Patti's tiny flat. The space was only about 10' square and dark for a lack of electrical outlets; a run down dollhouse in a mews lit at street level with a single light on wet cobblestone. It was like an empty movie set once the garage downstairs locked up at 6pm. The analog home studio was stacked around the room and a spaghetti ball of cords ran behind everything. It was a punk clubhouse, one of a few; we all made the rounds to each of them. To this day I remember the location of every cigarette machine in a one-mile radius of that mews. John and whomever he was running with functioned like an off-stage clack, providing a distracting and on-going commentary. It was smart and droll, like Beckett; it filled in the hours of nothing to do, while holding endless cups of tea.

As with anyone and virtually everyone who was informed as events unfolded in the Lydon Vs. McLaren saga, I am firmly with Lydon on all counts. John is the artist here; manipulating other people is not an art; selling is not an art - whether it's snake oil or skinny rubber t-shirts - it's a knack; at best, a skill; useful for the artist to be aware of, but the notion of the deal as 'art' I find ludicrous. It can never be said too often that if Malcolm was the artist, he could have fronted the Sex Pistols.

I would love to see John Lydon turn his hand to all the things that catch his interest; he's game and always engaging. His recent *I'm A Celebrity, Get Me Out Of Here!* and *Megabugs* television series suggests he's more open than ever to give things a 'go' - but battling with Malcolm McLaren, long before any issues were dragged

through the courts, was surely exhausting. Being deeply involved with someone, professionally and financially, whom you don't trust an inch, fearing to even blink in their presence, cuts seriously into your time and quality of creative daydreaming. If he has stepped back, away from the fray, to ride a bicycle along beach roads, it is understandable. He's been through the machine.

Like John Lydon, I am very familiar with the 'No Dogs, No Blacks, No Irish' signage. They had those signs in Boston too. Being of Irish descent in mid-70s London was not an advantage for anyone, but back then very few people in London thought of Americans as having an underlying ethnic identity, so I never mentioned it. Lydon and I share a background in the Irish Diaspora. I'm also aware his, like mine, traces back to Galway. Undoubtedly we

were told the same famine stories to keep the rage warm. There is no emotional compensation to be had in being at the survival end of your DNA chain. Almost everyone in Punk was descended, within one or two generations, from some social injustice somewhere. A sense of such probably explains why waves of Punk keep coming, even 30 years on, as yet there is no shortage of social injustice. Sub-Saharan Punk will be an exquisite confection of disenfranchised anger, something to really look forward to. Punk is always the gristle that doesn't break down in the crucible of pop culture.

I still do not really value anything that is decided by committee; maybe that's Punk. For the first wave, hitting the shores of being 50-plus, it's not the end but rather the second act. 'Refine not Recant' is a good way to proceed. Since Punk I've come to understand the power of not having secrets. Privacy in the 21st century has certainly been revealed to be as much a wishful human construct as safety. One is never 'safe'. If you run and hide you will be chased and hunted down. Punk even then was a para-dynamic model of a just society. In Punk everything happened late at night among children. You subscribed to a code of morality where a fall from grace is guaranteed a swift punishment and exile. In London, at least, Punk was predominately vegetarian, humanist, but also survived only by the fittest. It was violent; it had to be. I have no patience for the notion of 'street cred'. Because my own background was grim enough that my street credibility was never in doubt, I feel obligated to be the one to insist that England works best without false class wars. Gutter roots don't make you special any more than upper class roots do; you just have different skill sets. If you are street smart, you protect others. If your luck was wealth, you pick up the tab or buy time. There was a lot more diversity in Punk than the history you've heard would lead you to believe; everyone had inherited both a destiny and demons of diverse kinds. I believe more 'Punk ethos' has been scattered throughout the world than is immediately apparent.

The whole Punk-Reggae sensibility was unique to the British strand of the form. This commanded the bridge leading a multi-racial generation from analog to digital. Making sure that everyone has web access worldwide is what is crucial now. Reggae's influence on humanizing punk is well known, but it is only now that Punk's influence of strengthening Reggae is becoming clearer. We were never media naive. For those of us who rode the first wave, there was both the exhilaration of being on camera in a televised social war and the discomfort of being under a microscope, handled with tweezers in the hands of the enemy. We were studied like fleas because we did not own power outside of what destruction we were capable of doing. The feeling was that you were in the center of a very small world that mattered, where events were unfolding faster than they could be analyzed or spun. We hardly paid attention to the

feedback outside ourselves and were in fact purposefully uncooper-
ative in a world where others had press agents and queued up to get
15 minutes of strobe light bounced off their teeth. Our poverty was
somewhat shocking to rock stars of an earlier era that had aspired
to never having to do things for themselves. However, simply put,
if you decline to make money off the backs of others, there is less
money to be had in 'immediate reward', but in a long artistic career
of slow accumulation, there is always enough.

To this day there are not many intimate photographs of the period. What you have seen are nearly all taken on the street or at gigs.
The quality of what has emerged is mostly low because it was either
commissioned by the record companies or limited to band shots and
people sucking microphones on stage. There is very little information in the background of the picture. There are many images yet to
come, cannibalized from sequential stills or digitally reconstructed
into that 'as yet un-named media' (a phrase everyone crosses out in
contracts). All new technology is magic (with all the inherent cargo
cults) until you understand it. There are probably plenty of images
still trapped in boxes on closet shelves, archives, or in garages in the
countryside, because people fear the cropping or the cannibalization
of their personal memory. My guess is that there will be no deathbed
confessions and no stories told for free to some young magazine
hack. We've all rolled over into the age of blogging, self-archiving,
citizen reporters or whatever you want to call it; the public does not
automatically get to know everything. Punk reserves the right to be
unreasonable 'in perpetuity'. It is not an end game, no one cares
about 'putting the record straight'. Since nobody else owned a camera, Don Letts' work is what is known best right now and it can only
be judged as a dog that sang the Marseillaise. Still, I don't remember professional photographers other than Don and Kate Simon ever
being welcome to hang out 'off the record' after the gigs and ligs.

There was no party line on the exclusion of press. There was
only a self-protective stance to keep out anyone who would take
advantage of you; but it wasn't inflexible. If someone was old, fat,
smart, rich, and powerful, it was up them to be irresistible company.
I adored a few crankies who fitted that profile. Lydon was intuitive
about who should be kept at arms length. You had to personally feel

Don Letts

what was real; there was no guiding voice. Johnny didn't really buy into agitprop revolution or the class struggle motif that was being foisted on Punk; Nora was hardly a waif. I suspect that it wasn't a Lennon imagined working-class-hero that he wanted to be, but a *classless* hero in a world of equal access.

It was always hard to get a candid photograph of Lydon. He was aware of the camera and played it like a harp, even if he wasn't looking to lens. I saw one picture of him glaring at Malcolm, who is clearly engaged in something else. It is a narrative staged with complete self-consciousness, to be enjoyed in print later. The only other person I can think of who could pull this off as well as Johnny, was Princess Diana.

This might be a good time to mention that the 'who ripped who's T-shirt first' debate regarding timelines of London and New York punk, is absolute rubbish. Plane tickets were cheap and both Brits and Yanks moved back and forth. There was no nationally isolated development. At best you can say English language punk came first. American punk was not underpinned by any socio-political thought, which is what defined London punk more than clothes or songs. There is ultimately no point in a comparison made of apples and pears. Importing the Heartbreakers and Nancy Spungen into London was like exposing Native Americans to Europeans in the 17th century. Payback. The outcome was inevitable. The New York scene was infected with the same drug, race and gender issues that had seeded cultural failure over and over. Too many of its key figures had been close to the 'skin trade'. This connection is part of a continuing American entertainment lineage running through the brothels, slavery, porn, mob influence, and so on; it still holds true. The Arts and Humanities are not highly valued by the American government. UK punks can be thankful that their government's threadbare socialism at least allowed for squats and dole cheques – making the lure of the Earl's Court rent boy circuit less inevitable.

Before all that happened, the only Yanks most of the London crowd really knew well were Chrissie Hynde, Patti Palladin, Kate Simon and me. As different as we were from each other, we were all benevolent influences compared to what was to come. Even if drugs were certain to cull the herd, it was not possible to keep the punk era in a hot house with just beer, pot and a few uppers. Touring involves exposure to the rest of the world. By the time the first wave had disintegrated into drunks and junkies, the disappointment was palpable. It would be almost 15 years before I would run into Al-Anon theory and go back and re-read the photographs of John, as Sid was disappearing into heroin and inching closer and closer to death. Malcolm might have been too young himself to be fully aware that the interesting spectacle he was driving forward had consequences. Sid covered with blood, dazed and iconic, was matched by Johnny suffering, pinched and hateful. The Sex Pistols had become a living example of the family life Yeats described as 'too much hatred, too little room'. The coming retribution after Sid's death would fester with an Irish patience until John was old enough and strong enough to drag McLaren through the courts and out into the scrutiny of public opinion around the world. But look at the pictures; it started then. He was smoldering.

John revealed a less guarded self to women; he liked them. He liked female company. He set the tone of equality on the street. Punk, at street level, held total equality between males and females. Punk girls wore and said whatever they wanted. If they chose to walk around in garters, it was not an invitation to harass without expecting a violent response. Lydon was an equal opportunity offender, which is all women ever really asked for. He was very comfortable to be around; he didn't seem to have anything to prove. Women were around him all the time but it wasn't a harem, it was more like a palace guard. You'd be hard pressed to find a female who had been around him then that would testify against him today. The subsequent gender inequality in punk was injected by the record companies' mistreatment of female artists.

Malcolm McLaren and Vivienne Westwood's agenda of pandering to the carriage trade, with their expensive designer clothes, was pretty obvious early on. This crowd of malcontents was unlikely to go in for what Ian Dury called 'new boots and panties', with the same lust for ruffles and rollers as bands of the 60s had. Punk would not be bought off that easily. Palladin and I called out Vivienne's intentions with a couplet in an early Snatch song, 'Where's that blond bitch, she's always lookin' a fight? Out selling her Mao T-shirts, 20 quid. Alright!' She returned the shout with an inept fistfight at 10am one morning, and by the failed gesture of sending immigration to my door. There were a certain amount of Sex shop clothes circulating on the streets, but I never knew anyone who actually bought them. You wore some of it whenever it fell into your hands, just for a bit, and passed it along. Now, when you see the photographs, it is not obvious that you're looking at different people in the same pair of trousers. The Pistols had the all the Sex shop gear they wanted, but the full retail price was allegedly deducted from their wages. I remember Jonesy stripping it off and throwing it in a bag, then getting on a pushbike after the gig and peddling away in a boiler suit. He looked like Robin Asquith in the 70s soft porn flick *Confessions Of A Window Cleaner*. A fluffy mohair sweater wasn't worth being beaten up for when you were moving through enemy territory.

I was never personally convinced that Glitterbest (McLaren's limited company through which he 'managed' the Pistols) hadn't

set the band up for a beating to keep them in line and provide an irresistible press op. There's no loyalty when you're just a product; the Sex shop had been called Let It Rock, flogging drape suits and brothel creepers to Teds under the same ownership, before Punk hit. It was just business. Johnny's own style is always what he looked best in. Tricked out in rumpled suits and shredded sleeves with an old great coat thrown on top, that's mostly how I remember him.

After he hit the papers, I don't recall ever seeing him walk alone; Nora had a car; Palladin had a car, Viv Westwood had a car and Andy and Sue Czezowski (from the Roxy club) had a car. The rest of us kept street mufti fairly low key and home made. I never had much interest in bondage trousers; I'm not into having my knees tied together. I have got a slide of myself at the Roxy wearing one of the kiddy-porn Tees, but it must have been either Kate's or Chrissie's. I have never bought anything from Westwood and McLaren on principal.

The boat ride on the Thames was a pivotal event in the whole Sex Pistols saga. I didn't even consider getting on a launch that I couldn't get off for four hours, knowing Malcolm's penchant for orchestrating outrage. I just looked at the pictures in the papers next morning, showing Viv fighting with the cops, and shrugged. It was all so predictable. Twenty years later, when it came up in conversation, Bertie Marshall (Berlin) said he wasn't there either. Since then I have asked others out of curiosity. Kate Simon wasn't on the boat. Patti Palladin and Chrissie Hynde weren't. I've yet to ask anyone who said they were. I do wonder who exactly was afloat that day. Film extras? Immediate family? Industry stiffs? Members of the press, certainly. A saturated Richard Branson in all the photos. I'm guessing that Jubilee day 1977 was ironically when being in the band became a job. Johnny must have felt like he was cornered and they'd sent in the clowns!

'Holidays In The Sun', about slumming in the third world, has a sentiment I often think about even though I've never taken a holiday without work being involved. We all sensed we were on the threshold of first world implosion without exactly knowing what came next. It was a difficult idea to share; there was no language to discuss it

openly, but there was a quality in what we had made that you knew couldn't be for everyone, although everyone was encouraged to start a band. 'Starting a band' was the metaphor for changing yourself, like 'hitting the road' had been for the Beats. Malcolm successfully branded punk, tried to control it and inadvertently found that all the historical referencing in the world (remember, he wasn't at the Paris riots, he just read the books) couldn't make life into his private theatre. McClaren was always perfectly suited to work in advertising because ads are in memory 'single frame'. Usually it's the last frame in a commercial that is memorable. There is, inherently, an inability to control a social idea in an unfolding timeline. That sort of unfolding is best described as 'enantiodroma'. This is a great word I picked up reading Bruce Sterling; it describes how something folds in on itself endlessly, like kneaded dough, or ribbon candy oozing out of a tube. Manipulation of the event can't construct a 'single frame final history' anymore accurately than the point of view of a single eyewitness.

John Lydon's birthday is the 31st of January; mine is on February 1st. It was the late night of his birthday and the early hour of mine when Sid Vicious died. That night was not about Sid coming to grief in a foreign land. Lydon knew everyone involved, I did too. The mule that brought the smack from England, the money that bought Sid's hit and the guy who copped for him were all part of the London scene. You could say, 'bad luck has a long reach'; or you just accept the idea that you cannot outrun the consequences of dumb decisions and unhealthy associations.

I've recently seen a picture of Sid Vicious and myself reprinted in a book on CBGB's. I remember the moment. I remember letting photographer Joe Stephens know he could have one frame, because Sid was off duty. I felt protective of Sid, much as Johnny did. I also felt the frustration of being unable to stop the nightmare that Vicious was in. Like Lydon, I have a low flash-point and a sobering ability to avenge. It's all part of the soldier-poet riff, that Irish thing. It was his rage that makes me remember him as angular. I wasn't close enough to understand exactly what the point of the manipulation was to get Glen out of the band - since *he* could actually play - and replace him with Sid, who couldn't. How did John

imagine this would develop or was it a Glitterbest manipulation
that blind-sided him?

I used to follow Formula One racing. I didn't go to the track or
anything, but I kept up with it in the papers, read a few books and
looked at the cars when I could. I've found old scraps of newspaper

in my diaries of the period. James Hunt was driving on the McClaren (no relation) team and Niki Lauder ran the Ferrari 312. I'd carefully note their qualifying times and their triumphs. In Formula One I think I've found the perfect metaphor to explain my subliminal feelings about the music business. The odds of surviving a driving career were stacked against you; about one out of five drivers crash resulting in death or permanent damage (or at least they did then). When you regularly hit 200mph you assume you have a dangerous job. When you pick up a guitar to make music you don't think you are in much danger. Your chances of seeing a ripe old age if you are in a successful (or even just a well known) band are about the same as driving Formula One. This happens generation after generation and I don't accept it can be explained as 'only suicides, addicts and lunatics are drawn into making music'. The pressure to surface in grinding poverty, endless scrutiny, dashed hopes and legal manipulation is emotionally deforming. The final realization is that no matter how careful you are, you will be ripped off, cut down to size and shamed for stupidity. For most artists, each 'pressing' numbers just enough to make a chase through the courts with a 500-an-hour lawyer financially unproductive. If too much money (to hide) accrues on the books, the recording is licensed to the next label, where the routine (or some variation) starts all over again. Finding the royalties is a book keeping frustration that provokes self-medication in all types.

John Lydon's duality of being a loner and a leader is oddly hypnotic. To engage with him makes you feel like you're torturing him but the fact is he is holding you there. He is an authentic stage presence; power crackles off him like static electricity. I was spared all of the really bratty behavior, but the bristling energy he gives off when he's put upon matches his mouth, and he could be cutting. There was not that same kind of charisma among the punk bands who kept touring, even if they became very professional by doing so. They'd forgotten the earlier tradition that most UK punk performers followed, meeting and interacting with their audience; an unheard of approach to live events prior to 1977. It's a method that may return through necessity and prove to be the key to surviving, now that recordings are almost giveaways and the whole gig is a 'meet and greet'.

I've seen several bands and performers lose themselves in the big blast of fame. It's not pretty and most are never worth knowing again. There are probably those who feel this way about Lydon; he's not wedded to the devil in the details, quite a bit of what he says is self-conflicting, but the larger gesture of what he is willing to stand for has never wavered. Even when he's overwhelmed, he won't back down. It's a tendency to run screaming into certain death if you know it is the right thing. If you don't see that, well, as Johnny is so fond of screaming, 'You're just not paying attention!'

Johnny has retained a love of echo throughout his career; sonic expansiveness, a landscape that acknowledges the void is with you always, not just when you're stoned. His love of reggae was, if not instrumental, then certainly paramount in the music he produced post Pistols. In the early 80s, when the scene had moved on, the Jamaican habit of piling into the kitchen, passing the duchie and cooking up a stew with rice - resplendent with coconut - and with the music cranked was *de rigeur*. Before that, Punk cuisine was limited to bags of crisps, fish and chips, canned beans on toast and that foul concoction known as a chip buttie. For those who have never run into one, the ingredients are chips (fried potatos, for my fellow Yanks) between two slices of 'mother's pride' (cheap nasty white bread) slathered with salad cream (a vinegary, low grade mayonnaise). The first time I was offered this delicacy was at The Slits' hang out. We had all just gotten instruments which we'd no clue how to play. It was a room full of girls and unimaginable noise. I wanted so much to feel included that I closed my eyes and swallowed the whole thing in about five quick bites. The attempt to find a new 'comfort food' wasn't very successful but the reverb that I associate with this period is still deeply imprinted.

Lydon gained much more creative bandwidth during PiL's early phase. In a sense, Keith Levene fearlessly manifested the softer side of John, a quality burned out of him during the Pistols. PiL was essentially a great idea, whether or not it went as far as it could have. Personally, I think PiL has proven to be Lydon's finest hour, most notably with the first and greatest line up, Levene's contribution was as important as Lydon's. They built new forms out of very different influences. If they'd had more time, less industry attention and hadn't squabbled so much, they could have created another huge wave of music, and evolved into an umbrella organization to shelter other projects for a very long time. One problem I saw was the ongoing connection to Virgin. If it were resurrected today, PiL wouldn't need record company involvement of any kind.

I had first meet Adrian Sherwood at Jeanette Lee's, after Keith recommended his work to me. Adrian and I were able to develop a studio blend of content and form that sounded good to both of us. This collaboration produced the *Pal Judy* recordings, released as a - now impossible to find - LP in 1982. Many of the songs on *Pal Judy* had been toured and played live in NYC, where I was considered part of the 'No Wave' scene. I could only use a very basic Roland Space Echo on stage because it was all I could afford. Once re-corded in London, the production we did brought these songs much closer to what John was up to in PiL. The stylistic connection has never been made, I feel, because my vocal performance was very American.

John Lydon's experience of fame has been a weird one. He became a jackass magnet. Even people who should have known better (they were famous themselves), fawned and drooled. He's been rewarded in money and access for the 'news rape' that comes with 30 years of media attention, but anyone he enjoyed hanging out with was certainly not going to endure *this* circus. Interesting people cross your path and move on when they suss the set-up. Hanging with animals is a solution. Some of the best relationships in my life have been with *actual* dogs. Taking the stewardship of the animal world, seriously, is the first baby step toward the love of humankind. I never had the sense that Lydon loved humankind *per se*. Maybe he's doing better with animals.

The last time I saw John Lydon was in some stinky, sticky dump of a nightclub in New York, where he was obligated to promote his book. He was immediately surrounded by students (and I use the term loosely) who wanted him to sign their army jackets (these are possibly on eBay as I type). Nora complained, over some B-strain of disco inferno, she couldn't get a fresh squeezed orange juice (seemingly unaware in this kind of joint you only drink from a sealed bottle). Lydon was bored, and no bloody wonder, I felt like I was talking to a fly trapped in amber.

I was delighted that, in early 2006, the Sex Pistols blew off going to their Rock 'n' Roll Hall Of Fame induction. The sort of fame they achieved was not something that the industry is ever going to be allowed to bestow and shape in its own image as a 'billable'. It's not all about entertainment, its control and business. Beside which, the satin baseball jackets they were handing out to inductees are surely red flags in front of a bull. They remind all of us of the tour jackets worn by the full figured A&R men with expense accounts and ponytails who populated the record industry in the 1970s.

An ending point here is that Punk launched an interesting set of people into an iconic continuum. It's as 'not over' for them as it is 'always new' for the recently interested. When I first moved into my apartment in NYC, I used to watch John Cage come by and pick up the sculptor Louise Nevelson. They'd stroll around the neighborhood and then hang out on her rooftop, under a rattan pavilion she'd built. The rafters were hung with hundreds of bamboo wind chimes that made a particular clicking sound in the breeze. I could lie on my bed and see them framed in my window. She'd sit in one teak chair facing south, wearing a dark flowing kaftan and a Kelly green riding hat, looking like a Henry Moore sculpture. Cage sat in another chair facing her. Towards the end of his life I would describe Cage as a philosopher and a gardener more than a working composer. Forcing tulips in his refrigerator and composing music were meditations. They're both gone now, they're both remembered as a layer of New York City, the same way as John Lydon will always be a part of London. I think about Cage and Nevelson. I couldn't hear them up there on the roof and I don't get all I want from studying their work.

Intergenerational cooperation between artists is important; we didn't get it, are we able to give it to people who come after us? The weirdest thing about being part of an idea that keeps coming, wave after wave, is the paralyzing replay effect. You can distract yourself with breeding or making money but there is as much need to change the way things play out at the end of your life as there was at the beginning. Yet the beginning is what is publicly replayed, over and over and over.

© *Judy Nylon 2006*

Judy Nylon

Brit-Punk insider Judy Nylon was born in Boston, Massachusetts, USA. An early friend and colleague of Brian Eno and occasional vocalist for John Cale ('tis she who's the subject of Eno's 'Back In Judy's Jungle', and who plays temptress on Cale's 'The Man Who Couldn't Afford To Orgy'), Judy came to embrace punk as half of girl-duo Snatch with Patti Paladin. Part too of the 'Yank girls in London' quartet with Paladin, Chrissie Hynde and Kate Simon, Nylon took the 'No-Wave' route out of the style she was becoming tired of by 1978, and returned to New York, where no-wave was exploding.

She still lives in NYC and today is involved largely with art and writing. 'Nylon' was not a name adopted for its Punkish connotations, but had been a family nick-name, originally of her father's, for years before the big event.

Into The Mystic:
When Johnny Met Tommy
Interview by Tommy Vance R.I.P.
Additional Material by Kris Needs and Rob Johnstone

'I just like all music'. John Lydon

John Lydon's appearance on the late Tommy Vance's Saturday evening Capital Radio show (Britain's first commercial radio station, then available only to the Greater London area), broadcast live on 16 July 1977, caused a stir in more ways than one. Firstly, it came at a time when the besieged Lydon wasn't talking to the press. The Pistols were at the height of their Jubilee and label-hopping notoriety. Lydon had been attacked in the street and in the tabloids. He agreed to do Vance's show because he got a chance to play his favourite records and talk about music. For John, this came as some welcome light relief, although he still got to talk about his life and the incredible pressure on himself and his group. The other notable thing about the appearance was Lydon's choice of music. At a time when punk seemed to be already getting predictable and formularised, he displayed an eclectic range of records by artists he had liked since school and none by other punk bands.

Johnny

Tommy

Many of the artists he chose were mavericks, either considered to be 'out there' or ahead of their time. Captain Beefheart, Can, Kevin Coyne, Tim Buckley and Peter Hammill had always provided diamonds in the mire of progressive rock and pop pap, but to have punk rock's most infamous figure singing their praises was shocking, but to many of similar inclination, inspirational. Lydon's 'coming out' meant you didn't have to be ashamed of some of those albums acquired before 'Year Zero'. It also cemented the bond between punk and reggae, stoked by Don Letts at the Roxy. Lydon's selection - a statement in itself – also indicated that his diverse taste could well lead to something totally different in the future. After being introduced as 'Johnny Rotten - A Punk And His Music', Lydon kicked off with Tim Buckley's 'Sweet Surrender' and Vance started the interview. At the time it was fascinating and refreshing to hear Lydon in non-confrontational mode with the Media.

If you could start again, would you do it exactly the same way?
Yeah, it wasn't as laid out as that. We just did it. It was spontaneous. That's the only way you should do anything, 'cause it's honest. You find out in the future that's it's not such fun. It's fashionable to believe that Malcolm McLaren dictates to us, but that's just not true. If anything he's like the fifth member of the band. We have just as much say in him as anything (laughs). What really amuses me is the way they say Malcolm controls the press. Media manipulator. The point of it all is that he done nothing. He just sat back and let them garble out their own rubbish, and they did.

Somebody told me he's a fascist.
That's absolute rubbish. He couldn't be. He's a Jew for a start.

There's got to be a first record that gave you musical influences or turned you on. Any ideas what it might have been?
Oh God, no! I couldn't tell you anything like that. I've liked music since the first day I began living. I just like all music. I remember *Ready Steady Go!* when I was small. That was great fun. And I had a plastic Beatles wig. That's what started me buying records. I felt

a part of it. In recent years, over the 70s, I haven't felt a part of anything in particular. Like, Bowie was good for a while but you couldn't really get into it 'cause you didn't get the impression he believed in what he was doing. I dunno what he was up to.

Not even at any stage of his career? Do you think he was always phoney or putting on an act?
I dunno. He was like a real bad drag queen. Some drag queens are very good. He wasn't. Bad stuff. 'Rebel Rebel' was a good single. It's about the New York Dolls, I think.

Do you ever sit back – and under the circumstances you've got plenty of time to do that because...
(*Cuts in*) No sir... I ain't got nothing else to do but sit back. Not being able to play ain't much fun. Not when you're in a band and you want to get on with it. It's only for the moment. We're in limbo.

How do you propose to get out?
I don't know, I really just don't know. But we will. We'll never give up.

Whether you like it or whether you don't, you are a figurehead of a certain type of movement. Do you ever sit back and look at the movement, the way it's going?
Yeah, I do all the time. A lot of it's rubbish. I mean real rubbish, pathetic and just giving it all a terrible bad name. A lot of bands are just ruining it. They're either getting too much into the star trip or they're going the exact opposite way. Neither way is really honest. If you know what you're doing you can completely ignore the whole damn thing, which is what we've always done until some silly press man decides to ask us what we think of The Rolling Stones. They don't bother me.

Anything by The Rolling Stones you admire?
No.

Nothing?

Nothing! I've never really liked any of those 60s bands. They're all just a terrible scratching sound.

What would you do if someone came up to you and said, 'You're to blame for all this'?
I'd ask them to explain themselves. If someone gives me a valid reason I'll listen. I don't mind.

Here's an album by Fred Locks, *Black Star Liner*.
(*Assumes Northern accent*) And there's nowt better than that going round. (*Back to normal voice*) The only reason I like this album – it's pretty lame – is 'cause one of the songs is called 'These Walls', which is really good. It's about walls surrounding him wherever he goes. Paranoia.

You talk about paranoia with a smile on your face but paranoia, clinically, is something that knocks out the smiles in people.
If you live in London you're paranoid 'cause it's so depressing. I mean, how many times have you been stuck in your room wondering where you can go because you got all this energy to get rid of and you just want to have some fun? There's just nowhere to go... (*stops*) And this is amazingly straight. I hate talking into this mic. Is it right you used to do the reggae programme?

Yeah. I like reggae because for a long time I thought it was the only stream of music in which people were trying to do different things like overdubs, echoes...
They just love sound, any sound, right down to, to... like that Culture single - car horns, babies crying....And why not? It's only sound. Music.

Where did you go to school?
This poxy Roman Catholic thing. All they done was teach me religion. Didn't give a damn about your education. I mean, that's not important, is it? Just as long as you go out being a priest.

Which you haven't become.

Well, no. That kind of forcing ideas on you when you don't want to know is bound to get the opposite reaction. They don't let you work it out for yourself. And that's why I hate schools. You're not given a choice. It's not free.

Can you think of any better system of educating people?
No I can't! I just know that one's not right. I wouldn't dare. It's out of my depth. I have nothing to do with that side of things. I haven't been to university and studied all the right attitudes, so I don't know. (*Fades in Doctor Alamantado's 'Born For A Purpose'*) This is it – 'Born For A Purpose', right? Now this record, just after I got my brains kicked out, I went home and played it and there's a verse in it which goes, 'If you have no reason for living, don't determine my life'. Cause the same thing happened to him. He got run over because he was a dread.

That's a big pile of reggae records for someone in a white band.
Come round my place sometime! I was brought up on it, right from the skinhead days when reggae was going around. I like a lot of soul as well. I borrowed all my soul stuff. Just to get these was a real strain 'cause I ain't got a record player at the moment, so I have to pass them around, cause music's for listening to, not to store away in a bloody cupboard. Yeah, I love my music.

I get the impression you really know what you're talking about. Do you?
Well, I think so. I hope so! If I don't I'm in a real bad state. Yeah, I think I do, yeah. Yeah. What can I say to that? I don't know. I can't swear, or spit.

What I really mean is that you take it really seriously.
Yeah, I do. I take the band really serious. I'm not going to have people knock them for ignorant reasons. I'm annoyed that the majority of so-called intelligent people would rather believe what they read in the *Daily Mirror*, knowing that papers like that are rubbish.

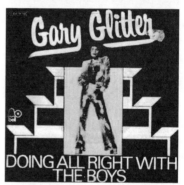

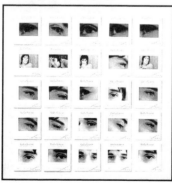

Scandal. It's stupid. I just thought everyone knew that. I was proved wrong. People like to believe the worst.

Do you resent the way people view you?
No, not at all. I don't care. If they get me wrong that's their problem. Just keep it to themselves. When they go out on the streets looking for me that's another kettle of fish. It's pathetic of them. Next question.

How many times have you been beaten up?
Loads. But that's just London at the moment. It's a violent town. Gangs strolling the streets. It's very easy to pick on one person and smash his head in. It's a big laugh for them.

I've only heard this next man's name – Peter Hammill.
He's great. A true original. If you listen to his solo albums I'm damn sure Bowie copied a lot off this geezer. The credit he deserves has just not been given to him.

This album is called *Nadir's Big Chance*. Can you give me a track?
Yeah. 'The Institute Of Mental Health Is Burning'. What's that other one? Oh God, the bastard hasn't written them in the right order. 'Nobody's Business'. That's it. That's really good. And it's about punks. He didn't mean it to be, but it's true. (*Sings*) 'You're nobody's, nobody's business'.

Johnny's Choice

1. Tim Buckley – Sweet Surrender
2. The Creation – Life Is Just Beginning
3. David Bowie – Rebel Rebel
4. The Chieftains – Jig A Jig
5. Augustus Pablo – King Tubby Meets The Rockers Uptown
6. Gary Glitter – Doin' All Right With The Boys
7. Fred Locks – Walls

8. Culture – I'm Not Ashamed
9. Dr Alimantado – Born For A Purpose
10. Bobby Byrd – Back From The Dead
11. Neil Young – Revolution Blues
12. Lou Reed – Men Of Good Fortune
13. Peter Hammill – The Institute Of Mental Health Is Burning
14. Aswad – Jah Wonderful
15. Captain Beefheart – The Blimp
16. Kevin Coyne – Eastbourne Ladies
17. Nico – Janitor Of Lunacy
18. Ken Boothe – Is It Because I'm Black?
19. John Cale – Legs Larry At The Television Centre
20. Third Ear Band – Fleance
21. Can – Halleluhwah
22. Peter Tosh – Legalise It

During the course of the show, the Sex Pistols' 'Did You No Wrong' was played (between Neil Young and Lou Reed), following Rotten's description of being beaten up in London. This was not one of his selections however, but added by the producers as it presumably appeared relevant to the topic of conversation. It had just been released as B' Side to 'God Save The Queen'. It was rather a strange choice for a Pistols' track because, although uncredited at the time, this song was written almost exclusively by Wally Nightingale. However, it should be remembered that this and it's A-Side were the only two Sex Pistols tracks available commercially at the time of the show - the 'Anarchy' 45 having been deleted when the band were removed from EMI. The Pistols debut album of course, wouldn't be released until October that year.

No More Mr Nice Guy:
The Brand New Us And Them
by Legs McNeil

When *Punk* magazine writer Mary Harron went to England to interview Johnny Rotten in the autumn of 1976, she returned to New York infected with Sex Pistols Fever, convinced that she had seen the future.

Before she went, Mary was also quite certain of the validity of the New York Punk scene, and was very generous with her praise of it – but still, it was nothing compared to her adoration of Rotten and the Pistols on her return, which made me sit up and take notice.

'Hey Mary, you actually like this guy?' I asked before I read a copy of her interview.

'Johnny Rotten's somebody who has a vision,' she told me, 'And for whatever reason, he's absolutely the center of this spinning, chaotic world – and he really does see it – because he embodies the thing that he is representing – that he is the spokesman for – and there was no bullshit. Johnny *was* the thing he was representing.

'He gave really clear and quite profound answers' Mary claimed, 'He's very smart, very confident, very funny, very young and he absolutely knows what's going on. I remember thinking while I was interviewing him, how incredibly smart he is. Johnny Rotten is one of the smartest people I have ever met.'

Of course. Harron went on to become the world famous film director of such movies as *I Shot Andy Warhol, American Psycho* and *The Notorious Bettie Page.*

But, before she found herself, Mary was a bit of a snob – Oxford-educated, theatre critic for *The Observer*, step-daughter of internationally famed author Stephen Vizinczey (*In Praise of Older Women*), step-daughter of Stanley Kubrick actress, Virginia Leith, and daughter of famed Canadian comic, Don Harron. If that wasn't confusing enough, one of Mary's stepmoms went on to marry playright Harold Pinter.

While I always thought it might have been John Holmstrom's sick sense of humour that sent Mary to interview Rotten, I must confess that I agreed with her take on Johnny.

'I was very scared when I went to interview him,' Harron confessed to me several years later, 'Because I was easily intimidated, and, after all – it was Johnny Rotten. The two scariest people I've interviewed were Lou Reed and Johnny Rotten. But actually, Johnny was wonderful, and very nice to me that night. He protected me from the others – Steve Jones and Glen Matlock – were kind of drunk and making rude remarks to me. Johnny told them, `She's alright, let it go, she's alright.'

Mary: What goes through your head when you're singing? What do you feel?
Johnny: It's like – (makes a face)
Mary: No, no, cut the shit. (laughing)
Johnny: I never understood why people are scared to go onstage, 'cause it doesn't take anything. You don't have to be drunk or out of your head. Just walk up there, that is if you feel like doing it.

'Like all the legendary events that I have attended in my life, the Sex Pistols concert was half empty,' Mary told me, 'The club was called Eric's, in Liverpool. It was quite a big nightclub, and it was half empty. There was hardly anybody there. There were about five people dressed like punks, and they all knew each other. If some movie director was filming this now, they would have everybody dressed like a punk.'

Mary: Did you ever have nerves before you went on?
Johnny: The first time, yeah. The first time I knew I wasn't getting it from a group.

'Did I tell you that I brought all these kids that were hanging around, into the interview with me?' Mary asked, 'I'd met all these kids in rubber trousers who looked terrifying in their fetishist clothing. Some of the Bromley Contingent were there, including Siouxsie Sioux, but mostly they were just hairdressers and art students from

Liverpool. Sweet kids. Their dream in life was to meet the Sex Pistols, so I brought them into the interview with me.'

Johnny: What's New York like, anyway?
Mary: It's really good.
Johnny: The New York groups, they're very into proving how good they are… how intellectual… I don't like that. I think that's silly.
Mary: What don't you like about it?
Johnny: You know, going on about social significance, blah, blah…

'When I first saw English punk,' Mary laughed, 'I thought, "Oh my god, oh my god, what have we done, what have we created?" I thought what we had done in New York as a joke – had been taken for real by a younger and more violent audience in England. It was like everything we had done ironically, in New York punk, the English took seriously.

Legs McNeil

'The English punk scene was more in your face and you couldn't help notice it,' Mary continued, 'There was a violence under the surface – it was much more kind of raw and real. You felt something could erupt at any moment; smashed glass, a real kind of violence. It was much more volatile and edgy – and more dangerous.'

Mary: But people are always saying your music is socially significant?
Johnny: BUT WE DON'T, DO WE? We want to be AMATEURS. Don't mouth your own philosophies, or you'll just get laughed at.

'I really liked the Sex Pistols as well,' Mary continued, 'I mean, that was a great show, I mean, it was bad – it was sloppy, but I loved the way Steve Jones played guitar. It was just like any good rock band, really. There was a little bit of casual heckling. I remember Johnny holding the mike and saying, "FUCK OFF SUNSHINE!" He was very sarcastic – and doing this weird kind of dance.'

Mary: How did you feel about the set?
Johnny: It wasn't a good one. We can do much better than that. We were in Wolverhampton last night. And Dundee the night before. Fuckin' traveling around in the back of a van is no fun. It fucks you up.

'One thing I was aware of sitting backstage,' Mary noted, 'Was that Johnny was very aware of what people expected of him – and he could play with that – or he could intimidate people if he wanted to. He already had that power. I don't think he could help it really, he'd already been written about – and he was kind of making fun of it.'

'My ex-boyfriend, who I'd dragged along with me, absolutely hated the show,' Mary laughed, 'He was just disgusted by Rotten and the Pistols and he told me, "I'm very sorry but the whole thing is just a con. It's all just hype! It's all been masterminded by their manager, Malcolm McLaren! It's a scam, and you're really stupid to have fallen for it!"

'He was just snide about it,' Mary continued laughing, 'And he found it hard to admit he was wrong.'

Mary: Do you think the anarchy thing has been misrepresented?
Johnny: People are trying to make it out as a bit of a joke, but it's not a joke. It's not political anarchy either, it's musical anarchy, which is a different thing.

I really felt the world moving and shaking that autumn in England, in terms of punk,' Mary confessed, 'I went to interview The Damned – I was supposed to do The Clash and that fell through – but there was definitely a sense of something big happening.'

Mary's interview was my first introduction to Johnny Rotten and the Sex Pistols, and it captures Rotten when he was still a fresh-faced, snot-nosed kid – his world spread-eagled before him with stunning possibilities. Johnny seemed like a sweet kid. Mary got him at just the right moment, before everything came crashing down on him.

By the time Mary did the interview in October 1976 and it was published in *Punk* magazine in March 1977, the interview was already obsolete. That's how fast things were happening.

In that time, the Pistols were signed to EMI Records, released their first single, 'Anarchy In The UK,' and then came the infamous December 1st 1976 appearance on the Bill Grundy television program. The Pistols, along with their entourage, 'The Bromley Contingent,' (including Siouxsie Sioux) appeared on the Thames Television Program, *Today*.

Johnny Rotten said, `Shit.'

Steve Jones told Bill Grundy he was, 'A Fuckin' Rotter'.

All in all, it was not as offensive as what is regularly seen on *The Jerry Springer Show*. Still, it was enough of a sin to snare the headlines – the *Daily Mirror* ran with the now infamous 'The Filth and the Fury,' while the *Daily Express* went with 'Punk? Call it Filthy Lucre.'

The Pistols were oblivious to the fuss they'd caused, and left the TV show to pick up Johnny Thunders & The Heartbreakers at Heathrow Airport, since the New York band was scheduled to open for the Pistols on their 'Anarchy In The UK Tour'. The Heartbreakers were there to lend the Sex Pistols some punk credibility, but after the TV show, they didn't need any.

'Someone called me in New York,' Mary explained, 'And said that she just heard that Johnny Rotten had been on this TV show and had said, "Fuck" or whatever. I had the number for Malcolm McLaren, so I called him in London and I could tell he was kind of shocked. It was Malcolm and Lee Black Childers, the manager of Johnny Thunders & The Heartbreakers. I talked to both of them. And I just thought, "Whoa-oh!" Because, quite in contradiction to the myth of Malcolm as a great manipulator, Malcolm said, "I can't believe what just happened!" I think they felt like they were on a runaway train.'

The resulting fallout from the Grundy show caused local authorities to cancel most dates on their Anarchy Tour – and as a hostile press slagged off the band – the Sex Pistols succeeded in becoming the world's first Punk band.

It didn't matter that The Ramones, The Damned, Patti Smith, Iggy Pop, The Slits, Richard Hell & The Voidoids, etc, were already going concerns. It the old music business dictum of 'Whoever gets the most press, wins,' the Sex Pistols captured the English imagination – and then the world's.

The Pistols and their ilk, looked disturbing, even to me. If you doubt this, ask yourself, 'What looks more shocking? A Johnny Ramone bowl-cut or a day-glo mohawk?' Suffice to say, it was in that moment, everything we had done in New York - the magazine, the music, the scene – were no longer valid. And what made it even worse was that the Pistols sounded *so good*.

Cheetah Chrome, the Dead Boys' lead gutarist told me, 'We were really happy with the first album that we had just done, when somebody put on the Pistols' first records and we went, "What the fuck?!"'

When the 'Anarchy In The UK Tour' finished up in near-riots – because of the cancellations – EMI was at a loss with what to do with the Pistols. So the boys in the front office decided to send their headaches to Amsterdam, while the negative press subsided.

It didn't.

Instead, Rotten and the Pistols became a bonafide snarling commodity after television crews filmed them drunk and disgusting in Heathrow Airport upon their return from Amsterdam.

EMI quickly dropped the band on January 27th, 1977 (it was my birthday. I was 21 years old). In the shake-up that followed, Glen Matlock was replaced by Johnny's friend, Sid Vicious, the ultimate Sex Pistols fan, and the band signed with A&M.

After a wild record signing party back at the A&M offices – Sid trashed the Managing Director's office and vomited on his desk – the Sex Pistols were dropped the following week from A&M Records.

All of this happened between Mary Harron interviewing Johnny Rotten in October 1976 and the interview being published in March of 1977. Whatever Johnny Rotten had been when he was playing to 50 people in Liverpool – he was now a household name in England.

The Heartbreakers

Was it particularly good for John Lydon or anyone else in the band? Probably not, but it was fantastic news for the brand names of 'Johnny Rotten' and the 'Sex Pistols', because they were fast morphing from a band into an argument.

Danny Fields, the manager of The Ramones, the discoverer of Iggy Pop, the editor of *Sixteen* magazine, among a dozen other credits too numerous to mention, has always told me that this was what killed The Ramones, and every other American punk band's chances of making it.

'Malcolm's strategy for the Pistols was the theory of chaos,' Fields said, 'It was out of control and had nothing to do with any-thing musical. It had to do with this phenomenon of terror that was coming out of England. They put safety pins in the Queen's nose and and they would vomit and curse and say it's the end of the world. I always say when the music moves from the music section to the front page of the newspaper, you're in trouble.

'It was news for the wrong reasons,' Fields continued, 'It was like, here's the Pistols making front-page news in England every time they burped and farted, which they did a lot. So it was reported in America, and it couldn't help but define punk rock, because as soon as something is on the seven o'clock news and on the front page of the newspaper, then *that* is punk rock.'

As right as Danny was, the Pistols' story didn't end there – in May of 1977, they signed to Virgin, their third label in 12 months. They quickly released their second single, 'God Save The Queen', during Queen Elizabeth II's Silver Jubilee celebration.

As some fans have noted, 'God Save The Queen' was an attack on the ideals and institutions of Britain, delivered in Johnny Rotten's trademark sneer. The song is summarized in the line "There is no future... in England's dreaming," which became a de facto posi-tion statement for British punk." (*England's Dreaming* is also the title of John Savage's great book on the Sex Pistols, which, if you haven't read, you should).

In celebration of the success of the record, Malcolm chartered a party boat, and the band sailed down the Thames – past Westmin-ister and the Houses Of Parliament – singing, 'GOD SAVE THE QUEEN, SHE AIN'T NO HUMAN BEING!' Since it was the week of the Queen's Silver Jubilee Celebration, upon returning to shore, the police immediately raided the boat and took Johnny Rotten and his entourage into custody. Again, the Sex Pistols made headlines.

What had started as an innocent publicity stunt, soon became an opportunity for Royalists and other English folk who didn't get the joke to get Johnny Rotten and kick the living shit out of him. The most costly incident happened when Johnny was assualted by Teddy Boys outside the Pegasus pub, making the headlines once again.

Never Mind The Bollocks, Here's The Sex Pistols!, the band's first and only album, was released on October 16, 1977. The album far surpassed every promise the band's singles ever made – and then some. Like every action the Pistols now took, there was a media reaction – the Sheriff of Nottingham gave the band more headlines when he threatened a local record store with prosecution for displaying the 'obscene' cover.

The *Sheriff of Nottingham*? Now they even had their own Robin Hood-style mythology happening – as the trial heard expert witnesses testifying to the origins of the word 'bollocks' – saying it meant a 'priest', 'testicles' and in this case, 'nonsense'. The case was thrown out of court, not before insuring that pre-release orders were so high for the album, that it immediately charted at number one.

Since it is every English band's dream to conquer America, Malcolm finally had the goods with *Nevermind The Bollocks*, and set out to declare war on the USA. Things started off on a bad note when the Pistols were denied entry into the US because of some minor criminal convictions. The tour was pushed back from December 1977 to January 1978, and in the process, they cancelled their showcase on the hit American television show, *Saturday Night Live*.

Elvis Costello & The Attractions jumped in and appeared on the show, undoubtedly selling more Elvis Costello records than Sex Pistols. Unfortunately, the Sex Pistols missed their one big chance to show America how great they were musically. Had they appeared, Johnny Rotten probably would have become the new Bob Dylan or some other kind of international hero.

Instead things only got worse.

'As the four musicians straggled toward the plane at London's Heathrow Airport last week,' *Time* magazine reported, 'It was clear

from their appearance that they were not just another Top 40 act. They spat in the air, hurled four-letter words (the mildest, 'scum') at the photographers and with malevolent glares set off shivers in their fellow passengers. Said one woman passenger in disbelief, 'What are we flying with – a load of animals?' No, just the Sex Pistols living up to their bad boy reputation as the prophets of British punk rock.'

Of course, since I was the resident Punk at *Punk* magazine, I was destined to meet the Sex Pistols. The moment came on January 17th, 1978 at the Winterland Theater in San Francisco. I had been in Los Angeles with The Ramones, when John Holmstrom called from somewhere in America, on tour with the Pistols, and told me it was my duty to meet up with him and *Punk* photo editor, Roberta Bayley in San Francisco for the last date of the Sex Pistols American tour. My immediate reaction was, 'I'm not going, this is stupid.'

My problem was The Ramones. If ever there was a group where each member believed in his heart that he was the star of the band – who never could give praise to anything except their own accomplishments – who were about to become even more bitter over the Sex Pistols success – it was The Ramones.

The Ramones' hatred of everything non-Ramones should never be underestimated. From day one, they set the standard for everything punk in America, which is probably why it took a bunch of bratty English kids to sell Punk to the world.

When I told Joey Ramone that I had to go see the Sex Pistols in San Francisco, he acted like I had stabbed him in the back.

'Yeah Legs, go hang out with your new best friends,' Joey snapped 'the Sex Pistols'.

Who could blame him? The Ramones had just released their third album, *Rocket To Russia*, and were headed for superstardom, they believed, when the train was derailed by Sex Pistols hysteria. Me and Joey watched on television as the Pistols crawled across America – and kids traded in their denim and flannel for black leather and leopard-skin prints – finally getting Punk.

'The Sex Pistols were at a soundcheck when the Variety '77 television show presented them on national TV for the first time,' John Holmstrom wrote, 'Alan King and Telly Savalas made a point of announcing their appearance every five minutes, 'Coming up soon, the Sensational Sex Pistols!'

It was amazing. The Sex Pistols did in ten days what we had been trying to do for three years. And what was so humilating – it wasn't being done because of The Ramones or *Punk* magazine, but because of these foreign creeps who got all the attention. And to add insult to injury, Warner Brothers, The Ramones' parent company, dumped all their promotion money into the Sex Pistols, while The Ramones were left high and dry, once again.

It was hard to admit, but America didn't want The Ramones or *Punk* magazine. In fact, nobody knew that we even existed. And the media had chosen the Pistols because they were the most easy to ridicule – the target was already pasted over their faces.

Take this quote from *Time* magazine, 'Sure enough, the Pistols American debut was tame, almost a respectable happening. Johnny did not throw empty beer bottles at the audience. All he did was blow his nose a lot. Guitarist Steve Jones did not vomit, though in the past he has proven he has the stomach for it. Nor did bassist Sid Vicious sputter forth more than a few four-letter words. Sid did manage to draw cheers when he removed his shirt and revealed the torso of a 90-lb weakling. Both Vicious and Rotten sported hairdos that looked as if they had been blow-dried in a wind tunnel or plugged into a pre-amp.'

'The Sex Pistols were more authentic than the New York punk bands,' Mary claimed, 'They had to be. That was their purpose. Their art was to be offensive, kind of like Iggy was in the early days. Iggy was more like the Sex Pistols than he was like The Ramones, in the spirit of those early performances.

'The big thing that was happening in Punk,' Mary asserted, 'probably more so in Britain than America, was a real emphasis on purity and integrity. On *not* being a poser. Of being honest in a way – but if you made one wrong move, then everyone would pounce on you.

'But once everything you *do* is extreme and everything you *know* is extreme,' Mary asked, 'Where do you go from there?'

Since I was in Los Angeles to interview Hugh Hefner and hang out at the Playboy Mansion, I didn't think it would hurt my drinking to make a side-trip to San Francisco to see the Pistols, while I waited for Hefner to get back to me (he never did).

I picked up the receptionist at *Playboy* magazine, a beautiful brunette – and drove to San Francisco with a bunch of beer-drinking musicians who had to stop the van every twenty minutes to take a piss. We finally made it to the Miyako Hotel in Frisco's Japan-Town after ten hours, where a luxury suite was waiting.

The greatest thing about seeing the Pistols was the Miyako Hotel – eating crab meat sandwiches with English Muffins from room service – while floating in this green stuff you poured in the tub. Myself and the receptionist spent most of our time in the tub eating crabmeat, while chaos ruled all around us.

There were hundreds of kids in black leather and bizarre ghoul make-up, standing in front of the hotel, trying to catch a glimpse of their heroes. But the big problem of the Pistols tour was Noel Monk and the Warner Brothers roadies, who decided to distance Johnny and Sid, who were traveling on the bus – from Malcolm McLaren, Steve Jones and Paul Cook – who were flying to every gig.

It was Malcolm's promotional genius that dictated the band would play every backward American city, instead of going for the glamour of big cities, which is why they played Atlanta, Memphis, Baton Rouge, Dallas, Tulsa, San Antonio, etc.

The Ramones

The two-week American jaunt was an exhausting, badly-planned, dispiriting experience for all concerned (Vicious was beaten up by the bodyguards hired to protect him, Rotten had a fierce head cold, and the band's performances were plagued by bad sound and physically hostile audiences, mainly at unlikely venues in the South).

As Malcolm told *Rolling Stone*, "We never should have played Atlanta or Baton Rouge. How can the band write good songs when they are playing for college students? Next time we'll play Mississippi and Alabama, so we can see how horrible things really are. If we'd have listened to Warner Brothers, we'd have played New York.'

Next time?

While Malcolm was all for adventuring, he didn't want to travel on a bus to every backward American city. Therefore Johnny Rotten and Sid Vicious were sealed inside – with the Warner Brothers thugs – so television stations had something to film from their helicopters that followed the bus across America.

While Malcolm was busy trying to cause a teenage revolution, Noel Monk tried to steal the band from him. Of all the rock'n'roll assholes I have met in my life, Noel Monk was without a doubt the biggest. He had all the charm of a Hell's Angel at Altamont, and tried to subvert Malcolm and the Pistols at every turn.

175

'One of the English reporters complained to the tour manager, Noel Monk, about the treatment they'd received,' John Holmstrom wrote, 'Monk was standing behind one of his gorillas, leering down at this wimpy little reporter, shouting, "OH YEAH? WE'LL JUST SAY YOU TOOK A SWING AT US. IT'LL BE YOUR WORD AGIANST OURS, MOTHERFUCKER!" The reporter stood up to Monk, trying to reason with him, but after persistent violent threats, retreated to the bar.'

What was such a pity, was that the Pistols now needed a thug like this to keep the shit away from them. Being a Sex Pistol had become so physically dangerous, that they needed thug bodyguards to protect them.

'I was on the tour bus with Johnny and Sid.' Rock photographer Bob Gruen told me, 'And it wasn't only the the band who were crazy – the people who were supporting them were even worse. The Sex Pistols weren't violent people, but by shouting out their boredom and rage with everything, they attracted the most bizarre reactions from every side.

'One night, Noel Monk was asleep,' Bob Gruen continued, 'We pulled into a truck stop, like two or three in the morning, and Sid and I were up front, talking. We pulled into this place, so we jumped off the bus to get a hamburger. We sat down at the counter and ordered. I got a hamburger and Sid got some eggs. Noel came running in and said, "What are you doing? What's going on? What's happening here?" I said, "We're getting something to eat. Nothing's happening, you know?" Noel said, "Okay, well, come right back on the bus when your done."

'Everything was very normal, but then this big cowboy walked in with his family and took a seat at a table right next to us. The cowboy recognized Sid and started talking to him, and then invited Sid to join him at the table and eat with his family. Everything was fine, until I heard the cowboy say, `Oh, you're Vicious, can you do this?'

"I looked over just in time to see the cowboy putting a cigarette out on his own hand. Sid was just sitting there eating his eggs with his knife and fork. He looked up, unfazed, and said, "Well, I can, you know, hurt myself…" Then Sid cut his hand with his knife and it made a small cut in the skin. Not very deep, but the blood started seeping out, slowly working its way down until it reached the plate of eggs. But Sid didn't care, he was hungry and just kept gobbling them up.

'And the more Sid ate, the more horrified the cowboy became, until he completely freaked out, jumped up, gathered up his family, and started running for the door.'

Had Noel Monk been the diner at the time, he probably would have murdered the cowboy's entire family. You see, the Sex Pistols were so battered by being Sex Pistols, that they made a pact with the Devil so he would protect them – and like all Faustian bargains, there'd be no happy ending.

As soon as I arrived in San Francisco, John Holmstrom and Roberta Bayley told me that Noel Monk had accused Roberta of being a CIA agent and wouldn't let her into the show that night at Winterland. 'Okay, crazy-time', I thought to myself.

'Well, if Roberta can't get in, than I'm not going either,' I told Holmstrom, but he could see through my solidarity ploy as just an excuse to stay in the bathtub with my Playmate.

So I had to go to the show.

The Sex Pistols concert at Winterland sucked. During the early evening, Malcolm had tried to get some young, unknown bands to open the show, and it turned into a musical nightmare. Bad sound. Bad lighting. Bad vibes. When the Sex Pistols came on, it was just a continuation of the bad. Plus, they looked like the weren't having any fun. In fact, they looked down right miserable.

Johnny Rotten finished the performance by saying those now infamous punk rock parting words, 'Ever get the feeling you've been cheated?'

The only thing interesting about the entire performance, was when the band was leaving the stage, Sid paused, and nodded to the roadies – who pulled four young women out of the audience. That greedy Sidney. The girls were all knockouts too. I was jealous.

Right after the show, Roberta introduced me to Malcolm for the first time, and I told him the Pistols sucked. Malcolm agreed with me, saying he hoped he could find a new punk band to blow the Pistols away. Even their manager wasn't having any fun.

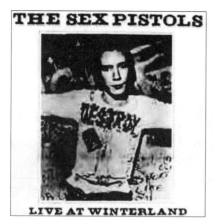

John Holmstrom found me after the concert, slapped a backstage pass on my jacket, handed me a tape recorder, and sent me to get a backstage interview with the band.

The backstage dressing room was a large rectangular room filled with old couches and green plastic garbage cans - filled with ice and Heinekens. Lucky for me, the pockets of my black leather jacket are ripped out, allowing me to fit an entire sixpack into my jacket.

On one wall, above the couches, someone had drawn, 'The Sex Pistols' in large, colorful letters, leaving me with the feeling that I was at some pathetic birthday party. I said hello to photographers Bob Gruen and Joe Stevens, both whom I knew from CBGB's, and grabbed a beer.

Sid was the first Pistol I saw, sitting in a chair, with his shirt off, surrounded by the four groupies the roadies just pulled from the audience. John Holmstrom and Roberta Bayley, had told me over the phone from Tulsa, 'You and Sid will get along great. He's just like you.'

I thought, 'Oh great, an idiot'. Sid didn't do much to change that image.

I watched him, a bit shocked that anyone would be offering themselves to Sid after *that* performance. Then I rememberd, it doesn't matter. The hype had done it's job.

Sid asked, 'Who's gonna fuck me tonight?'

One of the girls, a bit shy answered, 'How about a kiss first?' It was like a really bad porno movie.

'Poor Sid believed his own press,' Cheetah Chrome told me, 'He totally bought it, lock, stock and barrel. Sid was the perfect punk, I mean the guy came from fucking absolutely no musical background whatsoever, and just happened to be the best man for the job.

'Sid had to be the most attention-getting man in the world,' Cheetah laughed, 'Yeah, let's stick him in on bass,' and next thing he's an internationally famous rock'n'roll star, with like lots of money and no manners. No anything. If you put Sid and Peter Frampton, who was the biggest star of the world the year before, next to each other on a couch – Sid would have won hands down just by sheer force of personality. Sid was really rock'n'roll.'

Johnny Rotten looked a combination of embarrassed, painfully shy and angry, as the groupie said to him, 'Hi Johnny, how do you do?'

Johnny spat back a, 'Fuck you'.

The groupie turned red, and tried to smile. It was painful.

Johnny proceeded to go on a long rant about how, 'How do you do', was an invalid opening line. It was even more painful. Then photographer Joe Stevens introduced me to Rotten, who asked, 'What the fuck is a Legs McNeil?!!'

'What?' I asked, a bit pissed.

Johhny immediately went on to something else, flittering around the room, trying to come down from that debacle he had just orchestrated onstage. He looked like a duck on crack, except that he was wearing a beret and a long overcoat, so that he actually resembled a French duck on crack.

I sat on a couch, sipping my beer, when *Rolling Stone* photographer, Annie Leibowitz, came marching into the room, complete with an assistant carrying umbrellas and lights. Annie set up her photography equipment in a curtained bathroom, off of the main dressing room. Bob Gruen and Joe Stevens smirked to themselves at the idea of getting a posed Sex Pistols shot in this atmosphere.

At this point, Annie Leibowitz, realizing she wasn't going to have the band's cooperation for a posed shot in the bathroom, approached Johnny, who was now sitting on the couch alongside me.

'Johnny, will you sit next to Sid, so I can get a shot?' she asked politely, holding her camera.

'That fuckin' tosser can get over here then,' Johnny barked back.

179

Annie turned to Sid, still surrounded by the four groupies, and asked him if he would join Johnny.

'Fuckin' no way, tell that cunt he can come over here.'

This was going nowhere fast.

Sid and Johnny bantered back and forth, until Johnny turned to Annie and snarled, 'You wanna take my picture? IS MY HAIR AL-RIGHT?'

Then Johnny Rotten shot her one of his famous stock-crazy-faces, and I decided to leave. I said goodbye to Bob Gruen and Joe Stevens, as Annie somehow got Sid and Johnny a bit closer to each other, so she could get her picture.

As I walked out of the dressing room, my jacket full of Heinekens, I bumped into famed New York groupie Damita who was nine months pregnant. She had a hole cut in her t-shirt so that her naked, pregnant belly was exposed. I ripped off my backstage pass and slapped it on her swollen stomach, and said, 'Go get 'em girl!' And then I walked off, happy to be done with the Sex Pistols.

'Who could be bothered to listen to their music?' Danny Fields argued, 'Do you think Walter Cronkite was going to listen to 20 seconds of the music? There was no music on the network coverage of the Sex Pistols. It was simply that this sociological phenomenon from England that happened to play music, was playing here. What the Pistols did radical was in terms of music, which no one really appreciated. They were famous for the wrong reasons.'

Whatever Johnny had been when he played to those 50 people in Liverpool – he was now thoroughly damaged by the pummeling from everbody and everything

'It's unbelievable that a rock group,' John Holmstrom wrote, 'that played no more than 100 live performances (less then 50 according to guitarist Steve Jones) and existed for only 27 months , could become as internationally disliked as the Sex Pistols were.'

Little did I know, as I walked out of their dressing room, that it was the last time the Sex Pistols would be the Sex Pistols, for almost 20 years, until they would reform for another American tour in 1996.

Johnny Rotten would leave the band two days later.

'There's a fine line between the brilliant and the retarded,' Mary Harron claims, 'But in a way, both Johnny and Sid were the Id of Punk, they are the thing itself; you can't really separate them from it. They are these crazy destructive impulses – and they're primitive – but they're also very conceptual. Sid was very conceptual in the way he dressed – who is it that people want to look like? Sid became the very picture of punk. I know a Laotian couple who named their baby Sid Vicious.

'The Sex Pistols really couldn't continue as another band,' Mary continued, 'So I thought it was perfect that they broke up. I remember someone called me again to tell me that they had broken up and I was kind of like, "Oh, how perfect and true, they'll never disappoint us."'

Disappoint us? Never. Sid went on to be accused of murdering his girlfriend, Nancy Spungen, before he died of a heroin overdose himself. Johnny Rotten would sulk on the outskirts of the music industry, until he did his famous "I'm fat, I'm 40 and I'm back," tour of America 20 years after the fact. And so the Sex Pistols came to represent the long-dead era of Punk Rock.

But I always wondered what would have happened if the Pistols hadn't got all that attention and become such a spectacle. If they hadn't made front-page news every time they so much as burped. What if the music – instead of the antics – had gotten through?

If you want to know who the Sex Pistols really were, and what they might have become if they hadn't been chosen as the world's first punk band – hoisted out of the gutter by the media to be ridiculed and scorned, you only have to look at their final UK performance – at Ivanhoe's in Huddersfield, on Christmas Day 1977.

The Pistols played a benefit for the families of striking firemen, and as one critic wrote, "the gig was considered by some as a vindication of their anti-establishment stance when they were, for once, united with what might be viewed as their true constituency, the dispossessed British working class."

The Pistols did two shows, a matinee and an evening performance which, if it had been reported fairly, might have reversed some of their negative press. As one critic reported, 'Johnny Rotten mingled with the crowd wearing his pith helmet, and the good humour of the matinee – which was a benefit played for free – lingered on. Years later, the promoter of the evening show confessed that the Pistols never cashed his cheque.'

The Sex Pistols as naughty children, posing as bad boys, to raise money for striking firemen. It's a nice image, right? Johnny Rotten fixing a nice piece of cake for the old ladies in the corner, while Sid handed out turkey sandwiches?

The Sex Pistols were a bunch of scruffy street urchins who enjoyed a good time. That's the image I like to keep of them – getting drunk and playing at the Union Hall – while all the old ladies and gents looked on, disapprovingly.

(Johnny Rotten interview copyright 1976 by Mary Harron, used with permission of Mary Harron)

© *Legs McNeil 2006*

Legs McNeil

New York writer Legs McNeil co-founded the cult *PUNK* magazine in the mid-70s with John Holmstrom and another school friend. Indeed, the trio claimed to be the first people to ever use the word 'Punk' in the context of the brash new music they were then-writing about.

In more recent years, McNeil has co-written, *Please Kill Me: The Uncensored Oral History Of Punk*, (Little, Brown, 1996). In between, he has held the positions of Features Editor at *Spin* magazine and Editor-In-Chief at *Nerve*. He remains the foremost authority on the New York movement.

Goodbye and Hello:
Holding Court In Troubled Times
by Pat Gilbert

Johnny Rotten's emergence as a 21st century Renaissance Man seems to have surprised the British public – perhaps unsurprisingly, considering years of cartoon-ish portrayals in the tabloid press.

The fact Lydon is now an international, multi-media celebrity – famous not only for being the Pistols' most successful survivor, but also the star of reality TV show *I'm A Celebrity... Get Me Out Of Here!* and an accomplished TV presenter – places him in the curious position of outcast turned folk hero. He's probably the closest Britain has had in living memory to a Dick Turpin or Jonathan Wilde figure.

For years, Lydon felt misrepresented and unappreciated in the UK. His antipathy towards the British press ran deep, and explains in part his exodus to the States in the early 80s.

As recently as November 2001, when he was asked to accept an 'Inspiration' gong at *Q* magazine's prestigious annual Awards ceremony, he was privately expressing his concerns to the organisers that 'the press in Britain don't like me'. His perception was no doubt coloured by the unfavourable reviews of the Pistols' performance at Crystal Palace athletics stadium in June 2001; but it was also clear he felt (rightly or wrongly) there was a deep-seated and widespread hostility towards him.

But his relationship with his home country was soon going to change dramatically – and it all began at that *Q* Awards. After his memorable performance there, the public seemed to twig that Lydon's original views and fuck-you attitude were just what an increasingly corporate music business could do with. The nation didn't want the old cove as much as *need* him.

And what a day it was. Dressed in a cream-coloured suit and with an eccentrically shaved orange hairdo, John turned up at the swanky Park Lane Hotel in a rag-and-bone cart, accompanied by wife Nora and father John Christopher ('He's Steptoe,' he said by way of explanation, 'and I'm son.') The top-hatted doormen were somewhat taken aback.

Once inside, Rotten was in an impish mood. His party sat at a large round table towards the back of the hall and enthusiastically tucked into the free wine and beer. He was also accompanied by a handful of old Finsbury Park mates, including John 'Rambo' Stevens (also partner in his production company JSJL).

Lydon rattled the opulent chandeliers with an acceptance speech which went like this: 'Shut up! I've got a few words for you. Hello! This is the working class of England – I am one of them! And all you posh bastards out there too busy doing your fucking imitations know where it comes from. I want to say thank you to my family and friends. Stand up and let them know what a real Arsenal looks like! (To a heckler) Eh? You're a wanker!'

He went on to call comedian Keith Allen 'a turd' and praise Kate Bush – 'I fucking love your music'.

The funniest harangues, however, were bellowed from his table. As Elvis Costello opened the show with a solo spot, he shouted, 'Oh wonderful! Bloody wonderful! You were boring then and you're fucking boring now!' To the sartorially uninspired Starsailor he deadpanned, 'Nice of you to have made the fucking effort and dressed up for the occasion.'

A photographer was told, 'Fuck off you wanker! You've sprayed beer over my fucking shoes you clumsy cunt! What the fuck do you think you're doing? Fuck off!'

I, too, was the object of a verbal Lydon flailing. Once the awards had been distributed, I approached Rotten to ask him about his life-long heroes for a forthcoming issue of *MOJO* magazine. He told me he didn't believe in heroes. What about his favourite reggae artists, for example? No, he didn't want to mention any names, he didn't want to influence people – it was up to them to work it out for themselves.

Somewhat unwisely, I rose to the bait. 'Don't you think that's a bit conceited? Wouldn't they work it out for themselves anyway?' (Which, in retrospect, clearly wasn't what Lydon had meant).

'Look, you're the arsehole with the microphone,' he growled, 'sticking it in my face… Fuck off, little boy, or Johnny will give you a slap!'

The publicity that Lydon received in the papers the following day confirmed he was the star of the show. His arrival in the cart had delighted the press and his irreverent comments had shown he'd lost none of his old wit and fire. Lydon was suddenly now 'The Loveable Rogue' and a dignified, family-friendly punk survivor rather than 'Terrible Beast of Yore' – and like only a handful of other working class rascals turned national treasures – Keith Richards, George Best, Spike Milligan – he'd pulled off this feat without ever conforming to the expectations or rules of polite society.

The *Q* Awards was, then, the start of the nation's love affair with the then 40-something Johnny Rotten. But what it took to channel the prevailing affection for the man into an expression of widespread public admiration was his involvement in *I'm A Celebrity… Get Me Out Of Here!* – though he himself seems a little irritated that people regard the show as the key to his newly elevated public profile.

'I'd been around a long time before then,' he hisses when I interview him in December 2005. 'I damn well know that they did a publicity hype around that show… the way Granada (TV) manipulated the press was all about rubbishing your previous existence. This is what sells that show – you never really had a life beforehand. So be wary of that. Hello, I didn't just become invented by Granada TV! Of all people, Mr Rotten cannot be invented. Malcolm (McLaren) tried that cheeky shit and Granada are part two. It's nonsense.'

Yet there is no doubt that *I'm A Celebrity* did help shift a whole nation's perception of him. Many ordinary folk who knew him only by his Johnny Rotten *in extremis* persona saw for the first time the vulnerable, warm, witty and sensitive side of this staunchly working class curmudgeon.

On camera almost 24 hours a day for over a week, trapped with a group of other celebrities on a campsite in the heart of the Australian jungle, Lydon's humanity and bulldog spirit wooed a prime-time television audience often topping twelve million. His fellow inmates included model Jordan and ex-Aussie pop star Peter Andre (who subsequently married each other), George Best's former wife Alex and the disgraced peer Lord Brocket.

A spokesperson for ITV summed up public reaction when she said: '(Lydon) has been fantastic entertainment on the show and viewers and his fellow celebrities have found him to be an endearing, eccentric and sensitive character.'

Rotten was seen as friendly, hardworking, community-spirited (collecting wood for the campfire, killing rats, etc) and funny. His comedic, cracked-up face with its tooth-missing grin often filled the screen. In a 'Bush Tucker Trial' to earn food for his fellow campers he was viciously pecked by ostriches. He was also deliciously wicked about the contestants he thought weren't pulling their weight – namely, Jordan – and sent the ITV switchboard flashing when he said 'cunt' twice on air.

Jennie Bond, TV's delightfully posh Royal correspondent, seemed absolutely fascinated and charmed by the man who sang 'God save the Queen, she ain't no human being'. She looked at him with the same sense of wariness and awe that a domestic cat would look at a scorpion.

In a fascinating twist, it was revealed late in 2005 that Lydon was considering making a documentary about the Royal Family. It appears his attitude towards them is more complex that you might assume.

'Yeah, if it's there, it's there,' he explains. 'I do think they should be looked at properly. Janet Street-Porter did a thing on them and she's anti-Royal and I never knew that, and I've known her a long, long time. And they're ringing us and asking us to give them the rights to use 'God Save The Queen', and we're saying, "Hang on, right – who's the bloke who started all this discussion in the first place?" Don't you think I should have a say-so in it?'

Lydon adds that he *isn't* anti the Royals as human beings. He just doesn't understand how the monarchy can properly function as an institution – and doubts they do either.

Asked if there was anyone he particularly admired from that bunch of people; 'Charlie for hooking up with Camilla,' he smiles. 'I mean, at last he's married a car blanket! Super. But he clearly loves her. So at last in his daft existence he's found something he values. And that to me is *of* value, right? Now that's a good sign to me. That's how I look at it. He's put love above duty when he put duty before. How punishing it was marrying a gorgeous fairy tale bird!'

Princess Diana? 'Yeah… and was she a nice person? She couldn't possibly have been. She was a muck-raking, fucking jealous little bitch. Who married into a family knowing damn well that faith and love and truth, these are things that don't exist in that society.'

He goes on to praise Prince Harry for wanting to fight in the army and being 'of the people' and argues that the Royal Family represented a Britishness 'when there isn't much Britishness left. Where's the unity otherwise? I don't want a fake institution – I want them to be like us and us to be like them, but in a proper way.'

On *I'm A Celebrity*, viewers are invited to vote for their favourite contestant each day, and the one with the least votes is evicted from the jungle. Ten days in and with seven of the original dozen contestants left, Lydon sensationally packed his bags and walked out.

He didn't give a reason at the time, but later explained that the producers had failed to inform him that Nora had arrived safely in Australia from the States – despite an apparent agreement to do so. In December 1988, John and Nora were booked to fly on the Pan Am plane that crashed at Lockerbie when a terrorist bomb exploded in its hold: at the last minute they'd cancelled their reservation. Since then, they've made a ritual of telling each other of their safe arrival.

But there was a feeling among viewers that perhaps John would've left the set anyway: the fact it was a game show designed to mess with participants' heads didn't exactly make it a particularly Rotten-friendly environment. Since his dealings with Malcolm McLaren in the Pistols, Lydon has been trenchant about his unwillingness to be controlled or manipulated in any aspect of his life or in any situation: consciously or not, quitting early was the smartest move to make.

His exit completely wrong-footed the programme-makers and threw the game into disarray – very punk rock, very Rotten. It also transformed him into the hero of the piece. In the public's eyes he was the odds-on favourite to win who forsook his chance of glory on a matter of principle, leaving the crown to go to… homely C-lister Kerry McFadden.

The enthusiasm and empathy he'd shown for the jungle lizards and spiders had an unexpected effect: it immediately led to offers to front TV wildlife shows, including the *Megabugs* series (John going on the trail of various flies, ants, scorpions and wasps), plus *John Lydon Goes Ape* and *John Lydon's Shark Attack*. The latter, both shot in Africa, saw John, accompanied by Rambo, hanging out with gorillas in the jungle of Rwanda, and swimming with Great Whites off the coast north of Cape Town. The two Gooners' admiration for the African wildlife was matched only by their determination to buy a replica Arsenal shirt from a ramshackle wooden store in the middle of nowhere. It made great TV – Rotten in a swimsuit an' all.

Rumours later circulated that the singer donated his substantial *I'm A Celebrity* fee, reportedly around £100,000, to a chimp sanctuary in Sierra Leone.

Lydon is keen to impress that he takes the TV work extremely seriously. Previously, his series for VH-1 in the States, *Rotten TV*, had been taken off the air, reportedly because of its provocative content, though he also alleges there was a ploy by MTV (who own VH-1) to grab the 'Rotten' brand and 'use it for other people, like I don't count'.

He emphasises that he will not be scripted. 'What I do is free-form,' he explains, 'but it means your brain has to be so fucking in tune you really must be genuine in what you do. The *Megabugs* thingy, I mean, that's six weeks solid. There's not two minutes to spare – gruelling. I love it because I'm fully loaded inside.'

Lydon has also made a series of five programmes about British culture for Belgian TV with the Flemish historian Marc Reynebeau. It tackled the role of the Royal Family and other issues, including the infamous Mosque in his native Finsbury Park, which he found locked when he went to film it. God, he tells me, shouldn't come with a padlock attached.

So, here I am with Lydon in the week before Christmas in a posh suite at London's Savoy ('Hello, I'm at the Saveloy!' he beams). He will turn 50 next month, on 31 January 2006. Also present is Rambo, sitting in a chair next to him. There seems at first to be an element of Rambo chaperoning his old friend (for reasons that will become apparent later), but he soon melts into his seat, half-listening and occasionally chipping into the conversation to underline a point Lydon is making.

With Nora out in the West End shopping for gifts, we start by discussing Rotten's attitude towards his current status as household hero and national treasure.

The public perception of you seems to have been turned on its head – 'John Lydon: The Great Englishman'.
JL: But I see it as, 'By god, they've finally got it right' – that's all. Bingo. If I was wrong, nobody would be saying a word here. But I've been right. I'm more British now and I don't even live here! Maybe that's what being British is… I just like people – the good ones. I don't like institutions that create monsters.

But you were once Public Enemy Number 1, now you're something of a national treasure.
JL: And who was helping us? Nobody. (The Sex Pistols) were branded foul-mouthed yobs because a national alcoholic like Bill Grundy taunts us – shame on him not us. That's the society I come up from. Don't expect me to be loving that lot anytime soon.

That manipulation by the media must be very galling...

JL: Very infuriating, it really is. And it's a consistent burden to have to argue it – the more intellectual the publication, the more the compromise and bullshit and devious behaviour. I don't get any joy in talking to the media, I can tell you that for nothing. You know that.

For somebody who's meant to have a lazy nature, you seem to be doing a hell of a lot.

JL: I'd love to be (lazy). That would be my vision. I've tried hard to be lazy; I've really worked at it. I have to take huge breaks because my brain cannot handle it. At a certain point, I will start having seizures if I overwork myself (a legacy of his childhood meningitis). Big time. And that makes me very hard to work with, doesn't it John?

Rambo: Yes.

JL: There you go. I can't help that. But I'm far from lazy.

Was that always the way, from the beginning, that work ethic?

JL: None of this is a doddle or a breeze. I've made my life very hard in that way. But I wouldn't get any sense of purpose out of it any other way. I know what my ambitions are – I don't think I

can clearly define them because things that I value don't seem to be what most people understand or appreciate. I don't want to be famous – I don't have a need for it. I bloody like it – it's great – it's fantastic, but it's not the ambition. That's like being given a suitcase to carry your luggage in, but it's the luggage that matters. It's the content that matters.

So with all this TV work, and the Pistols still a going concern – are you now, well, happy?
JL: I like living. Every minute that I live is fine by me and it's not going to stop, even with the bad stuff. Like when I did time in Mountjoy prison (John was sentenced in 1980 to three months at the notoriously grim Dublin prison following a pub fracas; he was acquitted on appeal). I look back on it and think I did enjoy it there, this is new – what do I make of this? And I did exactly the same on *I'm A Celebrity*. I thought 'just be yourself', come what may.

And they liked you...
JL: Not always – who knows? But if they don't, then they're making a problem for me and I'll deal with that as it comes into my face. I'm not going to shy off from it. It's like Ireland – my family come from there so it's not a strange land to me. And every year we had to spend six weeks on a farm with no electricity. So Mountjoy was luxury! The annoyance of that was that my first night in was Friday, film night, and what did they play? They played a fucking punk rock film (Don Letts' *Punk Rock* movie). So there's (original punk scenester) Jordan wearing swastikas with her tits out and me goofing about and there's these blokes going, 'Is that you?' So I didn't die from knifing, I died from embarrassment! You think, 'Yeah, we are being a bit daft here'. So you take a double step and correct yourself. You've been told something, you've been warned. If you're not learning, you're cutting out other people.
It's the institutionalisation of prison. That's why I hate zoos. And here I am telling you: don't lock things up – just don't. Don't put bars around things. That doesn't solve criminality. Animals are violent in zoos, they've gone nuts. They're not designed for that. It's because of confines, lack of opportunities. Being put down, dis-

missed, left out of things. Poverty breeds crime – though the very worst criminals are the very wealthy.

When you go back to Finsbury Park, has the atmosphere changed?

JL: Sure - I'll say. It's very yuppied. The yuppies, they move into these working class areas and they don't do bugger all for the locals. They want them out. But they want to act like they're tough and they want to act like they're part of it. But they're buying their little weekend dreams. Weekend punks, and it's all shadowed versions of things. When they come into working class areas, they don't spread the money about. And there it goes, wicked.

Is there a working class anymore?

JL: No, because there aren't enough jobs. That's just basic common sense. I'm not talking 'knees up Mother Brown, 'round the old Joanna' working class, that's cornball. That isn't what I mean.

In your book, your father says you lost a lot of your early memories because of your childhood meningitis.

JL: Yeah. Bits and pieces have come back over the years but it's very odd – I can wake up one morning and remember something. So even to this day, I've still got bits of the jigsaw missing. And so I have that feeling of not belonging anywhere consistently.

Did your mum's passing in '79 change your perspective on a lot of stuff?

JL: I was numb, numb. She asked me to write a song for her when it looked like she was dying, for Christ's sake, (PiL's) Death Disco. That song's me screaming in pain and I don't even like to think about it. It's a very strange feeling to do it live, too, because I enjoy being that sad. Strange, strange thing because it's a release but my god you go through such agony in your head just re-living it. It's the same with everything I write. I mean every bloody word. I spend a long time thinking about what I do – it isn't just lazy-arsed shite. Although it's treated that flippantly by many journalists but that's their problem, not mine. I find people that don't do anything for a living hate me the most.

Your parents were quite supportive in their own way.
JL: Well they had to be, they had a loony for a son. I had no idea who they were. That's a terrible thing, innit? You bring a kid into the world and they go, 'Who are you?' (Laughs) What a burden that was. They were just basic Irish folks living in England. And that was bad. There was no doctors nor National Health to help so I ain't no romantic looking back at then, there was fuck all for you. Fuck all.
But bollocks to it – I love people. I'm a people person. I'm only really happy when it's out there in the field. Animals and insects, those are the things I understand. See how it operates with them. (Ironically) Thank God he's given us the burden of the seven deadly sins – greed, jealousy, etc! This is what comes with the gift of a brain and a higher intelligence. Well fuck that. (Points to his head) I want my bathroom sponge back. And on the other hand, I think it's marvellous what we are as a species. I think it's amazing. When you go out in the jungles and see that in the eyes of a chimpanzee when it looks at you, and you think it's going, 'Cor Johnny, I wish I was more like you.'

Lydon sits back on the settee and lights another Marlboro. This is the last in a whole afternoon of interviews and he's obviously starting to get tired. Earlier he'd complained to Rambo that his eyes were getting painful and were beginning to smart. Together with his bent spine, their sensitivity is another scar from his spinal meningitis, which laid him up in hospital for a year when he was seven.

In person, Lydon is unexpectedly friendly between his verbal tirades. Though he and Rambo resemble a couple of squatters in this palatial suite – magazines, books, discarded clothes and empty fag packets litter the ornate, striped upholstery – they also appear comfortable and relaxed. As with his bandmate Steve Jones, Lydon looks remarkably different from his younger self: in middle-age he has grown solid and stocky, and his lined face and missing tooth

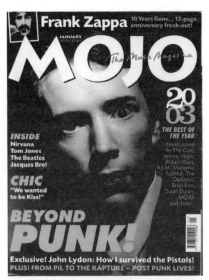

add to the impression of a rogue-ish, streetwise geezer. If you didn't know him as Johnny Rotten, you'd probably think he was a north London market-trader or virtuoso hairdresser.

When making a serious point, he looks anxious and thoughtful, punctuating his sentences with plenty of 'you know's and 'alright's, which don't invite dissension. When he's being impish, he'll refer to himself in the third person as 'Johnny' or 'Mr Rotten', hunch his shoulders and crumple his face into that leering, Old Man Steptoe grimace.

Lydon tells me he's taking painkillers, having dislocated his shoulder. 'How did I do it? (Laughs) Just being an arsehole in a comfortable bed. I do it a lot, put my shoulder out, and it just fucking sprung out at 4am and the pain was so, so fucking bad I thought, "Shit, I'll ruin this date," because I had this work to do and I've flown all this way and I feel obligated.'

There's nothing of the martyr about John – he seems genuinely pleased that he's pushed himself physically and mentally to honour all the interview commitments – but it does make you think about the many ignominies, if you can call them that, that he's suffered down the years, usually with admirable stoicism. Perhaps the most significant was the knife attack outside Wessex Studios in June 1977, at the height of the furore surrounding the Pistols' 'God Save The Queen' single. Rotten had taken refuge in a car, which was surrounded and smashed to pieces; one of his attackers managed to lean through a broken window and stab him through the hand with a stiletto blade.

After the incident, John became something of a recluse in his Chelsea house, wary of venturing out alone. At just 21, the media had transformed him into a semi-legitimate target for mindless violence.

Sadly, it seems, drinking in London still carries the threat of hassle 30-odd years later. I ask what the reaction would be if we popped to the pub across the road. 'It wouldn't work,' says Rambo.

'How would I know until I go?' adds Lydon. 'But I can tell you outright that any pub round here… safe as houses, I would think. That's until the arsehole accountant's had a few more and then the mouthy stuff starts. People generally just can't seem to butt out of your business. They see you in a newspaper or on TV and instantly seem to think they have a valued opinion about you. That's OK but keep it to yourself. Time out, mate. No one has the right to butt into your space. Some want to find the flaw and be the one that gets you that way. Others are just wickedly spiteful. And others think,

"Oh, isn't that what punks do, annoy each other?" To me, it means they're out of kilter with themselves.'

Later, I learn that John and Rambo had had to endure some wearisome remarks by a 'mouthy accountant' the previous night in the Savoy bar.

Worse still, Lydon explains, the media aren't much better. He doesn't expand on the theme – he doesn't have to. The group of journalists before me, dispatched by a middle-brow daily newspaper, steamed into the room and tried to goad Lydon into a slanging match. One of them called him a 'fucking cunt'. The party was bundled out of the room by John and Rambo; incredibly, the journo and photographer then went down to the Savoy's foyer and began ordering food and drinks on Lydon's room number. Naturally, the singer was extremely angry and upset.

Experience has taught Rotten to trust none but his own, which explains his tight circle of friends and family and the defensive aggression he uses to protect himself. I notice, for example, that whenever our conversation becomes too cosy, Lydon will suddenly switch into testy Johnny Rotten mode, reinforcing our relationship as journalist/fan and interviewee.

Tucking into the miniature whiskey bottles, our conversation continues.

You've talked about the Royal Family, do think a republic would work in a country like this?
JL: I'll fight for someone who'll fight for me. There it is. I ain't fighting for no cunt to have more expensive china.

What about living in the States? How does America view Britain now?
JL: As a piss-pot little country. As a place of insignificance; as a place run by a gormless idiot. Blair is seen as a gormless twat, right, and he's back-door Charlie to them. Rear entry, mate! The nonsense that he's whispering some common sense in Bush's ear – you read stuff like this. Oh yeah, is that how you ended up in Iraq then? Who's whose poodle?

A million people went out to protest on the streets of London against the War.
JL: If he'd have put his foot down and said, 'No, we need a good enough reason...' Before you kill anybody you'd better have a bloody good reason. And that vaguery, that nonsense (about WMD), wasn't a good enough reason. And so they go to war as war criminals. And these are dangerous words I speak – I go back (to America) on Monday. But I go willingly because I go with a sense of right in my mind. I'm not ashamed to say what's right. People have died because of these two cunts.

What was your father's perspective on all this stuff? Did he do National Service?
JL: I'm not going to say what my dad's perspective is. I'm never ever going to speak for him. Let's say he travelled a lot around conscription times (laughs).

What do you think was good about Britain in your parents' generation?
JL: People understood. People stuck by each other. They did. There was communities. When they started replacing pubs with wine bars, community went out the window. It's gone, it has. Football – teams, fans, it was community based. Now it's how much dosh you've got. Like the Highbury Library full of accountants, 'Oh come on you Gooners,' it's ridiculous. And I'm a season ticket holder – always will be, but I don't like what I have to put up with sitting around me. Years ago, you'd know everybody around you. You'd be somehow connected. And if you stepped out of line you'd get a smack on the back of the head and your dad would be told. But when the other lot came down your manor... hmm, they'd have to meet your manor on your manor. And that's important stuff. Those are not rules – those are common sense values that keep things proper.

Were 60s English TV comedies like *Hancock* and *Steptoe & Son* big influences on you?
JL: Influences? It's all there was on TV! You know, it was that or Panorama. Oh god, another Belfast documentary. I point these

things out and I don't mean to be… (tails off) that's all that went on in my life. I'm an avid book reader but that doesn't mean I'm a book. *Steptoe & Son* is the script. That was dialogue I could understand instinctively at an early age about things that were going on around me.

Was that humour reflected in the Sex Pistols?
JL: Oh, like totally. (Ironically) Yeah, like it's some dour, deep, dark thing with spiteful intent! Well it isn't. But the spiteful arseholes out there might think it's that way because that's how they are. Get it right. Don't try to reshape my history to accommodate your vision.

Changing the subject, in your book you say your family don't celebrate birthdays. You turn 50 in a few weeks' time…
JL: No, we've been quite loose about things like that. Which in a weird way has helped me have some sort of independence. You know, because we're not obligated by those things and don't see them as duties. And therefore when you celebrate you celebrate because you like each other and not because of an institution. That's why I don't believe in morals, I believe in values. There's a huge difference and I used to get the words confused and then I sorted that out. Anything that has a religious connotation goes. Except now, a contradiction of course is that they tried to take Christmas out of Christmas – I'm not going to gather round 'the Holiday Tree', that's dopey. Kids like Christmas, they like Santa Claus. Is Santa going to become the Gift Person – some politically correct, useless term?

Are you talking about America?
JL: In the States, but it's creeping over here. America's kind of running at the same pace as Britain now. It's beginning to get run down economically. They should call him the Great Leveller Bush.

How many of the Americans you meet in LA dislike Bush?
JL: A lot more than you would be led to believe by the media. People are people everywhere round the world, and I know that because I travelled it more than once or twice. There's good and there's bad but Bush is definitely not liked. You get this thing of block-vot-

ing Republicans – they don't actually vote, their vote is connected to being party members. They don't like him, even them, even the staunchest. It's seen as un-American to criticise him. It's almost like Russia years ago where they would have shot you for doing such a thing. You're just ostracised.

If you were around in the First World War, would you have been a conscientious objector? Would you have been conscripted?
JL: Yes, because I would be fully aware of the brutality of military prison. I'd rather take my chances in a trench, frankly. Why put yourself in a confined space to be brutalised daily? The bullets just might miss you, but the fucking truncheons won't. There's always common sense in these things. I do think it should be on a personal one-to-one basis whether you agree to go to a war or not. Hitler would definitely be a 'Yes, I'll be there', but this Iraq thing, 'No.' It's going to have to be run as a police state for god knows how many decades. You can't invade a country and solve its problems. You'll be seen as an occupying force. And it's mad out there anyway and they've run their lives that way too long to change it suddenly. You took the walls down in Russia – don't tell me that problem's solved. Afghanistan (laughs)! And you think Iraq's going to get any better? It's mental.

The interview is beginning to wind up. The photographer is setting up her equipment, and she and Rotten make small talk about her native Ireland. Having chatted all day, John doesn't seem in any hurry to stop. I tell him I need to use the bathroom, at which point he announces, to much laughter, 'I need a poo!'

Is it OK if I go first, I ask? 'Ha, ha!' cackles Lydon with head tilted sideways and an evil, comical smirk. 'Johnny Rotten has his *own* toilet…'

Lydon's brief absence gives me a moment to think about how, in 2006, he still exists in the public mind as a symbol of absolute rebellion – less the classic outsider who can't adjust to society (as you might imagine Sid Vicious would've been, had he lived; or Pete Doherty, if he survives), but someone who has unashamedly and intelligently played the system to his advantage. Yet unlike, say, the

Enron executives of this world, whatever Lydon does seems to be guided by a strong sense of moral purpose: he has a clear view of what's right from wrong.

Rotten remains, ultimately, *the* punk archetype. His individuality and unwillingness to conform define the notion of 'punk' better than anything or anyone else – next to him, the likes of Iggy Pop or The Ramones appear to have ended up oddly bourgeois. Lydon is also, perhaps, the last great English working class hero to come out of the grim, *Up The Junction* postwar years of poverty, bombsites, racism, poor diet and unravelling political Consensus. His mantra of 'don't accept what society tells you' is a creed worth handing down to subsequent generations.

In recent months, I've canvassed opinions about Rotten from his peers, and it's curious how they've reacted to his career arc. It's also interesting to see how they relate what he's doing to the notions of punk he himself established in the first place. (Not to imagine for one moment that Lydon gives a toss what they think.)

Steve Diggle of Buzzcocks, who still tour and record, thinks 'he does those programmes about lions and tigers really well and he's still really respected. But you've got to be careful you don't get all showbusiness, 'cos that's the antithesis of what punk was all about. I can't imagine Bob Dylan or Joe Strummer doing a programme on lions and tigers... what we did meant something and you must be careful to remind people of that. But Lydon's powerful and articulate and, the truth is, if it wasn't for him (Buzzcocks) wouldn't be here in the first place.'

Shane MacGowan, when asked if he and Rotten were the last true punks standing, wheezed 'I didn't know he was still standing. I thought he was kneeling down giving me a blowjob. He's only a little feller... But he's alright.' (Shane was, hard though it is to believe, completely pie-eyed at the time.)

The UK Subs' Charlie Harper argues 'it's great he's still out there doing it. I think his TV stuff is really cool. Why not?'

Lydon's ablutions sorted, we continue to talk, mostly about music and the future. The Sex Pistols – who in March 2006 would snub the attempt to induct them into the Rock'n'Roll Hall of Fame

– haven't toured now since 2001, and the last full Lydon solo album, *Psycho's Path*, was eight years ago, so…

Will the Pistols play again?
JL: No, we've done it. But there's been an offer in Japan – we might do it 'cause the money's great but secondly it can be filmed and that can be an end piece. We've done England. The hardcore were there (at Crystal Palace) and that's all that counts. And all those that weren't, like the other punk bands, can go fuck themselves. They missed out yet again. The Phoenix Festival was a stunner. In a weird way, putting out the singles (for *Best Of British Pound Notes*), we used samples to get an interest, I want them released. That's how it is. It's absurd. And distributed correctly, and I don't mean selling them down Camden Lock. Virgin isn't interested – the people who work there are fine but it's the hierarchy, they've lost the plot. They assume people know.

When the Pistols did the reunion in 1996 was there any sitting around beforehand saying, 'You called me a cunt, etc.'
JL: No, we all know it's all true so there's no discussion. We like the fact that we dislike each other and in a weird way that makes us like each other all the more. It's so brazenly in-your-face honest

between us. There's no problem at all with it. You know, I love being on stage with those chaps and I wouldn't be seen dead with them off. And they'd be the first to tell you the same about me. Alright. We're like that.

That's nice.
JL: (Laughs) No it's not nice.

Glen Matlock's taken a lot of stick from you over the years.
JL: Well, it's vice versa, too, you know, vice versa.

So you're all kind of in it together, you all know the score.
JL: It's still equal shares mate.

Was it better the second time around?
JL: The way we broke up, we all knew it was broken up for all the wrong reasons. And other people's manipulations. We reformed and it was the first time we actually got paid for what we did. Up to the end of the Sex Pistols we really hadn't seen much money at all. It had to involve court cases and all kinds of bollocks that went on for too long and in the interim period I went off and did PiL and they all went off and did their stuff and this cottage industry based on punk and the Sex Pistols built up and it didn't include us. No-one was offering us a fiver for the bootleg T-shirts. And so back we came and we were hated. 'How dare you come back!' Well hello, we've come back for our money! The money's not the big thing. I expected to be paid but the money wasn't great. I paid a few bills. It's the fact *we* now decide what we want to do, alright, and we made that very clear.

Would you ever get PiL back together?
JL: Which semblance of it? You know, 20-odd different albums, many different structures that I approached throughout all of that. But now I've put some of the Pistols and PiL songs together on that record, I really love the way they sound together – I've never done that before. I'm really chuffed with myself and with my brain and

how I've conceived music. It's anti-music throughout, really. And that makes it very, very musical.

What about children – have you ever wanted to do the dad thing?

JL: No, me and Nora… there was a mishap there a few yonks back and, yes, it broke both our hearts but there's always children around wherever I am, my brother's kids. One of the best jobs I ever had was before the Pistols looking after problem children. But they sacked me because I had green hair. So there was nothing else to do but become a Sex Pistol. The Sex Pistols wasn't something I was seeking, there was fuck all else left to do.

I still look out for kids with problems and I always will. I just have a natural affinity for the downtrodden, I can't help it. It's horrible and sad and it means your heart gets broken a lot. And there's so many of these pontificating, arrogant pop stars – their wonderful bloody Band Aid charity nonsenses. They do it in such a cold, businesslike way – they're removed from the problems, you know, they're not in there with the nitty gritty. The money I make, it goes all over. But anybody who thinks they can take it without asking, then they've got to walk.

Will there be a new solo album soon?

JL: I'm dying to get back and do that. I built my studio with (brother) Martin, we work really well and I can't be expected to know how every button works and Martin's very technical. I don't want to know how every machine works; I want to know what every machine does. And so we've found each other in that and that's great.

Finally, what of that tag on your website, 'John Lydon – army of one'?

JL: That's a piss-taker, the American logo. That's how they advertise that we're greedy – an army of one, and done in a John Wayne kind of way. That sounds like chaos, mate. So bingo.

And with that we pack up our bags and leave Johnny to inspect Nora's new purchases, and, interviews over, relax before their flight

206

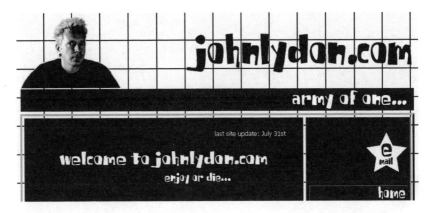

home. As we leave, the Great Englishman warns me: 'Be truthful with what you write.' Hopefully, the truth about Mr Johnny Rotten is in here somewhere.

Pat Gilbert

Pat Gilbert is the author of *Passion Is A Fashion: The Real Story Of The Clash* (Aurum, 2004) a book regarded by many as the last word on the Punk legends. He was editor at *Mojo* for three years, and during this stint also edited *The Mojo Collection*, a book which documents over 600 of the last century's most important records. He remains a well-respected commentator on punk music and popular culture in general, and continues to contribute to many music publications.

The Wrecking Ball:
Public Image Limited 1978 – 83
by Clinton Heylin

Rock (music) is an example of a youth cult that became mass cul-
ture over time: pest became host. Punk is an example, like Dada,
of a pesky youth cult that threatened to replace the host culture...
Whether observers are partisan to pest or host, the interest is in that
attacking moment when all risks are poised to leap. Such moments
lurk in the history of every movement and the clock never stands still.
But to leap is to exchange fluidity for power, inspiration for dogma,
and insight for wisdom. Pest becoming host, success becomes hollow:
'There's no success like failure.' Alternatively, when the youth cult
leaps and fails, there is no second chance. Instead, threat turns to
whimper and predatory forces digest it: 'Failure is no success at all.'
- 'Dadapunk', by W.T. Lhamon.

It is a supreme irony that the English punk movement should
take its name from a motley collection of US garage-bands from
the late sixties who drew their inspiration from the British Invasion
bands of 1964/5; because commercial success for any of these garage-bands was never anything but ephemeral. Even Lenny Kaye's
classic compilation LP of these outfits, *Nuggets*, must perforce remain a fleeting footnote in the history of pop music. The English
punk movement, though vastly more important than its American
precursor, also had an inbuilt self-destruct button.

The choices were as limited as the public image – spontaneous
combustion or inevitable dilution. It is debatable whether *any* of the
important UK artists who emerged in 1976 and 1977 ever improved
on their first records. In the case of the Sex Pistols, the band had
already arranged its own demise, sacking Glen Matlock in February
1977. Buzzcocks didn't make it further than their first EP, before
splitting in two; while the Damned lost co-founder Rat Scabies, and
all impetus, while rush-recording their second album. The Clash,
always professing a desire to overthrow the Rolling Stones, seemed
content to parody their mentors.

If punk was modern music's version of Dada-ism – 'a short-lived movement in art which sought to abandon all form and throw off all tradition' – then its second wave (starting in 1978 with a spurt of radical debut long-players), was punk's Surreal sequel. Generally confused with the New Wave, before becoming the no less definite post-punk, this second wave had its own vanguard, comprising the bands of Johnny Rotten né Lydon, Howard Devoto and Siouxsie Sioux, each a punk paradigm.

These leading lights of the second wave were all starting to think things through, and realised that the negative elements of the punk message could easily decline into nihilism, and considered those that feared progression as the new Luddites. In the case of Howard Devoto (with Magazine) and John Lydon (with PiL) they chose to curtail the pop sensibilities of their punk incarnations (Buzzcocks and the Sex Pistols) and start afresh. In the case of Siouxsie of The Banshees, the band managed to mature before recording any (official) album, and so emerged relatively untainted by their primordial origins.

For John Lydon – no longer Rotten – there had never been any question of a new music being created within the confines of The Pistols. By 1978, he had had his own epiphany – believing that The Sex Pistols were there to bring to an end the history of rock 'n' roll, blowing its artificial image up in everybody's face. His famous epitaph – 'Ha Ha Ha, Ever get the feeling you've been cheated. G'night,' - uttered at the end of their Winterland swansong, completed the act of immolation.

A sanctimonious exhumation of the corpse of Rock would certainly have flattered the fans and provided Lydon with his pension. Yet, throughout his days in a chilly New York in January 1978, to a sunnier Jamaica at the end of February, such a notion does not appear to have seriously crossed his mind. Keeping his cards close to his chest, he simply informed the awaiting press on his return to Blighty:

John Lydon: I've decided to become a parody of myself, because it's amusing. I'm looking forward to having six kids, a home in the country, a wonderful mortgage, ever so middle-class. And a

**Rolls-Royce – vintage of course. And a villa on the Isle of Wight.
P.S. I am now living with Norman Wisdom.**

Actually, Lydon galvanised himself into a frenetic enough bout of activity to recruit two old friends and an expatriate Canadian, for an entirely new band, and by the middle of May 1978 he was beginning to sculpt a new sound. As he typified it in a recent *Mojo* profile, he, Jah Wobble (né John Wardle) and Keith Levene (ex- of The Clash) 'were wanting to do something but didn't know what. The anger in us, different kinds of anger, kinda formed something... The little bit Wobble knew he knew well, and (what with) Keith's jangling over the top, the two formed such a lovely hook for me. It was like a gift from the gods.'

Jah Wobble was one of Lydon's oldest friends, having first met at Kingsway College of Further Education in 1971. Wardle was not initially impressed, thinking 'he was a Led Zeppelin fan. I was queuing up behind him and we had a bit of a quarrel about who was going to put their name down first. He just started crawling around after me, and I let him be my mate. He used to buy me drinks, though, cause no-one liked him then. He used to wind everyone up.'

Jim Walker, a 23-year old from British Columbia, apparently came over to Britain after hearing the wave of exciting music crashing over Albion, and spent a few frustrating months playing with his sticks before answering an ad in *Melody Maker* that read: 'Looking for a drummer to play on and off beat for rather famous singer'.

John Lydon: I went through weeks and weeks of rehearsing with everybody who bothered to reply to my ad in the music press. It said something like 'Lonely musician seeks comfort in fellow trendies...' I didn't use my own name because then people who didn't know how to play would have turned up, and that would have set me back another two years. But the people who did turn up were terrible. Denim clad heavy metal fans... Jim was the only person I liked from the auditions. He's amazing. He sounds like Can's drummer. All double beats.

Levene was the one band-member with any kind of pedigree in the new music. Having apparently received classical training in both guitar and piano 'well into his teens', Levene was a founder member of The Clash, but left when they started writing songs like 'White Riot': 'I said 'I'm not fucking singing 'White Riot', you're joking!' That "No Elvis, Beatles or The Rolling Stones" in '1977' was bad enough for me.' Levene put his departure down to band politics, the other members to his penchant for illegal substances. Whatever the case, Levene was then part of the short-lived Flowers Of Romance, which also featured future members of The Sex Pistols (Sid Vicious) and The Slits (Palm Olive and Viv Albertine), and then became Slits soundman while he pursued Albertine.

By mid-May 1978, when *NME*'s Neil Spencer – the first man to review the Pistols – became the first to interview Lydon's as-yet-unnamed combo, the band had at least two original songs worked up: 'Religion' (aka 'Sod In Heaven') and 'Public Image'. The words to the former had been written while Lydon was still in The Pistols; while the latter took its name and theme from an early Muriel Spark novel, *The Public Image*. Its 'composition' quickly became a *modus operandi* for the band:

Keith Levene: We were at rehearsal... We just got Jim in the band so we had a group then. We're playing away and nothing's happening. It's going really bad. Somehow we all managed to get onto something. Wobble was going da-da-da-da-da-da, da-da-da-da-da-da-da (the bass line for the song) and Jim was playing along – all I did was play the B chord all the way through. I went, *Stop!* Right, check this out – Wobble, do that bass line." So he did, and I played that (very) solo over it. I told John that he'd come in after we did it four times... (But) as soon as I heard that guitar line, I had it. (from Perfect Sound Forever website, www.furious.com/perfect - hereafter PSF)

Spencer also saw them rehearse two songs from the Pistols' repertoire, 'EMI' and 'Belsen Was A Gas', plus a song Wobble introduced as 'a vision I had last night,' which turned out to be The Who's 'My Generation'. Neil Spencer described what he heard as 'sound(ing) more like something from *Electric Ladyland* than your archetypal three-chord punk powerthrash.' Not punk then. Nor were the quartet a reggae band, despite Lydon and Wobble's love of all things dub:

Jah Wobble: Rock is obsolete. But it's our music, our basic culture. People thought we were gonna play reggae, but we ain't gonna be no GT Moore and The Reggae Guitars or nothing. It's just a natural influence – like I play heavy on the bass.

Another journalist central to punk's genesis also got to hear this post-punk progenitor in its embryonic stage. Caroline Coon had known Lydon since the early days of The Pistols, and called her article in a July *Sounds* 'Public Image', though the band remained unnamed, various joke monikers having been under none-too-serious discussion, including The Carnivorous Buttockflies, The Future Features, The Windsor Up-Lift and The Royal Family.

Asked to describe his new sound, Lydon told Coon it was, 'Total pop with deep meanings.' However, Coon's opinion of the band's progress was not quite so flattering as Spencer's: 'Ideally (Lydon said) he'd like to start gigging in six weeks time. On the evidence of rehearsals I've heard, however, that seems somewhat optimistic. With hard work and luck, the band could be ready in six months. Recording is another matter...' It certainly was. By the following week, the band were ensconced in the first of several studios recording their debut single, 'Public Image'. It was here that they really started to create a sound together, and found the band-name in a song they'd had all along.

Already the songs were coming with surprising ease, but attempts to work on a debut album were hindered by a habit PiL soon acquired of getting banned from studios at a rate resembling the Pistols' bans from concert venues. Among studios where recording came to an abrupt halt were Advision and Wessex Studios, the ban at the latter (where *NMTB* had largely been recorded) apparently following 'an altercation with an engineer... After the dialogue got a little heated, the engineer rather mysteriously launched his head at a bottle which, not unnaturally, broke.'

Meanwhile, the new band found they had to address the question of how they marketed themselves. The Sex Pistols had been able to rely on Jamie Reid's eye-catching ideas for logos, sleeves and adverts, all reflecting a common purpose. Public Image now needed to present themselves as something different, but equally important, and to proclaim their autonomy. The first requirement was a company logo. The now well-known PiL logo, a pill-like design with a black strip down the middle and the letters PiL in black, white and black, was introduced in press adverts for their eponymous debut 45. Hello, hello, hello....

Keith Levene: The PiL manifesto was... no managers, no producers, lawyers when we need them. We're not a band we're a company, think up your own ideas, total control. I guess we thought we were a bit important. (PSF)

When the 'Public Image' single appeared, wrapped in a mock newspaper, it included one of three separate ads, each featuring a different member of the band. In Lydon's, John asked, 'How come you're such a hit with the girls, Keith?' to which Levene replied in ad no. 2, 'I discovered PiL.' Wobble played up to his reputation as something of a hard-case with, 'I was wild with my chopper until I discovered PiL.' The parodic ads led some to think the music was also a way of pulling the critics' legs.

Already their determination to assert their independence was showing a counter-productive side. Due to appear on the punk-friendly TV show *Revolver* the week their single came out, only Levene turned up at the Midlands studio, accompanied by a mystified Virgin publicist. The other three had apparently absconded to Camber Sands. Producer Mickie Most sat and fumed, retorting, 'I think he (Lydon)'s done himself a lot of harm, as breaking your contract like that means an instant life ban on independent television. He's bound to need a television plug sometime in the next 20 years and he won't be able to get it.' Though Most was spouting drivel, it was an early indication of PiL's capacity for pulling itself every which way but forward.

Their live TV debut would have to wait a while longer. Meanwhile, they had filmed a promo video for 'Public Image' on a dimly-lit soundstage, for inclusion on London Weekend Television's *Saturday Night People* on October 21, drawing the single-word epithet, 'repulsive', from self-styled mordant wit Clive James. Though this was their only TV appearance to promote 'Public Image', issued on October 13, it still reached number nine in the singles charts, buoyed by a number of gushing reviews, including a mightily enthusiastic one from Giovanni Dadomo at *Sounds*: 'It will be a massive hit, and deserves to be'. Indeed, end of the year lists of best singles by *Melody Maker*, *NME* and *Sounds* placed the single first, second and second respectively (losing out in the latter two polls to the Buzzcocks' 'Ever Fallen In Love' and Patti Smith's 'Because The Night').

The song afforded fans their first opportunity to hear Lydon's new sound. And 'Public Image' contained all the quintessential PiL elements: Wobble's rumbling bass, Lydon's nasal whine and Levene's ringing, metallic guitar, while seemingly presenting a pop group fronted by punk's charismatic commander. But as Lydon sang, 'The public image belongs to me/ It's my own creation.' He

was determined to stand well outside any pseudo-Pistols niche others were still looking to place him in.

***

In fact, PiL were focused more on acruing and collating an LP's worth of songs, with which to truly stake their claim to post-modernity. An album was what was needed – one to match the likes of *The Scream* (Siouxsie & The Banshees), *Real Life* (Magazine), *Chairs Missing* (Wire) and *Live At The Witch Trials* (The Fall), all of which had appeared in the last six months, suggesting that punk could yet progress beyond the Ramonesian rant.

Highlighting the fact that the band were working on the album right up to the last minute, the front cover when it appeared listed only five tracks, the other two songs ('Attack' and 'Fodderstompf') having not been recorded when it had been designed. Lydon commented on some of the difficulties the band faced when their stance was still shiny new in a December 1978 *NME* interview:

John Lydon: We used nearly every studio there is. We ran out of them in the end. They're all so-o-o-o bad. They all cater for MOR sounds. If you want anything out of the ordinary out of the desks it gets really difficult. To get the sound that's on that album is so hard in those places. You have to go through so much bullshit. And all it is, is trying to get a live sound – the way any band should sound on stage... You've always got shithead engineers who won't show you the ins and outs of things and who scream blue murder when you turn anything up full.

Of the songs on the album – christened *First Issue* – it was the closer, 'Fodderstompf', which would come in for the most critical flak. Lydon told Chris Salewicz, 'You should've seen Branson's face when he heard that... He was furious.' The song, a seven-and-a-half-minute exercise in 'disco dub', seemed like a self-conscious device to stretch the album beyond half an hour. Yet what had come before was already radical enough, as Levene recently told Simon Reynolds:

Keith Levene: The first album is the one time when we were a band. I remember worrying a little at the time: Does this do too much what we publicly say we're not going to do? – meaning rock out. But what we were doing really was showing everybody that we were intimately acquainted with what we ultimately intended to break down. And we started that dismantling process with the album's last track.

'Fodderstompf' aside, *First Issue* was neatly divided between a trilogy of concise, riff-driven rants, à la 'Public Image', and a trio of lengthier excursions that gave full vent to the rhythm section's sledgehammer power and Levene's penchant for improvisation. Particularly disorienting was the album's opening track 'Theme', a largely improvised, nine-minute excursion into what it feels like when, 'it's dawn on a wet Wednesday in Chelsea and Britain's most powerful punk singer... is feeling like death.' Of all the tracks, it seemed like the one with which Lydon seemed most happy:

John Lydon: We did that about four or five in the morning. We'd already done a couple of takes but the machine was wrong. Really irritating. I think it sounds great. It's like there's a barrage of guitars all over the place but it's just Keith's one guitar. He's amazing – the racket he can get out of that thing! He's got all the madness that The Pistols had at the start.

Despite the pulverizing nature of the PiL piledriver, most reviewers still felt short-changed. Pete Silverton's review in *Sounds* was among the more misguided: 'A producer friend said it sounded like a band (who had) gone into the studio for the first time, and run riot with all the effects.' Nick Kent did his best to push the band in what he saw as a more productive direction, designating 'Public Image', 'Attack' and 'Lowlife' as 'musical territory that, given time and effort, will provide them with a strong and individual foundation for future focus and experimentation.' In fact, that direction was already abandoned, in favour of wilder, more dub-like extemporisations. Songs like 'Theme' sign-posted PiL's future direction, the collective nature of the sound reflecting PiL's communal approach:

John Lydon: In this band we are all equal. No Rod Stewarts. We all do equal amounts of work, we all produce equally, write songs and collect the money equally... We're just the beginning of a huge umbrella, we can each do our own solo ventures to our own amusement so long as they don't infringe on the band as a whole. I want it to spread out. I know that might sound a bit idealistic.

It was in these early album reviews that one first encounters the idea, expressed throughout PiL's creative five-year journey, that the band was some elaborate joke on Lydon's part (by the time he actually turn PiL into a joke at fans' expense, in the aftermath of 'This Is Not A Love Song', few were sure when the sniping began). One reviewer of *First Issue* concluded that Lydon was *trying* to lose his audience, that the album was deliberately anti-commercial: "Johnny Rotten is going to lose quite a few fans with this record, but... that seems to have been the purpose of it anyway."

Keith Levene: They all slagged (*First Issue*) because it was self-indulgent, non-simplistic and non-rock 'n' roll. Those are all good points. But that's the kind of music we intend to make. (1980)

Despite its share of critical flak, the album appeared at number 28 in *NME*'s list of the 'Best Albums Of 1978' (and at twenty-two in the charts). Kris Needs at *Zigzag* certainly cast his vote in the band's favour, writing about how 'PiL have already got their own sound, and this album has moments as biting as any Pistols song. No resting on laurels. No waste.'

If PiL was always supposed to be more than 'Lydon and lackeys', two solo ventures designed to reinforce this notion now slipped out of the Virgin vaults: Jah Wobble's exercise in dub, 'Dreadlock

Don't Deal With Wedlock', and a 12-inch EP called *Steel Leg Versus The Electric Dread*, featuring Keith Levene (billed as 'Stratetime Keith') Jah Wobble, and resident rapper at PiL HQ – Lydon's house in Gunter Grove, SW6 – Don Letts. Letts contributed lead vocals on the hilarious 'Haile Unlikely', while the weird and wacky 'Stratetime And The Wide Man' made further use of the same fire extinguisher found on 'Fodderstompf'.

Altogether more significant was the full cooperative's live London debut at the end of December. Two shows in Brussels and Paris were hastily arranged as warm-ups for dates at The Rainbow on Christmas and Boxing Day. In fact, the first gig in Brussels did not go too well, the band playing just six songs before the ubiquitous Belgian riot curtailed further extemporisation.

Thankfully the Paris show was more successful. The sound was suitably immense and the crowd responded enthusiastically. In fact, when PiL ran out of material they were obliged to play two songs from The Pistols' own repertoire, the controversial 'Belsen Was A Gas' and a one-off version of 'Problems'. When that still did not suffice, they ran through a couple of *First Issue* songs again ('Public Image' and 'Annalisa'). The success of this show convinced the boys they were on the right track, even if both Wobble and Lydon were already expressing concern regarding the band's likely reception in London.

Jah Wobble: Johnny Rotten is gonna lose, Keith Levene is gonna lose, Jim Walker is gonna lose. And all the kids are gonna watch us get our heads kicked in.
John Lydon: I'm going out of my way to even walk out on a stage, knowing that three-quarters of the audience won't be there just to listen to us, but to slag us off and survey and suss it out.

✳✳✳

The Rainbow Theatre. Christmas Day. The place is packed to the gills with fans awaiting the emperor's unveiling. As Wobble, Walker and Levene take to the stage, they launch straight into 'Theme', which fills the theatre with a crushing, monstrous, punishing sound. The stage looks fantastic. All green and black. Finally Lydon saunters on, carrying two overfull carrier bags, containing a supply of lager to get him through the forty-five minute set.

But this is a continuation of the confrontational Brunel show (the Pistols' last 'London' gig). Tonight is not about participation, even if Lydon first tries that route by handing the microphone out during 'Theme' for occasional, disorientating shouts of 'I wish I could die' from assorted members of the audience. After almost a quarter of an hour, the monumental sound finally dies down. At last the audience can make themselves heard: 'Submission', 'Anarchy In The UK', 'Pretty Vacant'. Lydon gets straight to the point:

'We're not gonna play any fucking Sex Pistols songs. If you wanna hear that, fuck off! That's history.' 'Lowlife'. Then 'Attack', which the NF skins, who have been an ominous presence throughout, take as their cue to start a fight. The band stop and Lydon shakes his head, 'You never learn'.

The crowd steadily becomes – as reviewer Keith Shadwick recalled – 'more and more confused and restless between numbers as their relationship with the band became more and more remote from the usual performer-audience axis, (while) Lydon would spend five minutes or more between songs in intense arguments with interjectors.' Some particularly phlegmatic punk at the front gobs right in Lydon's face. Lydon leans down and gobs right back, but his aim is untrue. He hits the guy in front, then calmly leans over and flicks the frozen phlegm off the guy's shoulder onto the Mohican-head behind.

Those at the front keep asking for Johnny to give 'em some lager. He finally obliges, dispensing several cans to the audience, only to get one back, unopened, full force, right in the face. Blood trickles down his forehead, where the can has hit him. Lydon stands over the stage, 'Come on mate. Just you and me. The bouncers won't touch you.' There is no response. By now, as Shadwick would later suggest, 'The real focus of the event was outside the music. It was in the battle between a man and his own public image, this being a microcosm of the central conflict in rock. Here was one of the great figures of his time desperately trying to state clearly his own control of himself.'

'Public Image' is the encore, though PiL never actually leave. Afterwards, Levene, Wobble and Walker sidle off the stage, as the immense sound dies away, leaving Lydon stage-right, crouched down, still calm. As he kneels, many members of the audience are refusing to leave. They want an explanation. Those crowding to the front are now in two camps, on the left PiL proselytizers, on the right those who came to harangue the man. Lydon is suitably snide, sarcastically putting down those content with their 'pink vinyl singles and Great Rock 'n' Roll Swindles.' The (admittedly futile) lecture continues. He has already left them behind.

221

Yet the reviews of that first London show were surprisingly un-sympathetic to Lydon's (and PiL's) predicament. Sounds – no long-er the paper of Savage, Suck and Sandy – devoted a whole page to a review of the show, written by someone who thought 'the album was disappointing (though) 'Low Life' and bits of 'Religion' were good', and who spent most of the second half of his review blam-ing the band for the fact that he couldn't get a taxi after the gig. Meanwhile, punk fanzine *Ripped And Torn* decided not to mince words with Lydon: 'You fucking pathetic little puppet with your to-tally indulgent wallowing mess of an album... and your wanky little statements about 'never being a punk'. I wonder where this one was standing at the end of the concert?

After all this controversy, the Boxing Day show was anti-climac-tic, passing without any real incident. Since it became the bootleg album, *Extra Issue*, but no real sense of the drama of opening night permeated beyond its immediate recipients. Public Image would not play London again for another five years and the ersatz PiL that finally played the Palais in November 1983 bore no resemblance to the idealistic band of yore. By then, the clink of the till had indeed triumphed.

* * *

PiL's volatile clash of personalities was already proving too much for drummer Jim Walker who, after four gigs at the sticks, called it quits in the new year, muttering what would become an increasingly familiar mantra, 'This is a business, it's not just sitting around a flat, taking drugs and being grey... But (the others seem) more interested in "communications videos" and sitting around and mismanagement.' Walker was to be the first of a procession of drummers streaming out of Gunter Grove. His departure broke the band's all-important unity of four. For the next eighteen months it would be a unity of three; then two; and finally one. The official line on his departure was surprisingly traditional – 'dissatisfaction with musical direction in the group structure.'

His departure made any further spreading of the word problematic. The band had planned 'a series of one-off appearances', the first of which, at the Dublin Project Arts Centre on February 16th, had already gone on sale. When the date for commencement of legal proceedings brought by Lydon against his erstwhile manager Malcolm McLaren coincided with the scheduled Dublin gig, he had the perfect get-out and the show was cancelled.

However, PiL still intended to proceed with a show at Manchester's King's Hall on February 23rd. In aid of the Race Today Friendly Society, it was christened 'Creation For Liberation'. Manchester, less fashion-conscious than London and already responsible for the most experimental punk scene in the country, was likely to be a lot more receptive than the capital. Now all PiL needed was a drummer. One seemed to be to hand in the form of Karl Burns, who had recently quit The Fall, the fourth member to do so. There was barely time to assimilate Burns into the set-up.

Lydon had spent much of the previous week wrestling back control of his work-to-date from McLaren, leaving little time for getting acquainted with PiL's latest recruit. Indeed at the Manchester show 'Belsen Was A Gas' would collapse mid-song due to a lack of rehearsal, much to Lydon's amusement, 'Fuckin' egg on face

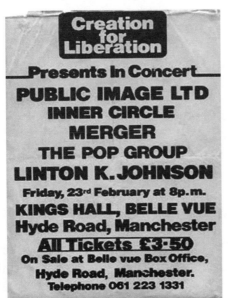

time.' The court case, which received considerable media attention from both the national and music press, finally concluded on February 14 when the judge appointed a Receiver to safeguard the assets of Glitterbest, pending their division among the four Pistols and/or their heirs.

It wasn't Lydon's only contact with the law that month. A police raid on Lydon's home at 6.30 am on February 13th was the second such raid in a month. Taken to Chelsea Police Station, Lydon was released without charge. Such petty harassment was becoming a regular feature of life in Gunter Grove, where the communal life-style and regular retinue of Rastas and known drug dealers knocking on the door gave the police due cause. Lydon's response was to ask his friend Dave Crowe to come and live at the house as the first line of defence, effectively making him the house bodyguard.

The Manchester show, where PiL were supported by the equally audacious Pop Group and Rasta poet Linton Kwesi Johnson, provided welcome relief from such incursions. Though King's Hall was something of an acoustical graveyard, Lydon was enthused by the reaction, later commenting that 'the sound is second to the atmosphere. Up north the shit didn't mean much. They either like it or hate it. They liked PiL. Only in London do we get Sex Pistols requests, ha, ha.'

Reviews were also more favourable than for the Rainbow shows. Paul Morley got it spot on, writing in *NME*: 'PiL play it blank and cryptic, offering no easy clues or anything tangible to grab hold of. They satirise, ridicule, delude and elude. It's a joke, a challenge, an indulgence, an assertion, a revenge, an adventure, a disturbance, a fascinating rock 'n' roll sound. You take it seriously or you don't. Whichever way, they're incredibly important.' *Sounds* reviewer and local lad, Mick Middles, also 'left totally convinced that Public Image are more than a major force in today's music scene.'

However, PiL didn't feel sure enough to play any new songs to the Mancunians, though they were soon back in the studio working on further material. Recording at Jah Studio, presumably with Burns on drums, the band taped what early reports called a 'modern version of Tchaikovsky's Swan Lake.' Lydon's mother had recently died of cancer, and the harrowing work (better known as 'Death

Disco') provided an anguished description of Lydon's feelings losing someone very close to him. The product of Lydon's cathartic grief and Levene's rich instrumental imagination, it plugged directly into the moment:

Keith Levene: I would play the E chord and it would be like breaking glass in slow motion ... The whole thing was in E. That opened it up, 'cos it was all literally in one note. I realized that this tune that I was bastardizing by mistake was 'Swan Lake.' So I started playing it on purpose, but I was doing it from memory... When he'd stop (singing), I'd play 'Swan Lake'. When he'd sing again, I'd go back to the harmonic thing and build it up. (PSF)

The song had first been worked on with Walker, but was the solitary solid statement to come from the Burns-era PiL. By the time of its release, he had been replaced by ex-101'ers drummer Richard Dudanski, summoned to the Townhouse studio to sit in that spring, without explanation or advance warning:

Richard Dudanski: The next ten days, we recorded like five songs. The tape was just left running. Basically, me and Wobble would just start playing, and maybe Keith'd say something like double-time. But it was a bass-drum thing which Keith would stick guitar on, and John would there and then write some words and wack 'em on... once we'd got the (basic tracks). I think the first day we did 'No Birds Do Sing' and 'Socialist'. Then we did 'Chant', 'Memories'.

Dudanski, who had been brought in after someone apparently thought Burns was a verb, says, 'I was really thrilled when first joining PiL. I shared the whole (idea) of wanting to do something different and not controlled by the industry.' He also found Lydon to be a true music lover, listening to everything from 'a little madrigal, or Renaissance music, a lot of Irish folk music... (to) Bulgarian voices, Indian stuff, a lot of Islamic percussion stuff.'

225

As a mildly humorous interlude – and one more way to debunk his status as pop icon – Lydon agreed to be a guest on the BBC's revival of *Juke Box Jury* during June, hosted by the faintly nauseating Noel Edmunds. Asked at the outset what music he listened to, Lydon replied, 'My own.' Acting throughout like a delinquent modern-day Groucho Marx, he eventually grew bored of the whole fiasco and made one of his famous impromptu stage-exits.

With Dudanski now fully ensconced in PiL, the band played its second gig of the year - returning to Manchester. This time, though, it was a secret gig at Russell's Club, organized at the last minute by Tony Wilson, with PiL playing to barely a couple of hundred punters. On June 18, in one of Manchester's dodgier districts, Hulme, PiL debuted over half of their forthcoming album. Indeed, in their one-hour set, the band featured only two songs from the first album, 'Public Image' (which they did three times, before getting it right) and 'Annalisa'.

The five new songs were all long, droney and opaque affairs. 'Chant', 'Death Disco', 'Memories', 'And No Birds Do Sing' - into which Lydon interjected several couplets of 'Arsenal 3 'Nited 2' to taunt the few United fans there, his team having beaten Man United 3-2 in a memorable Cup Final weeks earlier – and 'Albatross' were like nothing this audience had heard to date, even those who had caught earlier shows at the same club by Joy Division and Magazine.

Eleven days later PiL released 'Death Disco' as their second and third singles, giving fans two versions of the song, and two alternate b-sides. Its 7" guise came with 'And No Birds Do Sing' on the B-side; while a more langorous six-minute 'Mega-Mix' of this modern *Swan Lake*, on a 12-inch, came with an instrumental version of 'Fodderstompf (entitled 'half mix') on the other side.

Melody Maker's Chris Bohn called the extended 12" version 'the most awesome and complete musical experience since Can's *Tago Mago*. Most importantly, though, it's the one dance single of the year to define its own style, without shaping someone else's to suit its own needs.' If the single suggested that the group had set their controls towards the organised chaos of 'Theme', it still managed to chart, thanks to another bout of favourable reviews and an appearance on *Top Of The Pops* (where they performed live in the studio).

The band also appeared on a new Tyne-Tees pop programme, *Check It Out*, at the beginning of July, performing a live version of 'Chant'. After this powerful preview, though, they were again subjected to a cheap publicity stunt. The presenters introduced a film of Mond Cowie of the not-so-Angelic Upstarts, bad-mouthing 'Johnny Rotten' – without PiL's prior knowledge – and then asked for a response. Needless to say, Lydon told the unprofessional presenters that this was 'a cheapskate comedy interrogation act, and it just ain't on,' and duly walked off – again.

Jeanette Lee - now Levene's girlfriend, and PiL's occasional mouthpiece – summed up the feelings of the PiL camp when she told *NME*, 'You can understand that the whole cheap affair was an attempt to goad John into doing his nut and giving the show a great deal of publicity. It was sickening.' The following month Levene and Lydon were interviewed, more civilly, for Radio Merseyside. Levene took the opportunity to comment on the prejudices the band faced at this point:

Keith Levene: At first they expected the band to be an extension of The Pistols and it wasn't, it didn't occur to them to pick up on what PiL was. Instead of that they became kinda intimidated by it again – just because we were something different. That's what

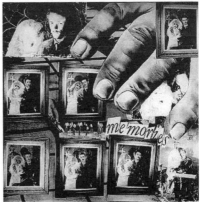

we get all the time just because they're not prepared. It doesn't occur to them to just pick up on what we are doing. They expect us to start gobbing and spewing up.

The whole band was starting to feel the overweening pressure of false expectations. Lydon in particular was constantly called on to defend his actions. But at this point he still believed he might prevail. In a letter to a fan in August 1979, Lydon spelt out his 'message': 'Anything soundwise that breaks the pattern won't even be heard by most and PiL are not a typical sound... PiL will win. Rock 'n' roll is dead. It all is... Music is collective noises, there must be no limits.'

Continuing to arrange a series of one-off concert appearances, rather than tour this tiny island, PiL were able to secure the greatest exposure for the minimum amount of effort. In August, they consented to headline the first night of the Leeds Sci-Fi Festival, to be held on September 8 at the Queen's Hall; sharing the same stage as Joy Division for the one and only time. It would be PiL's final UK show as a unit of innovation and improvisation – and the last featuring Richard Dudanski.

Leeds' response to PiL was as apathetic as their response to the Pistols, who had played the Polytechnic on the famous Anarchy Tour. If, by 1979, Mancunian fans didn't shout for Sex Pistols songs, they certainly still did in Leeds. As if this wasn't bad enough, one fan lobbed a full can of lager not at Lydon this time, but at Wobble. Lydon duly turned his back on the audience during the third song, remaining that way throughout the rest of the set, a gesture misrepresented in most press reports of the show.

The fickle music press again preferred to take potshots at PiL rather than condemn their 'fans'. Andy Gill – the hack, not the Gang of Four frontman – failed to identify most of the songs in his *NME* review, though only three of the nine songs remained unreleased ('Chant', 'Memories' and 'Another'). The Sounds reviewer, speaking on behalf of the Luddites of Leeds suggested, 'One measly rendition of 'Pretty Vacant' would have converted an expensive extravaganza into a rock n' roll concert.' Talk about missing the point! The most negative assessment of the gig, though, came from Keith Levene: 'We did a shit gig, to a shit audience in a shit place. We had a horrible time.'

Two related results of the Leeds gig were the departure of Richard Dudanski, and a decision by the band to avoid further UK shows, for the time being at least. Dudanski duly wrote to *NME* editor, Neil Spencer, to announce the reasoning behind his departure:

'Dear Mr Spencer,

In the absence of any statement from PiL, I would like to inform you that as from our Leeds gig I have ceased to be a member of that group.

My disagreements and inability to work with certain members of the group in particular, resulted in mutual satisfaction at my exit.

My only observation is that what could potentially be a great band, will probably do just enough to retain its guaranteed success. Perhaps exactly because of this guarantee, the really good ideas behind the band will never be more than just that. I hope not for JR's sake.'

Dudanski's departure threatened to disrupt the band's attempts to put the finishing touches to their second album, upsetting the finances of the band, at least one of whom now had a habit to feed. The high-strung Levene simply set about recording the requisite drum tracks himself. By this point he had his own idea of how he wanted to work and, as the one true musician in PiL, expected the acquiescence of others:

Keith Levene: With *Metal Box*, we became experimental very quickly... The way I saw it, the desk became an instrument. It was such a major part of the process. For the whole thing, the whole studio was becoming a big synthesizer... I told (the engineer) to record *everything* because we didn't know what the records are. So we didn't know when we were playing a tune or not. Sometimes we might have played something and it sounded like we were fucking around and it turns out to be something very serious. (PSF)

At this stage, he also maintained impetus by recording a pair of songs without any drums – 'Radio Four' and 'The Suit'. By the end of September it was announced that the second PiL album would consist of three 12-inch singles, "with an aggregate playing time equivalent to that of a normal LP" and would come in, "a cross between a film can and a biscuit tin" (much like the original 'albums' of records, which were sets of 78 rpm records in an 'album'). The set, which was to be entitled *Metal Box*, would be released on October 12, with a preview single, 'Memories', issued the week before.

'Memories' was certainly a good indication of the direction the band was heading in with their new album, though it was no more commercial than 'Death Disco'. The *Sounds* review summed up many people's disenchantment with Lydon's lot, 'Memories' is an apt enough title as this brings back memories of all their other rubbish.' But in *NME*, Danny Baker made the record 'Single Of The Week', while admitting that 'Memories' has no place within today's broadcasting set-up.' He was proven right when the single reached the none-too-dizzy heights of number sixty in the charts.

Both 'Memories' and its B-side, 'Another', had been recorded with Dudanski - also being performed at his Sci-Fi swansong – so the single, pressed as both 7" and 12", was in the shops on time. But it came as no surprise when the album was deferred until November 16 because, as Virgin announced, 'not all the tracks have been delivered yet.' The last track delivered also proved to be the audition for PiL's fifth drummer, Martin Atkins (Dave Humphries having seemingly come and gone in the interim):

Martin Atkins: It seemed that every time I opened a music mag PIL had fired another drummer - I'd call every time but someone else had filled the gap. One night I was sitting in my flat in Willesden... reading through old copies of *NME* - I found ANOTHER drummer had quit/been fired - actually I think that Karl Burns (yikes) from The Fall was actually set on fire... I called up Jeanette Lee... it was eventually agreed that I'd meet up with them the next weekend at the Town House which I assumed would be a rehearsal room. Errrrrrr. It wasn't - I walked in - to comments like — 'here's that northern git!' - and we wrote 'Bad Baby' (on the spot).

In the month since 'Memories' blipped across the lower regions of chartdom, advance copies of *Metal Box* (minus the tin!) had been sent to the music press, or played to the likes of Kris Needs and Vivien Goldman at the Gunter Grove grotto. In both instances, the

experience prompted an ecstatic critical response. Though the band maintained a highly ambivalent relationship with the UK music press – and vice-versa – *Metal Box* was to be the one instance where critics united in praising PiL's achievement. Angus MacKinnon in *NME* summed up the critical consensus when he wrote: 'All this forward flow in 12 months – it's almost frightening. PiL are miles out and miles ahead. Follow with care.'

Even *Sounds*, previously the most antagonistic of the major UK weekly music papers, devoted a page to the album; Dave McCullough not only giving it five stars, but attempting to evaluate its likely future importance: '*Metal Box* is a vital ending to seventies pop culture and a sizeable nod in the direction of a real rock 'n' roll future. The last laugh is with John Lydon and no mistake.'

Though the album came without a set of lyrics, press adverts corrected this oversight. Full page ads simply carried the band name at the top, the album title at the bottom, and the lyrics scrawled between, untitled and out of sequence. With the surprisingly effusive critical response Lydon faced a new problem - repeated questions as to what this or that song meant. 'Poptones', a story of rape viewed from the female vantage point, prompted more than most. He tried to deflect such enquiries when on BBC Radio One's *Rock On*. Asked how they write songs, he replied: 'We take a silly tune and strip it bare, and start again.' As for their chosen format, PiL went to great lengths to call it anything *but* An Album:

Keith Levene: It's not an album. You don't have to listen to the songs in any order. You can play what you want, disregard what you don't. Albums have a very strict format, the eight tracks, difficult to find, I hate all that – the quality is usually appallingly low, almost unlistenable. We can't get our sound on a normal record, you can't get the depths and heights.

Though there was no place for lyrics, the 'album's' insert found room for two additional members of the limited company, Dave Crowe and Jeanette Lee. By December, Levene was referring to the group as 'a unit of five, three public,' with 'the band bit of PiL as just me, John and Wobble... we have had various drummers, and they've always been told what to do and play. It's just one of those equal things.' Already history was being rewritten, at the expense of Walker and Dudanski. Vivien Goldman, a regular visitor and co-conspirator, suggested at the time that Jeanette Lee 'does the bulk of liaising with the outside world, as far as I can make out, though everyone in PiL refuses to say exactly what they do... Jeanette will (also) be making a film record, a kind of diary, of PiL.' Actually, she was now Keith Levene's girlfriend first, and everything else second:

Keith Levene: She was supposed to be in the band as the video person, but she hadn't done shit for ages. I got her in the band based on the idea that it was cool to get band members that didn't play instruments... I was crazy about her, I didn't know that she wasn't doing anything ... Wobble (had) said, 'What's she gonna do – be a secretary?' I said, 'No, she's gonna do video.' He hated her. (PSF)

Levene also informed a slightly sceptical Goldman, 'We're into vision - video - we've got this Super-8 camera... we want to use electronics as special effects, using electronics to condense the quality

of the Super-8.' Goldman summed up PiL's predicament at the end of her December 1979 *Melody Maker* cover story: 'PiL still haven't reached what to me seems the ideal stage: sending a constant stream of communiques, records or otherwise, that would remove them from the pitfalls of the "PiL album – an event – articles in the music press soon come" syndrome.'

For now, communiques remained confined to conventional media. In November PiL recorded three songs for a session on John Peel's late-night Radio 1 show. This 'Careering' gave the band ample opportunity to improvise new sounds, and for Levene to display his increasing preoccupation with synthesizers. The guitar was becoming increasingly sidelined as the synth became his instrument of choice. Part of the problem, as he later explained, was that 'once I got good enough to know the rules, I didn't want to be like any other guitarist.' Lydon, though, suspected a psychological uncertainty in his friend:

John Lydon: Keith really lacked confidence in himself. Such a shame. He was one of the most talented fucking guitar players I've ever known. He made a guitar do things that were not supposed to be possible. But he just didn't see the value in it. (2004)

'Careering', along with 'Poptones' was then performed on BBC-2's long-running *Old Grey Whistle Test*, now thankfully wrestled from the control of the somnambulant Bob Harris. New presenter Annie Nightingale called the PiL session the most powerful she'd ever witnessed, while Martin Atkins confirmed his position as 'new PiL drummer' - the most insecure job in rock music - by pounding the skins on both Beeb appearances.

With a one-song audition, a two-song *Whistle Test*, and a three-song Peel session under his belt, it was time Atkins experienced PiL live. On January 17th, he appeared with the three co-founders on stage at the Palace in Paris, for PiL's first gigs since the release of their landmark *Metal Box*. Both shows were being recorded officially; and reviewers were on hand to take notes.

NME's Frazer Clarke found opening night 'an alienating performance, but if it were John Lydon's aim to be a popular success he'd be singing re-treads of 'Pretty Vacant' (sic) ... We should be grateful.' The audience was not. Despite hearing the most lengthy PiL set to date - comprising 12 songs, eight from *Metal Box*, with live premieres for 'Careering', 'Poptones' and 'Bad Baby', plus 'Annalisa', 'Public Image', 'Attack' and 'Low Life' from *First Issue* - Frazer Clarke confessed he'd 'never before seen a band give an encore after having been jeered off.' Lydon later said that the tapes used for a live album, *Paris Au Printemps*, required 'some (additional) reverb to drown out the crowd booing.' The following night, the set lasting a mere seven songs, and concluded with 'Theme' (which never sounded quite immense enough minus the whomp of Walker). At least Atkins would always have Paris.

✶✶✶

"We're just not over-eager to do live gigs; you only get a lot of thickos who just want to hear rock 'n' roll, even though I know there are some good people out there who want to hear good music,

interesting music with subtleties and variations in it". Jah Wobble,
February 1980

With the band's continuing reluctance to gig, it was inevitable
that 'all this forward flow' would soon dissipate. Wobble, in particular, though towing the company line in interviews, was becoming increasingly frustrated. As an outlet for his own musical drive,
he spent the early months of 1980 putting together his first solo
album, *The Legend Lives On*, even recording enough for another
mini-album, *Blueberry Hill*, from leftover ideas. *The Legend Lives
On* allowed Wobble to make music more akin to the rhythms of life
than the soundscapes Levene liked. His use of the backing-track to
'Another', on his almost oriental remix, 'Not Another', would produce its own set of recriminations from the communications company chairman, but Wobble was unapologetic:

**Jah Wobble: I (just) wanted to put a sunshine record together,
but not be insulting ... I've got a happy side as well. I hope people tape it off Peel and listen to it by the sunny river ... It's partly
a political thing in one sense: making your stand. It's like with
PiL we have our own organisation so to speak. PiL is five people
really, six now with Martin. There's a girl called Jeanette and
Dave Crowe, both of whom are involved, coming up with ideas.
PiL is more than just a band; it's an all-embracing attitude ...
(But) in PiL strange things happen. You can be sitting about for
four months just soaking up influences. (1980)**

Reading between the lines, Wobble wanted to get back to making music. The 'all-embracing attitude' of others was getting in the
way. At one point Wobble took Lydon aside and said, 'John, fucking
hell, mate, the best thing to do would be to trust me, listen to me,
I'm speaking sense. Fuck these guys off ... Forget all the hangers-on
and let's do this band thing properly.' He admits now that he failed
to fully read the situation, 'I see now, in some respects, classic signs
of depression. He would spend an inordinate amount of time quietly watching videos, for hours on end. I remember feeling ..., "For

fuck's sake, John, come on!'" Atkins was equally non-plussed by the stupefying inertia at Gunter Grove:

Martin Atkins: PiL wasn't run like a business. It would take me five attempts of going across from Willesden Green to Chelsea before I could get anyone at Gunter Grove to open the door and give me my sixty quid. And I'd spend half of it on speed before I'd got home. If it was a Thursday, I'd probably stay at Gunter Grove until Sunday. We'd all be up watching *Apocalypse Now* (while) speeding.

At least there was the prospect of a trip to America, which was being organized by Levene and Lydon while Wobble put the finishing touches to *The Legend Lives On...* in London. It was here, after all, that Lydon's previous lot had imploded so spectacularly at tour's end. It was perhaps time to see if PiL could do the same. To sweeten the bitter PiL, their US label, Warners - who had passed on *First Issue* - had agreed to release *Metal Box* as a double-album called *Second Edition*, albeit begrudgingly:

Keith Levene: *Second Edition* was the Warners release. They said, "Forget any metal box, don't even go there ... Who do you think you are? You're lucky you're getting a cardboard box!' (PSF)

Lydon and Levene had flown to San Francisco at the beginning of March, as a promotional exercise coinciding with the US release of *Second Edition*, which received plentiful praise from Greil Marcus in his two-page *Rolling Stone* review. The pair also gave a press conference in a San Franciscan disco/new wave club called The City, which proved no less surreal than Dylan's, legendary San Francisco press conference fifteen years earlier.

If the US press found it hard to grasp the fact that PiL were not a rock 'n' roll band, Levene went one step further, denying that PiL were even musicians: 'Our music's got basic structure but it ain't music, 'cos I don't use chords on a guitar. Wobble does sing notes on the bass. They amount to sound. I do sound on a synthesizer. We use rhythm tracks for the drums. It's just different. It just isn't music...' Lydon decided to join in with the fun:

John Lydon: We don't make music - it's noise, sound. We avoid the term 'music' because of all those assholes who like to call themselves musicians or artists. It's just so phony. We don't give a shit about inner attitude, just as long as it sounds good. We're not some intellectual bunch of freaks. I think we're a very, very valid act. For once in a lifetime a band actually has its own way, its own terms - that would really make extreme music. We just want to make sure you have a choice. I mean, we can only be hated on a large scale.

Asked about a possible PiL tour, Lydon became impatient: 'We'll be doing occasional gigs, according to our whims and fancies. This is one band no one dictates to - ever. No routines.' Inevitably, though, most questions centred on The Sex Pistols:

Q: What is the connection between PiL and The Pistols?
A: There is no connection. The Pistols finished rock 'n' roll. That was the last rock 'n' roll band. It is all over. It's (in) the past.

Q: Why if the band is so contemptuous of the media did they consent to this press conference?
A: We need to promote our records. There is no point in hiding in closets and being arty. It is essential that everybody is aware that this band exists, because there is no competition. And I'd like that to be made very clear.

A handful of 'in-person' interviews were subsequently conducted at the Continental Hyatt Hotel in LA, to sympathetic journalists. Mikal Gilmore, rock journalist and brother of notorious murderer Gary Gilmore, there on behalf of *Rolling Stone*, asked Lydon what he thought of the endless questions about Lydon's previous band. He got the PiL manifesto in one sound-bite, 'All I can say is that Public Image is everything The Sex Pistols were meant to be - a valid threat to rock 'n' roll. In the end The Pistols weren't any more threatening than retreaded Chuck Berry.'

Because their first album hadn't been issued by Warners in the States - something that, in Levene's opinion, 'really fucked up our momentum' - Levene and Lydon were determined to emphasise the accessibility and danceability of PiL's music. Lydon, in particular, displayed a deep distrust of the critics, and was keen to downplay the reams of good press that had come PiL's way in the past six months:

John Lydon: Now all the critics love us. I don't trust all these people who praise us now. They're the same ones who waited until The Pistols were over before they accepted them ... I think our cause will be lost (too), but that won't be so bad.

Wobble and Atkins joined the other two on the east coast, in the middle of April. Though not booked to play night after night, they had arranged at least nine dates, spread over three weeks at the end of April and the beginning of May, in major US cities: Atlanta, Chicago, Boston, New York, Philadelphia, Detroit, Los Angeles, and San Francisco. Though it doubled the tally of PiL gigs to date, it was still not what their American label, Warner Bros, had had in mind. According to Lydon, their idea of a schedule was 'something like 60 days non-stop gigging in very, very small clubs ... cover(ing) every single possible part of America.'

PiL's first show - at The Orpheum in Boston - would be their longest ever gig. As with the first Paris show, they played through four months of road rust by performing everything they knew, excluding only 'Religion' from the full PiL repertoire. Aside from most of *First Issue* and *Second Edition*, PiL also featured 'Home Is Where The Heart Is', a song new to the live set, though it was something they'd been playing with for a while. The Boston show had been prefaced by two radio interview/phone-ins, both affairs being fairly good-humoured, though the WBCN broadcast largely consisted of the band abusing anyone foolish enough to phone in.

However, cracks in the 'public image' were becoming visible. At the end of this first US show, Wobble and Atkins played an instrumental continuation of 'Bad Baby' which did not appear to be rehearsed. According to *Subway News*, 'After Levene eventually stamped off stage in prima donna fury over the Orpheum speakers, and Lydon followed him to thrash things out collective style, Wobble allowed himself to have some ordinary fun with the crowd, mugging like a comic-book gangster and doing a little strutting, smiling and waving.'

Keith Levene: With me and John, we had this thing if we'd start a number and it just wasn't working, we'd stop. And then he'd do it again or do something else. The audience didn't much care, though sometimes we'd (have) really rowdy audiences, and we'd just wind them up even more. At this particular gig, they were just watching and taking it all in. It was just very, very flat ... Somehow John and I, at the same time, just had it with this fucking gig. I stopped by hitting my master power switch and turning everything off ... John just gave me a nod and we walked off ... So we stopped, and we're behind the stage and they're (still) playing. I said to John, 'I wonder how long Wobble's gonna do this?' (PSF)

These spring shows proved a memorable introduction to Brit post-punk for many US fans still catching up with the elements of punk interested in progression. Indeed, it is a great shame that the official live album PiL issued at the end of the year was from the lacklustre January shows, rather than one of the US shows - indeed, the live album was prompted by the release of the far more satisfactory double-bootleg, *Profile* from the May 5, 1980 Los Angeles show. The New York gig, two days after Boston - filmed and recorded professionally - could easily have been issued as both a sell-through video and an album. For PiL fans back home an enthusiastic review of the gig in question, in *NME*, suggested that they were missing out on some punchy performances:

'The show does defeat the expectations of a rock band performance in many ways: their approach to pacing is neither the classic strong start, slow down, big build-up-at-the-end scheme, nor the punk pull out all the stops approach. Instead there are long lulls when the music almost becomes a monotonous flow; then comes the peaks, redeeming everything - not through virtuosity, but through daring. ... After a while, Lydon starts bringing kids up on-stage to be guest vocalists. When a crowd of nine or ten punky-looking kids has massed, he hands a music stand and lyric sheet to one of them and joins the kids in the crowd onstage, just bopping around, grinning broadly. Tonight, his plan to share the stage with his audience causes the set to finally self-destruct - a conclusion which to PiL is probably more than acceptable.'

If the New York show played to an audience for whom 'no wave' had already provided a reasonable introduction to horrible noise, the Los Angeles show brought its own horrors, none of them musical. When Lydon took to the stage, it was to an audience the like of which even he had never encountered. As Mikail Gilmore has written, 'Lydon was plain transfixing, but the audience that assembled to celebrate the band's appearance, a crowd of thuggish-looking jar-head punks who eventually became dubbed the area's "hardcore" subculture, very nearly upstaged the show. It was the first time this audience had made its identity felt in such a large, collective and forcible way.' *Slash* editor Claude Bessy, who had done so much to push the punk revolution there in L.A., also sensed a parting of the ways:

'The kid is lifted to the stage and John starts whispering in his ear (no doubt professional tips on stage presence) while handing him a notebook of lyrics. The song is 'Bad Baby' and soon the 'don't you listen' chorus is being sung by the new vocalist over and over again, first with John and then alone. The hecklers, the fans, the spitters - everyone is standing, at a loss for an appropriate response. John sits grinning by the drum set, puffing on a cigarette, while the rest of PiL endlessly repeat the riff. The spitting has stopped, this substitution of targets being after all very upsetting and most unlike the way things had to be. And to the dismay of a mob that can't wait for the various roles of star and audience to be reinstated, so they can go on being idol and fan, things don't go back to normal ... Lydon skanks, laughing, enjoying this holiday, spots a clinging figure to one side and helps a second junior punk to the stage. Number two understands the new game and immediately struts about giving the finger to his mates, spitting on top of their heads and arrogantly skanking and weaving in the Huntingdon Beach Downhill Racer fashion. Two more minutes and a third edition who specialises in the worm style of dancing, the three extras taking turns banging on Keith's synthesizer. Lydon announced, "That's it, we've had enough", and bids farewell to Los Angeles.'

For all his debunking of punk, Lydon remained in command. As Kristine McKenna wrote in her *Rolling Stone* review of the show, 'What a show it was. The music was immense and primitive, the crowd was horrifying, and Lydon was staggeringly in control every second.' Lydon was determined to articulate his performance aesthetic (because that's what it amounted to). For him, it should always be 'free form. We decide what songs we do as we do them, as we're inspired. I couldn't bear a fuckin' format.' He also insisted on an element of positive audience participation.

During their LA sojourn, *Sounds'* US correspondent Sylvie Simmons asked Lydon whether he shouldn't be offering something more to the audience: 'In other words dictate? No. I merely offer my point of view *and Wobble offers his* (my italics); and you either appreciate it or hate it, simple, but don't slavishly idolise it. I'm not saying I'm totally right.'

That Lydon and Wobble were at odds with their respective approaches was no longer such a closely guarded secret. All this talk of spontaneity disguised deep divisions in the PiL camp. Wobble, in particular, thought that it had become an excuse for not rehearsing, not working at what they had. If he generally kept his thoughts to himself Stateside, even when a participant in radio phone-ins, after his departure from the set-up he portrayed this American visit in terms clearly critical of Lydon and Levene:

Jah Wobble: The gigs in America, playing for 20 minutes and getting into this corny audience conflict situation – it wasn't leading anywhere. A performer has got a responsibility, especially in ritual music like PiL played. It's give and take. (1982)

After the LA performance, PiL headed on to San Francisco for their final two US shows, at the Oakland Coliseum and San Francisco's Market Centre. The day of the last US gig the band again participated in a phone-in, on San Rafael's KTIM radio station. By now the image had clearly cracked, if not for Wobble, certainly for their

disillusioned drummer. To the acute embarrassment of Lydon, Martin Atkins took the opportunity of KTIM's live radio programme to launch an attack upon 'the PiL attitude'. Asked about the solo single that he had recently recorded as Brian Brain, he let rip:

MA: I just wanted to do something that was slightly professional.

DJ: Are you implying that the work you do with PiL is not professional?
MA: Yes. I would call it unprofessional. I would call it the emperor's new clothes.
Lydon: Go on, Martin. Keep waffling.
MA: We are the emperor's new clothes but no one is saying that we are. We are it.

DJ: Is Johnny the emperor?
MA: No, nobody is the emperor. We are it. I'm just waiting for some fucking asshole to say that we are not wearing any clothes. I just wish somebody would have the fucking guts to do it.

DJ: What makes it unprofessional?

MA: The attitude behind it. The promotion. Lack of management.

DJ: You manage yourselves?
MA: We don't manage ourselves. We mismanage ourselves.
Lydon: Are you still waffling?
MA: Before a gig we unsynchronise our watches, which is the whole crux of it. We cock-up everything there is to cock-up. We constantly underachieve.
Lydon (in childish voice): Can you put a record on, now, now, now?

Later on in the show Lydon refers to Atkins as 'the embarrassment of our little group'; but Atkins is no longer cowed, 'Yeah, 'cause I'm professional.'

***

Not surprisingly, Atkins was given the boot - for the first, but not the last time – on their return to Blighty. According to Atkins' own statement, 'Jah Wobble might be leaving the group as well.' A Virgin statement insisted that Wobble was still very much part of the organisation, but Atkins was 'not working with the band any more as they don't need a drummer, because they're not gigging any more.' The statement went further, depicting the PiL organisation as 'very much alive... (and) working on other visual and aural projects, the fruits of which will be seen and heard shortly." It was the same righteous blather they had been spouting for two years now.

Whatever the official Virgin line, PiL the band was clearly self-destructing. The statement that they would be playing no more gigs was probably the last straw for Wobble. When Levene and Lydon again flew out to the States, at the end of June, to discuss a possible film soundtrack (first mooted during their previous visit), and to appear on NBC's *Tomorrow Show*, compered by Tom Snyder, Wobble decided to leave them to it, and get back to making music. Wobble's rift with Lydon never entirely healed, and their years of friendship came to an unpleasant end. Looking back on his departure, a couple of years later, Wobble had this to say:

Jah Wobble: Public Image was always Rotten's vehicle. I figured that out. It took about nine months for me to decide to leave and it was finally because I couldn't stand the pretentiousness of it all... It was supposed to be an umbrella organisation, which it never became. The video, our own label, none of that ever happened. I started to feel embarrassed. (1982)

Wobble promptly recruited old PiL drummer Jim Walker for a new band called The Human Condition, with a view to developing some of the ideas left still-born by PiL after the brave new world of *First Issue* and *Metal Box*. Meanwhile, Lydon was telling Snyder that he considered gigs nowadays to be 'a bunch of gits on a stage with all these idiots standing in the pits worshipping them, thinking they're heroes. There should be no difference between who's on stage and who's in the audience. And we've tried very hard to break down those barriers but it's not working... (weary tone) So we have to think again. In the meantime, we'll put our attention somewhere else.'

The *Tomorrow* show exchange started out a bad-tempered affair, and got worse, with Snyder prodding and poking, but continually being blanked. Lydon seemed determined to put Snyder down, even when he asked a perfectly sensible question; while Levene just sat there pin-eyed – pilled to the gills, or jet-lagged, or both. When The Pistols were mentioned, Lydon stage-whispered, 'I wondered when you'd get to that.' During the commercial break Synder apparently exploded: 'What the fuck are you doing? You're making a fool of yourself.'

Lydon later contended that he'd been set up, but his boorish behaviour on national TV was not well-received by American press and public alike. *Rolling Stone* reported that, 'Snyder, for once, was right on the mark,' for calling Lydon a 'fucking fool'. So, not a particularly successful exercise in the art of communication from this so-called communication company. And yet the whole exercise in mutual incomprehension has come to be seen as a classic clip, a confrontation celèbre. Indeed, when Sony recently released a DVD compilation of Snyder's New Wave guests, it was given prominence in all the accompanying blurb and artwork.

But there was disturbing news from home. And so, the day before flying to New York - for further 'meetings' – Levene organised an interview with *NME*, intended to abate mounting speculation over the band's future. The front-cover of the paper still bore the headline, 'The PiL Corp to cease trading?', suggesting that editor Neil Spencer was unconvinced by Levene's rambling justifications of the way that PiL seemed to haemorrhage members. Levene again mentioned his desire to do the musical soundtrack for director Michael Wadleigh's forthcoming film, concerning the 'similarities between wolves and Red Indians -their outsider sensibilities, pack hunting and instinctive behaviour.'

Keith Levene: I met loads of guys in America who spoke about PiL, but he (Wadleigh) was the only one who knew what he was talking about. He's the only one who could pick up on those 32 levels 'of different things you can get off in PiL music...' I was talking of earlier; he could pinpoint and talk about them on certain tracks. He offered us a third of the soundtrack and I hope that we impress him enough (so) that we can do all of it. He wants us in our music to possibly find sounds for what a wolf sees and hears and smells when it sees a human and so on. We might just end up doing vocal sounds through John and treating them.

Though he could not read music, and had no experience of scoring a film, or working to a schedule set by the studio, not the twilight world he increasingly inhabited, Levene remained optimistic about the project. But the mention of Wobble prompted an attack on his extra-curricular activities, using the (oft-quoted) charge that the bassist had misappropriated PiL backing tracks for his solo album:

Keith Levene: We can all do solo work, yeah, but it comes under PiL, not Jah Wobble. We always knew that Wobble was mak-

247

ing the record, but we didn't know anything about it, so I don't see that it connects with PiL at all – whereas I see any of the stuff I do as always connecting with PiL. The thing that Wobble did was a mercenary act. I didn't like him using backing tracks from PiL that I didn't want people to hear. (1980)

Yet Wobble was not replaceable, and even the terrible twins recognised this. Levene and Lydon chose not to try, though they were unclear about how the communications company could maintain any kind of public profile without a rhythm section of any description. For now, their immediate recourse – both to maintain that public profile and to fund future ventures – was an industry cliche: the stop-gap live album.

With no studio album on the horizon, they decided to provide a potted history of PiL the occasional live band. Lydon was quick to point out that the release of *Paris Au Printemps* – on the first anniversary of the release of *Metal Box* - was essentially an anti-bootlegging exercise: 'It's a hell of a lot cheaper than the bootleg and much better quality – that's it.' However, this was no budget release; despite marginal production values, and the fact that just seven of the thirteen songs performed at the two Paris shows were included. The alternative – a more ambitious audio-visual package from the New York show in April – just seemed to require too much effort from two souls increasingly disconnected from the world at large; in Lydon's case, because of undiagnosed depression; in Levene's, the result of persistent drug use.

The reviews of this thin live album certainly gave concerned critics an excuse to vent on the unfulfilled potential of PiL, thanks to the sheer mundanity of the issued item. The review in *Sounds*, coming from the man who praised *Metal Box* to the skies, Dave McCullough, was all the more damning for his displayed disappointment, 'An album of blank noise would have said more about PiL, been more redeeming than this lifeless lump of rehashed vinyl.' Ex-*Sounds* correspondent Vivien Goldman – now defected to *Melody Maker* - remained close to the band but still couldn't help commenting on 'Wobble's steady bass, teetering on the brink of nimble jazz runs', before proceeding to ask the $64,000 question 'raised by the *Paris Au Printemps* time capsule... What will PiL be minus Wobble?'

And yet, it was the one positive review of the album – Lynden Barber's in the same paper, which called these soundscapes 'dangerous nightmare music that'll make you worry, lifting the stone of normality to find the dirt lurking beneath' - that drew Lydon's ire. Commenting on this review to Goldman, he said, 'Well, that's enough to turn off anyone. I mean would you buy a record that promised to sound like that?' Maybe he was embarrassed by any praise for such obvious product. Yet when it came to filthy lucre he had no shame. As he wrote a couple of months later, 'At the moment PiL's financial situation is desperate. But there are all kinds of ways of making money dear boy. Hustle, hustle, hustle.'

***

While Levene searched for a possible future musical direction that could be achieved without a rhythm section, Lydon elected to join his brother for an October weekend in Dublin. Though it was expected that the odd pint of Guinness might be consumed, Lydon couldn't have envisaged that he would spend the weekend in Mountjoy Prison, charged with assaulting a pub owner and his assistant. Lydon, who later claimed that he had been considering moving PiL enterprises across the Irish Sea to avoid harassment by petty officialdom, found that he was just as great a target in the not-so-quiet land of Erin.

Lydon claimed he had wandered into the Horse & Tram pub on October 3 with an anonymous fan, who had offered to buy him a drink. After being refused service, the landlord alleged that Lydon became abusive and physically assaulted the pub's owner and assistant – both of whom were 'seven foot tall and six feet wide', according to Lydon. Lydon's own account of the incident directly contradicted the testimony of Tweedledee and Tweedledum:

John Lydon: This man asked me for an autograph out in the street and offered me a pint of beer. Well, we went up to the bar and asked for two pints of lager and were told 'no'. When we were told to get out, I asked him, Why, was I black or something? He just told me to get out. Then, when I was walking out I got smashed in the back of the head... I have never been in any sort of affray like that. (1981)

After a District Court judge, Justice McCarthy, turned down three pleas for bail on Saturday morning Lydon was forced to spend the whole weekend in Dublin's notorious Mountjoy Prison. On the Monday afternoon he was peremptorily sentenced to three months in jail on the hearsay of two Dubliners of dubious provenance, at which point a Virgin representative produced the necessary bail, pending an appeal against the decision, to be heard in December.

The affair contributed to Lydon's increasing sense of disillusionment with life in the British Isles. Though insisting he would not write about his weekend in jail – 'That would be too corny. How could I write about me like that? Who would want to listen to me whining in self-pity?' – 'Francis Massacre' on the next album, ostensibly about the life sentence given to Francis Moran, retained as its refrain, 'Mountjoy is fun/ Go down for life.'

At the beginning of November, Lydon and Levene headed for Virgin's Manor Studios in Oxford to start work on the follow-up to the monumental *Metal Box*. Everyone was waiting to see where they went, without Wobble. Though supposedly there to record some demos with producer Mick Glossop, they had no finished songs to demo, just ideas, fragments, lines that they hoped might evolve sponaneously, just by setting up in the studio:

Keith Levene: (Initially) it was just me, John and Jeanette in the studio. We were booked into The Manor for 10 days and it was like we knew we were doing a new album, and we couldn't do anything for days – we couldn't do anything. It was like this horrible mental block... We'd turn up there and go through the process of setting up the instruments. And nothing was happening. Nobody was doing anything. It was the third day we were there and still, nobody was doing anything... By the fourth day, I set up this really fucking weird situation in the studio where we've got these 36 channels in and I'm using eighteen of them for the drums and this weird bamboo instrument I had set up in the drum booth. I was just on a high-energy pitch and said, 'We got to record something! I'm going into the fucking drum room, we'll do a quick mic check, then I want you to just put me into record.'... So I made that tune 'Hymie's Hymn.'... I had been offered to make this film soundtrack for *Wolfen*... I came up with 'Hymie's Hymn' as my pilot for the score for the movie. (1981/PSF)

Levene had spent the first two days at The Manor trying to redo 'Home Is Where The Heart Is', using a loop of four notes to replace Wobble's original, more melodic bass. Though the song ended up as the B-side of the 'Flowers Of Romance' single, this was an exercise in treading water. Finally, Levene made the call to Martin Atkins.

Martin Atkins: I was excited to hear what they had done in the preceding two weeks up there – NOTHING! I dove in and worked on a few rhythms, Mickey Mouse watch loops etc., for 'Four Enclosed', trumpets from this little battery powered trumpet thing that played 3" plastic discs etc.

251

Three songs featuring Atkins *were* recorded – 'Four Enclosed Walls', 'Under The House' and 'Banging The Door' – at the remaining Manor sessions. According to Atkins, talking in 2004, 'John also told me recently that I performed (and co-wrote) the 'Flowers' track - I just let all of these ideas flow, then left them with the ideas and went off to tour the USA.' Still some way short of an album, sessions continued at Townhouse Studios in West London. Chris Salewicz, sent there to interview Lydon and Levene, described the scene that greeted him:

'John is hunched over a 32-track mixing desk that dwarfs his slight, unexpectedly studious figure. He is mixing PiL tracks recorded the previous day for a new studio album. Between takes, from time to time, he peers up at the television that is set in the wall above his head.'

It was at the Townhouse that the duo decided they would try a surfeit of minimalism. Though at previous stages of the recording process they seemed uncertain of how they wanted the final album to sound, Levene has said, 'We knew we were gonna concentrate on the drum sound.' After three weeks' further work, Levene realised the drum sound was fine as is, and that further overdubs were unnecessary:

Keith Levene: There were two weeks when we were doing this album at the Townhouse. We had this fucking great drum sound and we had all these tracks. I was racking my brains – what can I put on this? What can I put on that? And I kept listening back to them. On the last day, we knew we weren't gonna have any more time for it so we were finishing it off, it was then I realised – fuck it, that's it! There's no room for anything. And that was a track that might only have had, the drums, John's voice, and that's all... If you restrict yourself to labels like rock 'n' roll you're never going to get anywhere with PiL... That's my dilemma in the studio right now. Right this minute. The last album, *Metal Box*, **if you want to call it rock 'n' roll, it's the furthest you can go in rock 'n' roll... Now there's got to be a complete change. At the moment I'm designing a drum synthesizer that I'd like to put out on the market.**

The album they claimed to have completed by the end of November would not be released until the following spring, perhaps because Virgin were not yet convinced that what they'd delivered qualified as an album. Looking back on *Flowers Of Romance* 18 months later, Lydon admitted that it was recorded too quickly, and at a bad time personally for him:

John Lydon: I came straight out of jail in Dublin and came to London and recorded instantly... (A song like 'Go Back') is the way I was feeling at the time, and it shows badly. It's horrible to listen back to that kind of paranoia. (1982)

As it happens, 'Go Back' was a rare highlight of the album, sounding like an actual song and not a demo for Professor Levene's latest drum synthesizer. Confronting the paranoia Lydon had felt for some time, thrown into high relief by the sentence dished out to him in October, it suggested hard times ahead. In fact, when Lydon arrived at the Dublin appeal in December, it took only a five-minute hearing for the Circuit Court Judge, Frank Martin, to recognise a stitch-up, and to grant the appeal against the draconian sentence, stating that he was, 'satisfied of the petty nature of the incident and of the fact that neither of the publicans had been injured in the alleged fraças.' Thin tissue of lies, anyone?

Also in December, a select few journalists were allowed to hear parts of the new studio album, now deemed finished, pending its January or February release (sic). Ian Penman, whose preview in *NME* carried the immortal headline 'PiL's Ukulele Album', found a Lydon mightily pleased with himself. Apparently, it was all about 'minimalism. Everything just plays on dynamics. No tune is played, there is no melody going through any song. We just piled a load of instruments in the corner of the studio and thought, what can we do with this?' Despite this surprisingly accurate depiction of the process Penman felt that, 'the resulting noises certainly do not lack melody or discipline.'

In the same month Vivien Goldman further whet any appetite for the new studio album. At the end of her downbeat review of *Paris Au Printemps*, she suggested that 'PiL have done it again - broken another sound barrier. While half the world wants to sound like Chic, and the other half like Sly and Robbie – or like PiL, come to that – the Company's created a new kind of rhythm, a definite danceable rhythm not based on bass and drums... The meaning behind the moaning gets clearer all the time.'

After another review of the live album, Radio One's *Rock On* also previewed the promised platter with a lengthy snippet from the title-track, 'Flowers Of Romance', played at the end of another Lydon/Levene interview. It was a clever way of implying a wealth of activity when Lydon and Levene were struggling to cover up the joins. Unfortunately, PiL's relationship with Virgin – always an at-arms-length arrangement the label only tolerated because it was John Lydon's band – now discernibly deteriorated. Even with the most iconic frontman this side of Bowie, PiL had never been a commercial band, though their avant-garde approach made them darlings to a still-influential critical coterie. But Virgin considered much of the material on *Flowers Of Romance* utterly inaccessible, even compared with either *Metal Box* or *First Issue*. Lydon implied that this was part of their design to *Record Mirror*:

John Lydon: I'd have to say that if *Flowers* had made the top I'd seriously have to question: 'Why?' That sort of mass accept-

**ance can be an indication of 'Oh my God! – the world's caught
up with us, or we've gone three steps back'. (1981)**

Virgin's decision to delay the release of the album, though, made
no sense at all. Apparently, they considered the album so uncom-
mercial that they initially suggested re-releasing the group's 'Public
Image' 45, to stimulate interest in the band. When Virgin finally arranged for the album's release, they were only prepared to press half
the number of copies previously done for *Metal Box*, much to the
chagrin of Levene, who felt 'we were delivering a truly commercial
album that had a string of production values all the way through that
was consistent – because of the drum sound we had'.

In fact, Virgin had to hurriedly repress when the title track of
the album provided PiL with their third Top 30 single, reaching 24
in the singles charts – boosted by a particularly surreal appearance
on *Top Of The Pops*, with Lydon dressed like a defrocked vicar,
Jeanette Lee sawing away at double bass, and Levene resembling
a half-crazed medical student beating away at a set of drums. It
may not have made many converts but it sure livened up a by-now-
dead-on-its-knees programme! Boosted by the exposure, the album
charted at 11, seven places higher than *Metal Box*, though it only re-

mained in the charts for five weeks, suggesting that word of mouth among post-punks was hardly the friend it had been to its predecessor.

Reviews of the album were even less of an ally. At one extreme was Lynden Barber (again) in *Melody Maker*, who stated: 'Whatever your attitude towards PiL... it's an album that demands to be heard by everybody who claims to be concerned about contemporary music.' At the other was Jeff Nesin in *Creem*: 'Adrift and singularly unattractive without Wobble's resonant bass, *Flowers Of Romance* is a collection of nine skeletal cartoons and meandering notions of a possibly sinister, certainly unpleasant nature from a very cocky pop refugee turned art snob suffering from a lethal overdose of UK attention.' The majority of reviewers went the Nesin route, though the generally-hostile *Sounds* decided to give the album five stars, describing it as, 'the album mankind has been waiting for: Absolute Music!'

The most balanced review came from the Irish music paper *Hot Press*: "The best bits? They're good, but after this the most subversive thing PiL could do might just turn out to be producing something utterly ordinary." *New Musical Express* gave it to Ian Penman, presumably expecting the praise showered their way in his preview. Instead he voiced his fear at the direction Lydon and Levene were pursuing, and the pretensions they were assuming along the way:

'*Flowers Of Romance* is not a collection of film soundtracks – nor does it manipulate its graphic projection in a sufficiently groundbreaking manner to make this anything other than The New PiL LP, complete with Single Off The LP and interviews galore. PiL seem to be so retentively, forlornly hung up – to a blinding, neurotic degree – on their 'anti rock 'n' roll' crusade as to lose sight of where this crusade might actually be taking them.'

In fact, PiL were fast becoming so po-faced about their 'conceit' that the music papers began to dish out the kind of treatment previously reserved for the Queens and Roxy Musics of this world. The most glorious parody of the band's occasional pretensions was in *Hot Press*, which published a history of the corporation by the eminent Baron Seamus Of Marzipan:

'The firm of Public Image Limited was founded a wee while ago. Its authorised capital is not much, its shareholders are all drunk and the directors as dissolute a bunch of ruffians as I have ever encountered in a Watney's household... (The) charge is one of inconsistency, to wit, a lot said but a little achieved, activities likely to enrage and annoy revealing a lack of sympathy for the general populace and sheer bad manners.'

* * *

'I don't mind that (PiL) go on about rock 'n' roll is dead and it's gotta be killed off'; (but) that's just a load of words, what does it actually mean?' Joe Strummer, NME, 3/1/81

Lydon and Levene had already set themselves up for just such a fall. The repeated references to 'other projects' had still come to naught. And, as a peeved Penman pointed out in his review, 'In one breath Keith Levene scorns the idea of making an LP as being 're-ally boring' – then proceeds to bore you for about half an hour (or an entire PiL LP) about the ins and outs of one particular synthesizer technique.' Caught in the glare of their own contradictions, Lydon copped a plea:

John Lydon: (PiL is) a limited company... (who) have access to other things, like video and electronics, and hi-fi and books and painting and yes... even the theatre, (but has) piss-arsed about for far too long. It's more than fucking high time things got serious.

As perhaps an indication of the need to shake things up at Gunter Grove, the community expelled yet another slacker in the winter of 1981. Dave Crowe took his collection of cutthroat accoutrements and left the building. When asked what had happened to Crowe, Levene suggested he was just another one not 'on the program':

Keith Levene: John had known him for years, so any excuse would do to get him in the band, so we made him a secretary and he ended up kind of keeping accounts and receipts together and so on. But the PiL thing is that each person must take initiative and must have ideas and just go about them, not like the way Wobble did in a mercenary way, using the company, y'know. Crowe ended up wanting to be told what his job was, and... he was creating a lot of head problems, which weren't there.

Still hanging on was Jeanette Lee, whose ostensible role continued to be to expand the visual concepts of the band (though as she informed Gavin Martin, "I'm always present at studio mixes, (so) just the fact that I'm there means I'm contributing to the clash of personalities."). However, Wobble's persistent query to Lee, 'What exactly is it that you *do*?' stayed unanswered. The band even stopped making regular promotional videos (as previously done for 'Public Image' and 'Death Disco'), at precisely the time when the format was starting to sprout wings. Another project which seemed more definite than most had now fizzled out – the soundtrack for Michael Wadleigh's film about wolves and Indians, even though the film itself appeared, as *Wolfen*.

With *Flowers Of Romance* – and its UK promotion – complete, Levene headed for New York. If the album was not the direction most fans of the band wanted them to pursue, at least Lydon and Levene were still coming up with new ideas about the kind of sounds they wanted to produce. The off its axis pivot on which PiL pirouetted, though, tilted, after their next public appearance – their first in twelve months – at a midtown Manhattan club on May 15, 1981.

The whole affair started when Bow Wow Wow were forced to cancel their scheduled two-night engagement at the Ritz, due to visa difficulties. Via Levene, the Ritz offered PiL the cancelled dates, while he was weighing up the pros and cons of relocating the band to New York. Lydon felt it was one way to get out of his rut, and Levene hoped that New York would be more receptive to the assorted projects he wished to pursue, such as designing his drum synthesizer, building a porta-studio and scoring drugs. On the day

The Flowers of Romance

Public Image. Ltd.

a new long playing record.

of the show, though, he and Lydon apparently had their first major disagreement.

Keith Levene: I originally popped over here for a week; then I got John and Jeanette over here for this thing we really wanted to do, which was a live video gig at the Ritz. All I got from them was that I was treating them like puppets; the morning of the gig they had their suitcases packed, ready to go home. I said, 'Look, fuckin' go home, I don't really care, 'cos if we don't do this gig we'll get our fuckin' legs broken.' (1983)

The show went ahead, but in typical PiL fashion, with a patent lack of rehearsal-time wrapped in the rhetoric of spontaneity. As Jeanette Lee told journalist Tim Sommer before the balloon went up, 'I hope no one's been misled – no one said it was a gig. Everything is actually going to be done live – there's no preparation. The band will be live, the video will be live – it's all spontaneous. It (organising the gig) happened so quickly, and I'm interested in what we can do in a day – that's the exciting part. The whole thing about this Corporation is spontaneity.' Sommer was amazed. As he later wrote, 'Not to warn the audience that this was not going to be a gig, but a video and noise presentation... was a major show of gross negligence on the Ritz's part and gross arrogance on PiL's part.'

As paying punters entered the tatty ballroom, they saw the large video screen, that was usually rolled up to the ceiling while bands performed, was covering the stage. When PiL arrived, they disappeared behind the screen, and it was from this position that they began to play. According to the *NME* report, 'A video camera, also behind the screen, picked up their image which was simultaneously projected on to the screen. Levene stood at his synthesizer, Lydon sang sporadically and Jeanette Lee just wandered around. This simultaneous projection was intercut with old PiL promotional videos, the band in a rehearsal studio, etc.'

The band had gone as far as recruiting a drummer – so there *was* some intent to incorporate elements of live performance, albeit from behind the screen – and intercut video sequences (presumably 'organised' by Jeannette Lee) with shots of the band playing. The

'Flowers Of Romance' that opened proceedings, though, was clearly pre-recorded; and rather than segueing into something recognisably live, Levene indulged in assorted synthesizer doodlings while the video screen flickered. The audience grew restless. This was no downtown loft, and they hadn't been served wine and canapés. Finally, Levene's discernible guitar sound came through the speakers, accompanied by drums and synthesizer – intercut with the video of *The Tomorrow Show* on the screen – duly becoming a discernible version of 'Four Enclosed Walls'. All the while the band remained behind the screen.

At this point the audience realised that the band were not coming out. And this was the wrong crowd for this kind of performance art. As Richard Grabel stated, 'The Ritz on a Friday night... usually gets a hardcore rock 'n' roll crowd. They expect to be catered to for their twelve dollars and they usually are. The subtleties of a conceptual video performance – or whatever it was PiL thought they were doing – were bound to be lost on them.' Lydon, never one to shirk a confrontation, now began taunting the crowd, with inevitable results:

Lydon: Hello. So glad you're enjoying the show. That's right, get your money's worth, (background synthesizer noises... audience boos)... Boo! Boo! It's not fair. It's not fair. We want rock 'n' roll. Boo! Hiss! (sings in high-pitched whine), 'When the sun comes shining through/just for youuu... ' All financial donations accepted. Oh you're so wonderful. So nice to be here in your wonderful city y'know (starts 'Go Back', quickly grinds to a halt amid assorted cries of 'Fuck You')... Was I wonderful? Aren't you getting your money's worth? This is what rock 'n' roll's all about, maaaan. I'm so happy, so happy you've all come to see me. Ah I'm having so much fun. Would you like to know who's behind the screen? All right here's Sammy on drums. Well hello Sammy, how you doing? Isn't it pretty groovy? Now this is Keith Levene, you've heard of him – he's pretty famous. And now over here we have Jeanette Lee. Hi there, Jeanette, say hello to the guys and girls. ('Hello guys and girls') There, getting your money's worth. Go Back.

Bottles now started raining on the screen. Levene, underestimating the furore PiL were creating, further incited the crowd, 'I think you're boring. You're a boring fucking audience. If you destroy that fucking screen, we will destroy you. We have the power behind us. If you destroy the screen, you are destroyed.' Lydon stopped reciting 'Go Back' to join in with baiting the crowd:

Lydon: I'm safe... You're not throwing enough. You're what I call a passive audience. It's obvious you're all into peace and love ... Hey I can see you're having fun out there. (Assorted shouts of 'Fuck You', Lydon starts singing repeatedly in high-pitched whine). 'Happiness, Happiness/The greatest gift that I possess... Video killed the radio star/Video killed the audience again. Kill the fucking audience...' I'm so glad you're all into new ideas. Destroy! Destroy! Go on – destroy. It's The Sex Pistols all over again. I've seen it all before. (Sings in high-pitched whine) 'New York New York/Is a wonderful town'.

Twenty minutes after 'PiL' took to the stage, as Grabel worte, someone decided enough was enough and hurled a chair 'from the balcony, hitting the screen dead centre and smashing down on the stage. This was the signal for the true riot to begin.' As the audience grabbed the screen and pulled it down, the band wisely quit the stage, amidst shouts of 'Smash the fucking lens', the inevitable 'Fuck you' and 'Play some fucking music'. The perennial New York fights between fans and bouncers broke out on a stage already covered with the broken glass from bottles fans had been throwing at the screen. The evening 'ended with the block on which the club is located being sealed off by police, a mob of angry people gathered outside the doors, several injuries and thousands of dollars worth of damage done inside the club.'

PiL's label, Warner Brothers, going into PR-panic mode, organized a press conference for Tuesday of the following week, at which PiL could explain their *raison d'etre* to unknowing eyes. Instead, Levene showed those attending a video of the show, which the band had filmed, and informed the press, 'I am satisfied it had impact and we'll do it again, but it'll be altogether different.' Perhaps unaware how close he had come to being the gig's most serious casualty, Levene continued to justify the incident even after he left the band:

Keith Levene: Everyone I spoke to said it was brilliant. The American public, I hear, thinks it was some kind of rip off; I'm sure I would have found that gig worth my ten dollars. The idea that we weren't really gonna know what was going to happen. As you saw we didn't. We weren't trying to start a riot... that was the last thing we were trying to do. We had a boom mic over the audience. I wanted this communication between the audience. (1983)

Lydon, on the other hand, was dismissive of the audience that night – as well as anybody who sought to see some great artistic conceit in the exercise: 'They wanted some kind of rock 'n' roll band. Pity, 'cos that's not what they are going to get from us. Piss off to them, they have a pretty good idea what to expect next time we do a gig... I would not knowingly ever play to an 'Art' crowd. I hate arteests.' Actually, by the next time PiL were able to 'do a gig', they had reverted to recognisable-rock-quartet playing mostly familiar songs they'd actually rehearsed. The Ritz riot was not to be the shape of things to come, even though it was, as *Sounds* said at the time, 'The first time that PiL has actually done what they've always said they were going to do (and) actually lived up to and acted on everything they claim to stand for and have stated that they wanted to achieve.' It was also the last shot fired during PiL's original, anti-rock crusade.

* * *

By the time the dust had settled, the show had considerably limited their options. Warners were no more convinced by *Flowers Of Romance* than Virgin. Though they humoured the band for a few more months, waiting to see if the riot had a positive effect on their profile, by the spring of 1982 Public Image were without a US label. Lydon was free of Warners, free to do what he wanted any old time – as long as said activity was free, or close to it. Having left England – and Virgin – behind, the Ritz riot also left Lydon without the prospect of any US club willing to book his atonal anarchists.

In fact, the one offer of help in the aftermath of the riot came from a most unexpected source – the management of the Ritz – who, according to media reports were 'offering PiL large sums of money for a return, though probably not a repeat, performance.' The offer was not taken up. They couldn't pull the same stunt twice, and they lacked the apparatus or the personnel to actually perform a *Flowers*-like set live. Indeed, it would be a further 16 months before anything more would be heard from the PiL corporation, broken only by the occasional worrying rumour, such as one printed in *Sounds* in January 1982 that the band had 'disintegrated'. Lydon's response was, 'The tosspot was desperate for a story last week, so he made one up.'

Virgin – as in the dark as the rest of us – claimed that the band's failure to produce anything save hotel bills during their sojourn across the sea was down to 'the unavailability of certain new innovative synthesized and other electro-music technology.' The motherless child Lydon, fast approaching 29, still had a lot to learn.

The slothful side of the author of 'Seventeen', previously held in some kind of check, was given rein thanks to the on-call culture of New York, Levene's increasing debilitation-by-drugs, and the absence of any new ideas. If rock was dead, whither now? The inertia sporadically evident throughout his journey now consumed Lydon.

In the winter of 1981, Lydon had written a nominally humorous, but actually deeply worrying week-long diary for teenzine *Smash Hits*. In it, he showed himself to be a man with some deep psychological scars. He here described Tuesday as 'the only day I left the house'; admitted that he was 'a TV addict – it all started when I used to lock myself up trying to avoid people'; and when, at the weekend, he visited then-girlfriend (later wife) Nora, confessed he spent 'most of my time round friends' houses. I hate my own place. It's morbid. I can't bear it.'

Even when he wrote about his 'all-time favourite film', *The Lion In Winter*, Lydon's enthusiasm for it seemed to stem from its subject-matter – 'It's about this family who continuously wind each other up.' In the year after the Ritz, Lydon continued to catch up on his TV viewing, while flitting from hotel to hotel, settling at the Chelsea in the end (presumably not in the same room as the one where his old friend Sid Vicious stabbed his girlfriend, Nauseating Nancy, to death). Tim Sommer's report, 'Public Enterprises', in an October 1982 issue of *Sounds*, was the first media account of what had befallen the brave experimentalist/s:

'PiL did absolutely nothing as a band but drink beer and watch videos and hang out, any cohesiveness about the PiL unit/concept dissolved in a lazy haze. John put on weight, Keith (to some, but admittedly not to all) became an intolerable star/junkie, Jeanette Lee maintained the public profile of the so-called band, and the Lydon personality cult drew leeches and starfuckers like any personality cult would, some like Ken Lockie masking their groupie-ism with musicianship, others, like Roger Trilling and Bob Tullipan, masking it with 'management'.'

When it seemed that PiL as a creative unit was well and truly finished, a 'chance meeting' between Levene and Martin Atkins at the Mudd Club in New York provided the impetus for a rekindling of PiL activities. According to Levene, Atkins was playing the club with his band Brian Brain, and Levene 'invited him to stick around and work on a new PiL record.' This isn't quite how Atkins remembers it:

Martin Atkins: I was performing with Brian Brain at the Mudd Club – we were doing a version of Careering and when I turned around John was down the front smiling at me – it was weird – I should have had him come up onstage and sing. Later, in the dressing room, the new manager Bob Tulipan asked me to rejoin to work on a new album.

Tullipan was apparently one of a pair of businessmen who wanted to 'help' the group. He owned a small recording studio, South Park, and arranged for the band to get studio time when the studio wasn't booked, on the kind of basis usually reserved for a new act looking for a record deal. As far as PiL were concerned, it was the only game in town. Virgin were not prepared to fund further wastefulness, and the money had well and truly dried up.

Keith Levene: Virgin actually pulled our advance – they said, 'You have to deliver the record.' We said, 'How the fuck are we going to make the record without the advance?' So the only way we could get any money was by finishing the record. (PSF)

Desperately in need of replenished coffers, Lydon was obliged to accept an acting role in a new movie by Italian director Roberto Faenza. The movie, initially entitled *Psycho Jogger*, was to be shot in New York's Central Park and Rome. Lydon was offered a mere $10,000 to appear in it – as a jogging cop killer – but knew it was an offer he couldn't refuse. Again, it was suggested that PiL might provide the soundtrack music for the film. Though this did not in fact prove to be the case, Levene worked up a couple of instrumentals, one of which bore the eventual title of the movie, *The Order Of Death*. Meanwhile, Lydon started writing lyrics again, one of which expressed his true feelings about this time, 'I am not an actor/I can-not hide away.'

While Keith and Martin spent their time in the studio, usually in 24-hour weekend-stints, Lydon was holed up in Rome. En route to New York from Rome, Lydon spent a few days in London in late July, during which he talked with a curious *NME* editor, Neil Spen-cer, about what was happening in the world of PiL:

John Lydon: It's been difficult because I've been away two-and-a-half months and that's a long time to be separated. Keith's been at work because we have a very good studio deal with some people we might be amalgamating with. He's been banging down rough ideas and I've been sending over lyrics. (1982)

In fact, the album Levene and Atkins had been hard at work on suggested that PiL had decided to exhume Rock, *Flowers Of Romance* being left in the graveyard, and the Ritz riot forgotten. Lydon's paranoia remained the one constant in a set of new songs most of which had a rocksteady beat, even with Levene preferring synthesizer to guitar.

PiL were also trying to put their business matters on a sounder footing, setting up their own record label – P.E.P. – Public Entertain-ment Productions, along with an organisation called M.I.C. (Multi-Image Corporation), which according to Levene would be, 'an ex-pansion of the original PiL idea, facilitat(ing) a multitude of people going in a multitude of directions. It also produces PiL's music and coordinates PiL's artwork.' It sounded suspiciously like an early 80s Apple – minus any of The Beatles' money. Needless to say, MIC came to naught. PiL, though, went back to Public Entertainment.

By November 1982 there was even apparently a six-track mini-album – *You Are Now Entering A Commercial Zone* – ready for release. The band duly organised another West Coast press con-ference, at glitzy Hollywood restaurant Le Dome, to announce a return to gigging. Lydon even went to some pains to insist that PiL were not an 'arty' band – 'I find it bloody irritating that people pay more attention to the sociological phenomenon of Public Image than the music we play.'

In fact, PiL had already resumed their live career on the east coast. It had just taken until November to venture west. Though Keith Levene had continued recording the majority of bass parts in the studio, Martin Atkins now provided PiL with a new bass player, a fellow member of Brian Brain, Pete Jones. And the band actually rehearsed some new material for their first series of dates in two and a half years – beginning in New York on September 28,1982.

At the fall shows the band premiered four new songs (though the first show in New York only featured two: the instrumental 'Lou Reed Part One' and 'Where Are You'). 'Blue Water' (which was originally scheduled to be the next PiL single) and 'Mad Max' (subsequently rechristened 'Bad Life') were soon added. It was as if the band had wholly written off the two years since Wobble's departure as an unproductive sideturn (only 'Under The House' from *Flowers* remained in the set).

Of the new songs, 'Where Are You' – according to Levene – 'was totally about Jeanette', who was no longer part of PiL, PEP or MIC. The exact reasons/timing of Jeannette Lee's departure were left unclear. Even Levene confessed, 'I don't know what happened between her and John when he went to Italy with her to make the movie, but she left after that. Who knows, who cares?' Actually, she was still with Lydon when he was interviewed by Neil Spencer in London in July, so perhaps she took the opportunity to stay put, recognising a band on its last legs. The song, like 'Public Image', opened with Lydon declaiming 'hello, hello, hello', but this time it sounded like someone on the end of the phone talking to no-one.

The 1982 shows, though, were good solid performances, albeit generally non-confrontational affairs. On the first night at New York's Roseland Ballroom, Lydon even allowed a reprise of 'Public Image' as an encore. In fact, the set featured five songs from the first album, though only two from *Metal Box* ('Death Disco' and 'Chant'). By the time they got to California, six weeks later, PiL were performing all of the first album with the exception of 'Fodderstompf', five songs from *Metal Box*, as well as the quartet of new songs. Anyone who missed out on 1981 might have presumed that this was the same 'old' PiL, with a new bassist. Levene was even playing some coruscating guitar licks. When the bootleggers put out the Pasadena show, it seemed like old times.

But both David Fricke's and Richard Grabel's reviews of that debut New York show deemed it a chanceless affair. Fricke gave them the benefit of the doubt, concluding that 'the safety factor of familiar material and the concentrated vigour with which they play it suggests PiL feel the need to redeem themselves as an active, battling unit,' but Grabel seemed to expect more, 'PiL put on a good show and perhaps it's sour grapes not to leave it at that. But... good as it was, this show was just coasting.' Without Warners, though, the band needed to re-establish its audience before unleashing new product.

The band had seemingly abandoned the idea of a mini-album, recording further material for a full follow-up to *Flowers*. Two more songs were now recorded, 'This Is Not A Love Song' and 'Solitaire'. The latter saw Levene pick up his guitar, gathering dust in a corner somewhere, after what sounds like a sustained listen to the first two Gang Of Four albums. But still there was no product reaffirming that long-awaited return to form.

Instead PiL continued playing occasional gigs in New York and New Jersey, shows at the Brooklyn Zoo in January, and Poughkeepsie and Staten Island in March, presumably intended to fund further studio work. But, according to Levene, '(Though) we charged as much as possible... because we were so disorganised we spent just as much hiring the equipment and getting there.' Relations between Lydon and Levene were also fast deteriorating. Levene's marital union with an American girl, Lori, was sowing the seeds of the band's ultimate demise:

Keith Levene: My marriage had a great deal to do with me leaving PiL, it was an integral reason. The way my wife puts it – which doesn't make me look too great – is that I was with a lot of bastards that were giving me a hard time and I was too much a nice guy to know it... The last six to eight months we were going around being everything we always swore we would never

want to be. I was aware of it. I had to see the scene through, but I had to say goodbye in the end. (1983)

The final split came over the mixing of the song now planned as PiL's first single in two years. Levene had grown to despise Atkins' 'buddy-buddy' act with Lydon. In his mind, Atkins seemed intent on driving a wedge between the pair of old friends, 'John was in LA by then... I went into the studio to remix 'Love Song'. I told them I've got to remix it, it is embarrassing. Martin called John in LA and told him I was in the studio – this was the major trump card in Martin's power play to be John's best buddy. John called up screaming that I should get out of the studio immediately."

Lydon had gone to Los Angeles at the instigation of one Larry White, some time sound engineer/road manager and general entrepreneur. He apparently told Lydon, 'You'll never make it with your sound; what a bunch of wankers! The people want to see Johnny Rotten, man. Do you realise what you've got in your hands?' White introduced Lydon to Westside Frankie & The Inglewood Jerks, a hopeless bunch of wannabes from New Jersey who 'knew the Sex Pistols repertoire by heart.' Lydon apparently rehearsed PiL material with this band and tried out the show at a small club in LA. The show ended with 'Anarchy In The UK'. The fans pogoed away.

So when Lydon started screaming at him down the phone, Levene went on the attack: 'I don't like what I've been hearing about you in LA. It's a joke! Singing 'Anarchy In The UK'... We're doing all the things we said we'd never do. Is that what you want? A sell-out?' Lydon hung up. Following previous models of PiL departures, there was considerable acrimony on both sides. At Lydon's October 1983 press conference in London, when asked why Levene and Jeanette Lee had left the group, he opined, 'They're quitters.' So, another journo enquired, why have there been so many quitters involved in PiL? 'There's an awful lot of weak people in the world.' A year later, he was asked about Levene's whereabouts on Melbourne radio, and replied, 'Dead – I hope.' Levene was no less caustic:

Keith Levene: I thought he had a unique talent but I don't think he's got it any more... John was my best friend for years.

I thought he was great, so great. It was me, John and Sid... Sid died... and John has now died as far as I'm concerned. I don't want the PiL name and I don't want to be associated with them any more. (1983)

Twenty years later, talking to Jason Gross, the hurt was still evident. Certainly, the portrait he paints of Lydon does him few favours. But then, it is hard to argue with the last sentence – an epitaph for PiL if ever there was one.

Keith Levene: He's such an annoying git because he doesn't do anything to help. He knows what the picture should be and he's got an idea what it is. When it doesn't work out, he just blames people. He likes to pretend that other people are weak and it's never him. The reason that things don't work out the way that wants them to is that he doesn't do his bit... anyone you got in, John just vibed-out so badly, they didn't want to do it, or it was such a drag that it wasn't worth getting them in... John just didn't like *anyone*. In retrospect, the fucker just did not work with anyone. (PSF)

***

Amazingly enough, with the original band having wholly ceased to exist, Public Image Limited gained the biggest hit of its bad life. Having finally resolved on a mix, Lydon issued 'This Is Not A Love Song' (actually with two separate mixes on the 12"), along with 'Blue Water' and - as a final fillip to fans – the original 'Public Image', still as fresh as ever; and in September 1983 he had a Top Five single in the UK, and a reason to carry on.

He even persevered with the 'Holiday Inn' version of PiL who had toured Japan in late June (Lydon had been offered nine-thousand bucks to play an eight-date tour). The tour centred wholly around Tokyo where 'PiL' played six concerts at the Nakano Sun

Plaza. While there, Lydon was offered the opportunity of recording a live album on one of only three Mitsubishi X-800 PCM 32-channel digital tape recorders in the world. Two of the last three shows were duly recorded, and also filmed for a possible video release, an irony presumably not lost on Lydon, given the band's failure to produce a single live video during its worthier years.

The actual material performed by the band was a cross-section of the real PiL career, including three songs from *Flowers Of Romance* (the title song, 'Under The House' and 'Banging The Door'), and three songs recorded for the unfinished *Commercial Zone* ('This Is Not A Love Song', 'Solitaire' and 'Bad Life', aka 'Mad Max'). Also performed, as an encore, was 'Anarchy In The UK', though thankfully this was not included on the resultant live album. What was left still wasn't worth the effort, and the reviewers were for once universal in their distaste. Particularly curt and to the point was *NME*'s Richard Cook, who described the album as, 'Lydon, the entertainer, in ghastly pieces... (while) PiL's sound has become as formal and inelastic as elevator music: it is, again, noise – without heart or flesh of any sort.'

Nevertheless, on the back of a Top Five single and a second live album, Lydon felt it was time to play the first UK PiL tour. In November 1983, Lydon finally gave those fans at the Rainbow what they wanted – a gaudy travesty of the public image he had now claimed for his own. Levene, though, was determined to have his say, and the following spring there appeared in America a nine-track representation of *Commercial Zone*, in a blank white sleeve.

Levene had told *NME* the previous November that 'the record is finished – I finished it. I guess that was against PiL's will, but they weren't doing anything about it... Personally, if I was John Lydon, I wouldn't have said the vocals were finished, but they said they were. I went in and made the best of a bad job. But the album turned out quite good.' It was better than quite good, even if the trio of instrumentals, save for the evocative 'Order Of Death', smacked of filler. Issued in 1980, on the heels of *Metal Box*, it might even have been a commercial hit. But even after the fact, Levene rightly felt that it was a necessary addendum to the PiL story:

Keith Levene: If *Commercial Zone* would have come out (properly), with maybe more of a contribution from John... that would have been the fourth record and made all the other records make sense. It would have shown everyone that all those things were fucking serious. (PSF)

It represented a strange twist in the tale that the surreptitious release of this official bootleg in non-Virgin territories should be a way to convince doubters that the PiL co-founders were – and always had been – 'fucking serious', ever since they had embarked on their original crusade to turn rock on its head. Lydon, though, was no longer amused, insisting on issuing his own version of much the same material on the lamentable *This Is What You Want, This Is What You Get* – which really was a very poor joke at the public's expense.

Lydon – ever on the run from his own demons – was determined to rewrite history again. The travesty of 'This Is Not A Love Song' issued on *This Is What You Want* was mysteriously transmogrified into the 'hit' version, appearing on a subsequent PiL greatest hits, a 4-CD PiL box-set and even a *Now That's What I Call Music* 80s compilation *as the hit single*. It was as if Lydon hoped this risible wreck of a record could actually inveigle its way into the charts *retrospectively*. But history is a hard thing to rewrite when people insist on retaining those useless memories of the real McCoy. Oh, and those thunderous original PiL, which records still remained in the racks. Lydon was left with the name, and a nominal career. When he couldn't even sustain the pretence that PiL now became, he decided to trade on his rotten image as Mr Punk Personality. Reality TV beckoned. But that, as Subway Sect frontman Vic Goddard once wrote, is a different story.

Thanks to: Jason Gross at Perfect Sound Forever for use of his definitive Keith Levene interview; Jean Encoule at Trakmarx (www. trakmarx.com) for use of his Martin Atkins interview; Sean Body at Helter-Skelter and Richard Dudanski. This article is a (largely) revised version of the text to my 1988 history of PiL, Rise/Fall (Omnibus Books). Thanks to Chris Charlesworth.

Clinton Heylin

Clinton Heylin is the author of From *The Velvets To The Voidoids: The Birth of American Punk Rock* (Penguin, 1993 / Helter Skelter, 2005), *Sex Pistols: Never Mind The Bollocks - A Classic Album* (Music Sales, 1998), *PiL: Rise And Fall* (Omnibus, 1988), *Bob Dylan: Behind The Shades Take Two* (Penguin, 2002) and numerous others. He recently edited *All Yesterdays' Parties: The Velvet Underground In Print 1966–1971* (Da Capo, 2005), a collection of reviews and articles about the band.

Time Loves A Hero:
The Fury Returns
by Nigel Williamson

Four years ago, on the occasion of the 25th anniversary of the release of the Sex Pistols' 'God Save the Queen', I wrote a provocative article in *The Guardian* - a 'think piece' in newspaper parlance - questioning the historical significance of the punk explosion in the annals of popular culture. From this brave, if not foolhardy, messing with the cherished memories of a generation, a mischief-making sub-editor then extracted the article's most inflammatory phrase and came up with the eye-catching, tabloid-style headline: 'FACE IT: PUNK WAS RUBBISH'. Underneath there ran a somewhat more reasoned expression of the article's central contention, with a strapline that read: 'Sure, it had energy and attitude. But punk's importance has been hugely exaggerated, says Nigel Williamson.'

But the headline had done its job and it brought down a torrent of anger, abuse, and metaphorical spittle upon my head. I make no complaints about that. The piece had been intended to provoke a debate but I didn't realise just how virulent it would get. I suppose I should have taken more notice when the paper happily predicted that I would get crucified. 'This will keep the letters page busy for a week,' my commissioning editor told me approvingly.

He had underestimated. I was roundly denounced and abused by the paper's readers for the next two weeks. Then it got silly. Someone wrote in to say that nobody with a name like Nigel could have ever made a credible punk, and somebody else then wrote in to wonder where this left XTC's 'Making Plans For Nigel'. At this point the letters' editor wisely declared the correspondence closed, although it continued to rage for months on various websites and message boards, where calls for me to be hung, drawn and quartered - or worse - appeared with alarming passion and worrying regularity.

Someone even wrote to the editor of *Uncut*, another title for which I work regularly in a freelance capacity, demanding that I never be allowed to appear in the pages of the magazine again, and threatening to organise a reader's petition if I wasn't banished forthwith. On the other hand, there was also some support. Several prominent

REF

SEX PISTOLS.
c/o SEX
430 KINGS RD.
CHELSEA
LONDON. S.W.10.

01-673-0855
01-351-0764.

(MALCOLM)

TRACY COOKLIN
Ravensbourne
College of Art.
Walden Road.
Chislehurst.
Nr. Bromley.
Kent.

Dear Tracy
          This is a short note
to confirm that the SEX PISTOLS
will appear at your college
on the 9th December and play
at 9 p.m. for 1 hour maximum.
They will arrive at 4 p.m.
and endeavour to sort out
any problems about playing
time and equipment with
the other band FOGG. We do
have our own P.A. etc. and
everything should run ~~perfect~~
          smoothly. Free beer for
the band would be welcome
    Look forward to seeing you.
then. remaining yours faithfully
                    which ever.

fellow hacks emailed to commend me on my 'guts' (which I took to mean they probably agreed but weren't going to say so in public) while one reader wrote to express appreciation that someone had finally taken on 'the Stalinist/*NME* view of musical history'.

When asked to revisit the debate for this book of essays, my first act was to look up that original, notorious article from 2002. In describing it as 'notorious', I hope I'm not guilty of self-aggrandisement here. But in the four years since the piece first appeared, I would estimate that I've been reminded or asked about it at least once a month. Like Siouxsie's swastika or The Rolling Stones pissing up a garage wall, it was a social *faux pas* which in certain quarters shall never be forgiven or forgotten.

The original piece, of course, was written in a racy, polemical style, deliberately geared to get a rise out of readers, so inevitably it represented a simplified and short-handed version of my views. But in reading it again, I can't really say that I would wish to disown anything I wrote, even if I might have expressed some of the more contentious views with greater diplomacy. With apologies to those who read it at the time (and no doubt reacted as angrily as I'd intended), this is a summary of the argument.

I saw one of the Sex Pistols first gigs on a cold and cheerless Saturday night in December 1975. We were drinking in Henekey's Wine Bar, on Bromley High Street, and wondering whether we could be bothered to move the short distance to Ravensbourne College of Art to see a band nobody had heard of, or whether to stay put and get steadily drunk. In the end, we went and paid an entry fee that I seem to recall was 50 pence. Within minutes of the band taking the stage, we wished we'd stayed in the pub, for there seemed more future in getting mindlessly obliterated on pints of Newcastle Brown than in listening to such a racket.

The Pistols could barely play their instruments. Each tuneless thrash that passed for a song sounded the same as the one before. While the spotty, undernourished front-man knew how to sneer, he certainly didn't know how to sing. I don't think we bothered to stay until the end and after retrieving our Afghan coats from the cloakroom, we shuffled off into the night, back to our squat to skin up a spliff and listen to the new Little Feat album.

Not everyone who was present that night shared our dismissive judgement. Also in attendance was 18-year-old Susan Dallion. She and her mates decided they had witnessed the future of rock 'n' roll and went on to form punk's notorious chapter, 'the Bromley contingent'. It wasn't long before Dallion was fronting Siouxsie & The Banshees, one of the more imaginative and interesting bands to emerge from the punk scene.

We thought no more about the Sex Pistols until a few months later when we set off to see a great little pub rock outfit called Roogalator at the 100 Club. When we arrived, they had cancelled due to illness and the replacement was a band called The Jam, playing one of their first London gigs. They were even worse than the Pistols and we asked for a refund. I'm sure we got our money back too.

Yes, you could say I never really got punk. I was 22 years old in 1976 - younger than Mick Jones and Joe Strummer and the same age as Elvis Costello - and by rights I should have loved punk's iconoclasm. Instead, I hated its lack of imagination, its absence of musicality and its empty nihilism. Yet today, it has become heretical to point out that punk actually wasn't very good.

Rotten with 'The Contingent', Siouxsie second right.

I still go to gigs and talking to younger fans am frequently told how lucky I was to have been around during the punk era. I don't have the heart to tell them how truly awful most of it was. Sure, it had energy. It had attitude. But so does a pub-side full of no-hopers playing soccer on Hackney Marsh every Sunday. The honest truth is that the reverence in which punk is held some 30 years after it first rattled the bars of youth culture is based on a series of myths and misconceptions.

First: it is now received wisdom that by 1976, popular music was so complacent, self indulgent and moribund that punk was a reaction that had to happen. True, we could have done without the tedious triple live albums from Emerson, Lake and Palmer. Alongside this the pretentious gatefold concepts of Yes, and such boring old farts as Barclay James Harvest, probably deserved to be swept away. But punk threw the baby out with the bath water.

You'd never know it from the punk version of musical history, but the mid-1970s were actually a golden period for rock. David Bowie released *Low*, Roxy Music made *Siren* and Led Zeppelin produced *Physical Graffiti*, the heaviest album of their career. In America, Bruce Springsteen had just released *Born To Run*, Dylan had returned to form with *Blood On The Tracks* and Tom Waits was finding his boho voice on albums such as *Nighthawks At The Diner* and *Small Change*.

Second: punk, they say, was responsible for launching the most prolific crop of great bands since the 1960s beat boom. Really? The Sex Pistols made one studio album - although admittedly this did turn out to be an all-time classic. The Clash made a handful of great records and Siouxsie had a certain style when she got over the swastika. But can anyone seriously claim that Sham 69 or Slaughter & The Dogs have stood the test of time? Of course there was Ian Dury & The Blockheads, but the great man was in his mid-30s by the time punk came along and had, by 1976, been peddling his inspired songs for half a dozen years in Kilburn & The High Roads. Only that was called 'pub rock' and we were meant to despise that, weren't we?

Third: we are asked to believe that punk not only rescued rock 'n' roll from its deathbed, but also gave birth to the 'new wave'. In fact, the so-called new wave happened not because of punk but de-

spite it, as those who could write proper songs and had some genuine musical ability began to reassert more traditional values. Elvis Costello may have astutely adopted some of the 'fuck you' attitude of the era, but he always knew more than three chords and hardly needed the example of Johnny Rotten and his ilk to make albums such as *My Aim Is True* and *This Year's Model*.

Fourth: we are regularly reminded that punk ensured music would never be the same again. In fact its influence was largely ephemeral. By the end of the 1970s, punk's self-styled barbarians at the gate had exhausted themselves and pop music went back to its same old ways. Only some of it was even worse as the 1980s were drowned out in tinny synthesizers and boring drum machines programmed by men with risible perms. What of the old farts the punk hordes promised to consign to the dustbin of history? They just go on and on as if nothing ever happened.

Then with a rhetorical flourish, I appended the infamous final paragraph that gave the piece its eye-catching headline: 'Let's face it. Punk was rubbish. But perhaps that was the point. It was always meant to be.'

It was controversial stuff and trenchantly expressed to be sure, and the reaction was as swift as my commissioning editor had predicted. To be fair, much of the debate that ensued was intelligent and informed. Harvey Johnman from London was the first into print. 'Nigel Williamson's vision is still obscured by his joss sticks,' he wrote. 'The best bands that followed all took their call from punk: Wire, Gang of Four, Joy Division. The fall-out is still happening, from Nick Cave to Nirvana, Primal Scream to Leftfield, the most exciting and original rock and dance artists, all sparked by punk, continue to fight the cause. Face it, with his Afghan coat in 1976, Nigel was really too old to get it.'

James Martin Charlton, another London reader with a clearly utopian bent, then tried to claim that it had been perfectly possible to like both punk and traditional rock in 1977. He clearly wasn't around at the time, for my recollection is that you'd actually have been safer wearing a Spurs shirt to a match at Highbury than turning up to a punk gig with long hair and an Incredible String Band album under your arm. 'It wasn't against the good things Nigel mentions - Springsteen, Dylan, Led Zeppelin,' he insisted. 'It was for artistic expression, kicking open doors and expressing bliss in sharp bursts.'

Then - shock horror - a brave chap called Paul Flewers wrote in to agree with me. 'Punk was awful. Apart from its musical ineptitude, it was deeply misanthropic. Its anti-authoritarianism was that of the yob who spits at anything of beauty, subtlety, and genuine humanity,' he blasted. That wasn't really what I had meant at all, but thanks for sticking up for me anyway, Paul.

More measured support came from David Ash, an ex-pat who emailed *The Guardian* all the way from Singapore. 'I was 18 at the peak of the punk movement in 1977 and was caught up in the whole idealism and music at the time. But there came a point when a bell rang in my head that caused me to stop and take a closer look at the whole sorry mess,' he reasoned. 'I'm not sure what caused that bell to ring but I have a feeling it was the start of 1978 and an article in *Sounds* about The Damned being the future of rock 'n' roll. Huh? I remembered them playing Croydon Greyhound two years earlier and thinking they were a reasonable pub band. Was this the same? The future of rock 'n' roll? Did I miss something? Sadly, yes, and to see them in 2002 reforming to tour again with god knows who in the line up makes me glad I moved 6,000 miles away. Every month I look at *Q* magazine and I see who's reforming/playing. Siouxsie, Buzzcocks, Pistols, UK Subs (did they ever go away?) and I shake my head. I can maybe, just maybe, understand the Pistols getting back together for a gig for the Jubilee but the rest of them sound like one of the those 60s revival tours with The Hollies and The Drifters. What next? The Lurkers at Pontin's? Nigel, you were right, most of the bands were shit but the attitude was the order of the day and that was the most important thing.'

I also enjoyed this response from Bob Kemp who brilliantly managed to articulate his teenage passion a quarter of a century earlier: 'In 1975 I was 13 and punk was nibbling its way into the provinces in the shape of a school weirdo whose name was Kev. He dressed in a mac, had dyed hair and oddball make-up. Meanwhile the charts were full of disco like - The Real Thing and similar works of the devil. Guitars were played without distortion. When the Pistols were(n't) on *Top Of The Pops* the clouds cleared (they were filmed in some echoing hall, well away from the BBC no doubt). A moment of catharsis equalled only by Otway and Barrett's power chords and yowling vocals. Happiness was a warm fuzz box. Two chords could be an elegant quip. The Pistols produced one good album – who cares who played on it or how overdubbed it may have been? Punk wasn't the sound of the suburbs – it was the sound of a tinny TV speaker, of your dad's stereo when he'd gone to do his dinner party duty, of a tape from the radio with plates clanking in the background, of a song you couldn't hear 'cos no-one would play it. The rock 'n' roll *dream* Nige, geddit?'

Mike Nelson emailed the letters editor with another intelligently argued response. 'Nigel Williamson misses the point by a greater distance than John Lydon could spit,' he began, before going on to point out – quite correctly, I am forced to admit – that 'Tom Waits could have released a wonderful album once a fortnight without ever affecting the lives of Britain's dissatisfied youth.'

Costello, he claimed, was not a typical example of those who rode to prominence on the crest of punk. 'Try instead The Stranglers, XTC, Blondie, The Boomtown Rats, The Police. Without punk, none of these bands could get past the front desks of a record company's offices. After punk, they all found audiences amongst the young and reckless (i.e. not 22-year-old, Afghan-wearing, Little Feat fans).'

Someone styling themselves 'Fred Ramone' then wrote in to say: 'Yes, there were good things going on in music but they were scattered, many of them underground and their appeal was to adults. What did a 13-year-old like me want in 1976 with Bob Dylan or Tom Waits? I like it now but then! I wanted *energy*, I wanted *passion*. I'd come out of loving the Sweet and Wizzard, what did I want with Little Feat?'

Steve Vanstone from Purley began by agreeing with my thesis, but subtly shifted the ground of the argument by claiming that crap music could still be great (a view with which I can only agree and which even Noel Coward recognised when he once had a character remark on the potency of 'cheap music'). 'Of course most of punk was rubbish and, of course, little of it has stood the test of time,' he admitted. 'But punk was all about adolescents making their own music very cheaply, and if they were lucky enough to get their three minutes (or less) of fame via the John Peel show, then most were happy and moved on. Punk music was instant, disposable pop but that doesn't preclude any of it being excellent, inspiring and exciting. The world would have been a more miserable place without the likes of The Buzzcocks, The Nipple Erectors and the Snivelling Shits. So what if it was only two or three chords?'

Then, to my delight, the mighty Captain Sensible from The Damned wrote in to denounce me as a 'berk' (and, if you will forgive my cynicism, also to secure a free plug for the revival tour his band of punk geriatrics were about to undertake). 'Nigel Williamson seems to have missed the point,' he railed. 'Punk was never just about the music – although some of it was pretty spectacular in its aggression and pure cheek. No – it was about the *attitude*.

285

The 'punks' sang relevant songs about previously taboo subjects (republicanism, animal rights, etc) while overturning the ridiculous mid-70s 'cock rock' music scene with its limos, groupies and coke-fuelled sexist rock stars writing meaningless songs about wizards, pixies and the like. And for a couple of years you didn't need to have vast amounts of cash, a flashy sports car and a wardrobe full of Italian fashion crap to be the trendiest person in town. No, even rich folk were wearing dodgy clothes from charity shops and bin liners – you had to laugh! And if you were lucky enough to be able to finish the look with a few spots and some bad teeth then you had it made. Just what was Nigel Williamson doing listening to boring American nonsense like Little Feat and Bruce Springsteen in Britain's finest hour? Berk!'

Fantastic, I thought – there really are old punks out there who still think Little Feat are the enemy, and believe in 'year zero', just like those mythical Japanese soldiers still hiding in the Asian jungle not aware that WWII is over. But I took the view that I'd had my say and so never responded to any of the debate. I was more than happy to wear, as a badge of honour, the names assigned to me by a middle-aged bloke who still clung to the punk moniker he'd adopted in his early 20s. If I'd thought, there was even a great t-shirt in it: 'Captain Sensible Called Me A Berk'.

Despite the provocative headline, my main intention had been less to argue that punk was worthless, and more to question its myths and some of its more preposterous manifestations. I was always particularly offended by the Pol Pot-style dumbness of the 'year zero' mentality. In 2005, I asked Kris Needs, editor of *Zig-Zag* during the punk years and fellow contributor to this collection, if such an absolutist attitude had been necessary. He admitted that today it looked foolish but still argued that it had been vital at the time. 'I think you had to wipe the slate keen,' he insisted. 'The Sex Pistols did that by saying every band that had gone before was crap and Joe [Strummer] for a while wiped his slate very clean too, and wouldn't acknowledge his past. What you have to remember is that rock 'n' roll was a taboo phrase.'

I still have a problem with that sensibility, and what I also wanted to explore in my original article was whether what fired punk was

Captain Sensible

really much different from what fuelled any other generation finding the music of its elders outdated and dull, seeking its own new and rebellious forms of expression.

When Elvis Presley walked into the Sun Studios in Memphis in 1954 and recorded 'That's All Right', he wasn't aspiring to be a fat millionaire who would play Las Vegas. When the teenage Mick Jagger was sending off to Chess' mail order department in Chicago for obscure R&B records, which he would then try to copy, he wasn't thinking about a knighthood. Likewise, when Robert Plant joined Led Zeppelin, he wasn't dreaming of becoming the god of cock-rock. Nor, and we include him simply because his band became a kind of emblem in the original debate, was Lowell George imagining stretch limos and silver coke spoons when he formed Little Feat.

287

All they were thinking about was making music. In this, I continue to argue, such luminaries as Joe Strummer, Nick Lowe and Elvis Costello who came to prominence on the crest of punk were no different from those who had gone before them.

What's more, had the likes of Jagger, Plant and others been coming of age in the 1970s rather than the 1960s, they would surely have been part of the punk revolution. When I interviewed Robert Plant in 2005 and asked him how he had responded at the time to those who denounced him as a dinosaur, wishing to consign his band to the dustbin of musical history, he insisted that he and Jimmy Page had both been delighted. 'The punks reminded us of what we were when we started out,' he claimed. 'Punk was marvellous, especially if you discounted the lack of originality in most of it. But they were right. There had to be some spit and some sputum. You don't always know you're becoming remote and missing the point. You get comfortable and you think that's it. But then again, you can't be in the youth club forever.'

Conversely, had the likes of Strummer and company been a decade older, they would have been in bands like the Stones and Zeppelin. As it was, punk was what was happening at the time they were emerging and they rode on its coattails expertly. Yet it would be hard for anybody to claim that without punk we never would have heard of Elvis Costello, Paul Weller, Sting or Joe Strummer, or that Patti Smith, the Ramones, Blondie and Television would not have reached our ears from the other side of the Atlantic. Such talent would have blossomed in any era and the argument that, without punk they would never have got past the receptionist in the record company's plush front office does them a disservice. However, there is probably one notable exception to this rule. Without punk, there surely could not have been Johnny Rotten – although arguably there might have been a Sex Pistols, led by Steve Jones and Glen Matlock. They'd probably have done quite well as an amiable pub rock band playing covers of numbers by The Who and The Small Faces too, for as future Pet Shop Boy Neil Tenant put it in a letter to *NME* at the time (albeit, inaccurately), before Sid's arrival the Pistols were 'three nice clean middle-class art students and a real live dementoid.' What's more, without Rotten's unruly behaviour and extraordinary attitude, there probably would have been no punk movement at all in the UK, as every such phenomenon needs its icon. When rock 'n' roll emerged, it was Elvis Presley. In the 60s beat boom it was The Beatles. In the 1970s it was Johnny Rotten who served as the figurehead, with a charisma that the likes of poor old Rat Scabies *et al* could only dream about.

Rotten was also unusual, if not unique, in that he knew or cared little about musical history. He had his odd and quirky passions for Captain Beefheart, Can and even prog misfits Van Der Graaf Generator, and he was also partial to a reggae rhythm. But he didn't really give a toss about where it all came from. By the mid-1970s, rock 'n' roll was already more than two decades old and had developed a powerful sense of its own legacy. Most of those forming bands – even punk bands – knew that rock music was part of a chain with roots in blues, R&B, folk and other earlier forms. Joe Strummer was so consumed by this heritage that at one point in his pre-Clash days he named himself after Woody Guthrie and would answer to no other name. Patti Smith hung out with Dylan in Greenwich Village and was 30 years old before she made her first groundbreaking album; and Costello, despite his indefensible dissing of Ray Charles as 'a blind ignorant nigger', was another who was acutely aware of his place as the inheritor of a rich and profound musical legacy.

But John Lydon was a different kind of animal. He despised the past. He denied its validity because all that mattered was the here and now. He wasn't about to embrace Pete Townshend because he wrote 'My Generation'. He had only contempt for him as the writer of rock operas. Rotten admired the New York Dolls, who had been managed for a short while by the Pistols' svengali Malcolm MacLaren. Yet if he was aware that they had started out trying to copy The Rolling Stones (who were then hated with a rare loathing by every punk in town), he didn't care. He was even less interested in knowing that the Stones had in turn found their sound trying to copy Chuck Berry. To Rotten, it was irrelevant that Berry begat the Stones who begat the Dolls who begat the Pistols. So fucking what? It sounded like something out of the Old Testament. Also, unlike the more musical members of the Pistols, Rotten wasn't interested in playing covers of songs by The Who and The Small Faces. They were the past. History was bunk, every second of it, and to Rotten and his group of camp followers – including Sid Vicious – 'year zero' was totally for real. They *knew* that everything that had gone before was worthless and boring and they proceeded to trash the past at every available opportunity.

They did so verbally, but they also did it brilliantly on record, most notably in the case of Vicious' extraordinary version of 'My Way'. Of course, the record was trash. But it was trash of the most subversive kind. Your mum and dad hated it, not just because it was noisy and vulgar but because it mercilessly mocked their own tastes and lives. Funnily enough, the song's writer Paul Anka came to recognise the validity of Sid's statement. More than 30 years later, I asked him what he had made of the indignities punk had served

upon his composition. To my surprise he paid tribute to the integrity of the cover. 'At first I went "what?"' he confessed. 'But then I got it, because I think the guy was sincere and for him there was no other way to do it. You've got to respect that.'

In a way it helped that the likes of Vicious and Rotten had no real musical skills whatsoever. The latter couldn't sing but he made a virtue out of it and he knew his talents lay elsewhere, as a controversialist. McLaren, who Tony Wilson once wickedly accused of wanting to create an outrageous version of the Bay City Rollers, may have said: 'I was taking the nuances of Richard Hell, the faggy pop of the New York Dolls and the politics of boredom and mashing it all together to make a statement.' But that certainly wasn't what Rotten was doing. He wasn't going to be McLaren's puppet. He was just enjoying getting in people's faces - mostly for the sheer hell of it. As he told *NME*'s Neil Spencer at one of the Pistols' early gigs: 'We're not into music. We're into chaos.' Although that sounds suspiciously like one of McLaren's lines, it also happened to be true.

For many - including Strummer and Costello who deliberately contrived to 'lose' not only their sense of history but their own chequered musical past - 'year zero' was little more than a career tactic. Others, such as The Stranglers, were even more blatant bandwagoneers. Yet for Rotten and Vicious, 'year zero' was both an expression of an ineffable truth and an article of faith. Consequently, it was because they believed in it to the bottom of their punk hearts that *Never Mind The Bollocks* remains the most potent and genuine expression of the late '70s punk ethos.

Despite my early contempt after seeing the Pistols in Bromley that night in December 1975 (and I would summon former *Melody Maker* editor Allan Jones as a witness to confirm how terrible those first gigs were – he wrote after one hapless early appearance that he didn't think we'd ever be hearing from them again), it was the realisation that they were genuine barbarians, who really didn't give a flying fuck, that eventually endeared them to me.

Strummer, too, realised this in what was a moment of epiphany when the Pistols supported his band The 101ers at the Nashville Rooms in April 1976. 'The difference was we played Route 66 to the drunks in the bar, going "Please like us". But here was this quartet who were standing there going, "We don't give a toss what you think, you pricks…", it took my head off. They didn't give a shit.'

It was that quality that led me to buy *Never Mind The Bollocks* on its release – a rare punk purchase on my part – along with a few select singles that seemed to possess the same feral quality; X-Ray Spex's 'Oh Bondage, Up Yours'; a clutch of more sophisticated American 'punk' albums such as Patti Smith's *Horses* and Television's *Marquee Moon*. But I pointedly refused to buy the first Clash album. If the Pistols were the real thing, The Clash – and I know this is going to bring down a fresh round of abuse on my head from the Strummerites – seemed to me to be nothing more than posturing hypocrites.

I had seen Strummer's pub rock band playing Route 66 and I knew his musical history. Observing him parade his new group as the most uncompromising, sea-green incorruptibles in punk's militant army of scorched earthers just didn't ring true. Nor did the dangerous image that the band so carefully cultivated, quite match up with The Clash who took a £100,000 advance from CBS and went on songwriting vacations to Jamaica, or The Clash who flew in American AOR producer Sandy Pearlman – on Concorde, incidentally – to oversee their Westway-inspired musical graffiti. Rotten knew it was fake too, which is presumably the reason he never liked Strummer. In fact, he once claimed the only member of The Clash he had ever been able to have a conversation with was Keith Levene, who left after only half a dozen shows and with whom Rotten would later team up in Public Image Ltd.

Strummer was also at times capable of some mind-blowingly preposterous bullshit. If you reckon that's heresy, try this piece of arrant nonsense: 'There's nothing better, if you're having an argument which won't resolve itself in any other way, than smashing somebody's face in'. Or this, from his first major *NME* interview, delivered while idly toying with a flick-knife: 'Suppose some guy comes up to me and tries to put one over on me and I smash his face up. If he learns something from it, that's creative violence.'

Presumably it was all part of Strummer's striving to be a 'real life dementoid' like Rotten. But from an intelligent, well-educated human being who had grown up not in a squalid tower block with a broken lift but in a world of comfortable middle-class privilege, such calculated dumbing-down seemed not only idiotic and crass but cynical and dishonest. Years later, it occurred to me that such statements could actually serve as a cipher for American foreign policy post 9/11. Nobody would pretend such sentiments were clever coming from George Bush, so why should we kid ourselves that such nonsense was cool just because it came from the mouth of Joe Strummer?

In later years, via a mutual interest in world music, I got to know a very different and far more avuncular Strummer; I subsequently assisted his band, The Mescaleros, with press bios and a promotional film. I never asked him about the 1976–77 period, but I formed the distinct impression that he would have been profoundly embarrassed

The Mescaleros

to be reminded of some of his dafter pronouncements about the pleasures of smashing up people's faces because they disagreed with you.

Similarly, although I didn't know Costello, I did know Jake Riviera, his manager and Stiff Records supremo. When I first encountered Jake around 1972, he was managing country-tinged pub rock hopefuls Chilli Willi & The Red Hot Peppers. As an 18-year-old, I used to follow the band around such pub rock venues as the Hope & Anchor in Islington and the Tally Ho in Kentish Town, and after he'd noticed me at gigs a few times, he introduced himself. One night when I was going to miss the end of their set in order to catch the last train back to Bromley, he invited me to stay the night at his Notting Hill flat. There we stayed up until dawn with the Willis' guitarist Martin Stone, smoking dope and listening to country-rock albums. I distinctly remember him playing John Stewart's *California Bloodlines* but I'm pretty sure he also gave Little Feat's *Dixie Chicken* a spin.

Therefore, when Riviera and his protégé Elvis Costello emerged as self-appointed spokesmen for the safety pin generation, I was deeply suspicious. When I listened to Costello's early albums, all I heard were great songs, properly played by a band which included

Little Feat

such pub rock veterans as former Chilli Willis' drummer Pete Tho-
mas. Apart from a certain snarl and mannered venom in the vocals,
I wondered what the hell Costello had in common with an idiotic
bunch like Sham 69, getting drenched with spittle every night. As
if to prove the point, four years later he was in Nashville making a
country album with Billy Sherrill. This was a great move in my book,
but one that only made his earlier punk posturing look phoney.

But if Costello and Strummer were essentially career musos,
Rotten genuinely didn't give a fuck – about record deals or anything
else. Strummer's musings about creative violence seemed to me to
represent 'attitude' of the most transparently calculated and fake
kind. Yet the Pistols' infamous TV appearance on Bill Grundy's
show proved that their recklessness and defiance was entirely real.

Of course they were sometimes manipulated by the media savvy
McLaren. But they didn't give a fuck about that either. As long as
there was a supply of booze and sulphate to keep them happy they
were up for anything. However, the most revealing part of the Grundy show appearance was that it was not one of Malcolm's stunts at
all but a spontaneous outburst. Indeed, it's been reported that when

the Pistols left the television studio, an ashen-faced MacLaren wondered aloud if this time they had gone too far. 'But the cunt deserved it,' was the alleged riposte from Steve Jones, in a typical example of the irrefutable logic that underpinned most things the Pistols did at the time. According to our old friend Captain Sensible, after the TV appearance, the band went back to the Roxy in Harlesden, where McLaren continued to berate the band, telling them: 'You fucking idiots, you've ruined everything. We're finished.' But while he fretted and fussed, Rotten beamed with pleasure, for he knew that even if it had finished them, it didn't matter because immortality awaited in the 'filth and the fury' headlines that would greet them the next morning.

It was the ultimate expression of what dear old Captain Sensible meant in the one intelligent thing he said in his letter to *The Guardian*: 'Punk was never just about the music – although some of it was pretty spectacular in its aggression and pure cheek,' he wrote. 'No, it was about the *attitude*'. The Pistols, and Rotten in particular, had front, aggression and attitude in industrial quantities. While others cleverly and often convincingly faked such qualities, like a school of punk actors, the Pistols had no need to dissemble. That's what made them great.

It also meant that when Rotten slagged off everything that had gone before, it was hard to take offence. He hated everything pre-punk simply because it was old. That was crime enough in his book and he really didn't give a flying fuck about tracing the music back to its roots or any of that shit. But what really cemented the Pistols as heroes in my estimation was the release of 'God Save the Queen' in May 1977. Workers at the CBS plant where the record was being pressed threatened to walk out because of the disrespect to Her Majesty. Radio One banned it from its daytime schedules. Record chains refused to stock it. But the more the authorities tried to bury the record, the more determined fans were to buy it - 150,000 of them in the first five days.

At the grand old age of 22 I recognised this was why I had fallen in love with rock 'n' roll in the first place. From the protest songs of Dylan to the 'lock up your daughters' outrage of the Stones, a major part of rock music for me was about sticking two fingers up at the 'straight world' and the establishment. 'Anarchy In The UK' had been a great piece of pop subversion, but I wasn't an anarchist. Rather, at the time, I was a card-carrying Marxist and fully paid-up combatant in the class struggle. That meant I was also a fervent anti-monarchist and 'God Save The Queen' with its Jamie Reid picture sleeve showing a safety pin through the loathed royal visage, warmed my republican heart. It was the perfect riposte to the one million loyal subjects who lined the streets of London to watch the Queen, dressed in frightful pink, make her way, in a golden state carriage, from Buckingham Palace to St Paul's Cathedral. Across Britain, millions more of her subjects tuned in to watch the 'pomp and circumstance' on television, and celebrated with their own street parties. What were they thinking? The country was going to the dogs and instead of protesting about it, most of the nation was celebrating the very symbol of everything that was wrong and fucked up about our society. I wanted to vomit and turned up the Pistols to full volume just to piss off the neighbours. Even Little Feat's latest opus could wait.

Looking back, it's hard to remember just what a horribly conservative place Britain was circa 1976–77. Racism, homophobia and sexism were rampant and the establishment was part of the conspiracy, for it wasn't just the Pistols who were being persecuted by the authorities. In July 1977 the courts found *Gay News*, and its editor Denis Lemon, guilty of 'blasphemous libel' following a private prosecution brought by Mary Whitehouse, the self-appointed guardian of the nation's morals via her National Viewers and Listeners Association. The charge related to a poem and illustration about a homosexual soldier's love for Christ at the crucifixion, that Lemon published in *Gay News*. The prosecution behaved like something out of the Spanish Inquisition, or from the days when you could be locked up for suggesting the world wasn't flat.

In public, the national anthem was played on every conceivable occasion. If you went to the cinema, when the film ended they played 'God Save The Queen' (original version). More than once I was threatened with violence for refusing to stand. But you didn't have to be a full-on republican to find the entire patriotic atmosphere of the nation offensive. Flag-waving had been given a further nasty taste by being hijacked by the National Front and its 'Britain for the British' mentality.

In August 1977 I joined an anti-National Front march in Lewisham, arranged by Rock Against Racism, an organisation run by the Socialist Workers Party. The NF were out in force on the streets, too, alongside a massive police presence. The cops, inevitably, sided with the fascists and for no reason whatsoever I found myself being chased, with around fifty other perfectly peaceful protestors, down an alley by uniformed thugs from the Special Patrol Group and had to escape via the roof of a multi-story car park.

Such events certainly demanded a soundtrack and The Clash's 'White Riot' was one contender:

*"Black man gotta lot a problems, but they don't mind throwing
a brick
White people go to school, where they teach you, while we walk
the street, too chicken to even try it
Everybody's doin' just what they're told to"*

Yet somehow it seemed phoney. I didn't want to throw a brick. But I wanted to stand up and be counted and for me it was the working-class irreverence of the Pistols rather than the posing of The Clash that gave the most effective riposte to what was going so wrong with modern Britain. There seemed to be far more genuine subversion and insurrectionary intent in lines like:

*"God save the Queen
the fascist regime
they made you a moron
a potential H-bomb"*

By the time the Pistols imploded in January 1978, the true spirit of punk was already on the ropes and it had degenerated into a bunch of nihilist copycat bands who imposed a uniformity that was the very opposite of what punk's DIY spirit had supposedly been about. Rotten knew this, and much has been made of his words at the band's final gig: 'A ha, ha! Ever got the feeling you're being cheated?' To me, his meaning was crystal clear. Everything in this life is a cheat. Unless you were part of the charmed circle of the establishment elite, you were cheated of your rights from the day you were born. Even when you made your protest and shouted it as loudly as punk did, someone would turn it into a product and market it and cheat everybody all over again. It wasn't the Sex Pistols who were cheating their fans. We were all being cheated by the capitalist society in which we lived. At least, that was my Marxist analysis at the time.

Which leaves us with the disputed legacy of the Pistols and punk. My view, that after a brief hiatus normal service was swiftly resumed and the old guard carried on pretty much as if nothing had ever happened, remains unaltered. In his letter to *The Guardian*, 'Fred Ramone' claimed: 'Without punk there'd be no U2, no Nirvana, no Cure, no Joy Division or New Order, no Smiths, no Police, no Simple Minds. Without punk there would have been no 2-Tone. Bang go The Specials and Madness. Without punk no electronica – thus no Human League, no Cabaret Voltaire, no Soft Cell.' Well, up to a point. I'm pretty sure most of them would have emerged in some shape or form anyway, but they might well have sounded appreciably different.

He also made claims for punk exerting a far broader impact on the zeitgeist beyond influencing a few bands. 'What about the effects on wider culture?' he wondered. 'Would Nick Logan have started *The Face* and that whole world of style magazines? Would Alan McGee have set up Creation? Would Irvine Welsh have written *Trainspotting*? No punk, no Factory Records, no Haçienda, no Mike Pickering, no house/E-Culture.'

On one level, of course, he was absolutely right. Every movement in popular culture has far-reaching ripples and every new development is shaped by what has gone before, even if is only as a reaction against it. Hence claiming house and ecstasy as a legacy of punk is no more or less valid than claiming it as the offspring of 1967's original summer of love. Equally, if we're going to credit punk with having spawned the Haçienda and Pickering's legendary acid house DJ sets, then presumably we also have to lay at punk's door the blame for the latter's involvement with M People.

Yet my argument was never that punk did not make any lasting impact. Rather, it was that that claims that punk represented some kind of unique sea-change or watershed in pop music are vastly overstated. Popular culture needs a kick up the pants at regular intervals – in fact, every time its latest manifestation gets lazy, formulaic and complacent – pretty much without fail, someone comes along to deliver it. In 1977 it was the Sex Pistols and *Never Mind The Bollocks*. But they weren't the first or the last to turn music on its head and, if we're lucky, there will still be several more such revolutions to come. Of course, there's another theory which holds that, having passed its half century, rock 'n' roll is now a geriatric form, like jazz, that is no longer capable of innovation or reinventing itself. But that's another argument, for another day – and another book.

© *Nigel Williamson 2006*

Nigel Williamson

Nigel Williamson began his career in journalism as a reporter for *The Tribune*, before joining *The Times* in 1989, then moving into music writing. Nigel is now a contributing editor to *Uncut* and writes on music for *The Times, The Observer, The Guardian* and other publications. He is also the author of *Journey Through The Past: The Stories Behind The Classic Songs Of Neil Young* (Backbeat, 2003), *The Rough Guide To Bob Dylan* (Rough Guides, 2004), and *The Rough Guide To The Blues,* which is due for publication in 2006. Currently, Williamson is writing a book about the making of the seminal Rolling Stones album, *Beggar's Banquet*.

MUSICAL EXPRESS

100 SECONDS THAT P*NK ROCKED FLEET STREET

THE GRUNDY/PISTOLS GRUNT-IN: COMPLETE AND UNEXPURGATED

WARNING: This issue may be incomplete at time of going to press. An industrial dispute interrupted our production schedule, and may result in some white spaces. We also apologise for lateness of delivery in some areas, but again this is due to circumstances beyond our control. "Taste and try before you buy, but BUY ALREADY!!!"

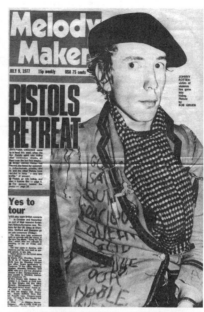

Melody Maker

JULY 9, 1977   15p weekly   USA 75 cents

PISTOLS RETREAT

Yes to tour

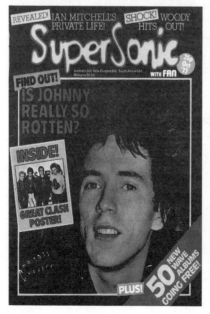

REVEALED! **IAN MITCHELL'S PRIVATE LIFE!**   SHOCK! WOODY HITS OUT!

SuperSonic WITH FAB

Australia 50c New Zealand 60c South Africa 60c
Malaysia $1.50

FIND OUT!
IS JOHNNY REALLY SO ROTTEN?

INSIDE!
GREAT CLASH POSTER!

PLUS! **50** NEW WAVE ALBUMS GOING FREE!

A-HA   BRYAN ADAMS   RED WEDGE

SMASH HITS

BELOUIS SOME   MIDGE URE   JOHN TAYLOR

LOOK OUT!

HE'S BACK! WHO'S BACK?
SEE PAGE 10

FRA LIPPO LIPPI   FEARGAL SHARKEY

45p 12-25 FEBRUARY 1986

Stir It Up:
Thoughts From A Mind Less Ordinary
50 Quotes by John Lydon

'I hate shit. I hate hippies and what they stand for. I hate long hair. I hate pub bands. I want to change it so there are rock bands like us.'

'I want people to go out and start something, to see us and start something, or else I'm just wasting my time.'
Sounds, April 1976

'The great ignorant public don't know why we're in a band; it's because we're bored with all that old crap. Like every decent human being should be.'
Sounds, October 1976

'There is a lot of violence when we play but I don't really try to start it. When it comes though, I like it because it isn't false like the reaction to all those boring old has-beens like the Stones and The Who.'
Evening News, November 1976

'I feel sorry for people who stand up for what they believe and get kicked in the teeth. That's what would have happened to me if I hadn't joined the Pistols. I would have been locked up, put quietly away, classified as insane... you have got to fight back or die'
Record Mirror, December 1976

"God Save The Queen' is not a direct personal attack on the Queen, it's what she represents. I happen to be personally all for royalty, and I feel that the Queen contributes a great deal to the country, but the band don't see it that way.'
Melody Maker, March 1977

'Maybe it was a good thing, us being banned from this country. It seems like it anyway.'
Stage announcement, London, March 1977

'We haven't written one song about how depressing it is to be on the dole. Getting money for nothing, ain't that depressing.'
Record Mirror, June 11, 1977

'I might completely change my mind tomorrow, hate everything or like everything. That's the way you should live.'
Zigzag, June 1977

'Give us a chance to play, so that people can decide for themselves whether we're a heap of shit. Don't take their right away. Then if the far-out audiences of our wonderful country don't like it, they can stuff it.'
Album Tracking, August 1977

'Music's about the only thing I have around me that's permanent. Until I get bored with it. Because things change, and so does your attitude towards certain sounds. And then you pass on.'
Sounds, August 1977

'He's one of my favourites, that geezer. I've got seven or eight of his albums. He's mad. He's great.'
Talking Captain Beefheart to Tommy Vance on Capital Radio, July, 1977

'...I don't care what anybody says about the way I look. It's the way I want to look and I don't care.'
Sounds, August 1977

'Listen, this band started by nicking every piece of equipment. I still sing through David Bowie's microphones. Punk fashions are a load of bollocks. Real punks nick their gear from junk shops.'
Rolling Stone, October 1977

'Our songs are anti-God, anti-Queen, anti the palsied values of present day society. I am a revolutionary... I want to stir people up to think for themselves. That's all.'
Daily Mirror, December 1977

'[Schools] try to take away your brain. To make you like everyone else – just one great mass that's easily controlled.'
The Sun, January 1978

'Ever get the feeling you've been cheated? Aha ha ha!'
Stage announcement, Sex Pistols' last gig, January 1978

'I'm sick of working with The Sex Pistols. I never want to appear with them again. We haven't had any rows. We had gone as far as we could go. Everyone was trying to turn us into a big group and I hated that.'
New York Post, January 1978

'I refused to go to Brazil. It stank of a publicity stunt.'
The Sun, January 1978

'What did Malcolm do to make us famous? I had the motivation, the direction, things that didn't occur to them... when I first joined they thought I was insane.'
Sounds, May 1978

'I don't think there is an organised campaign going to harm me, but there are people on the streets who oppose what I have done. And they're prepared to fight to prove their point.'
Record Mirror, May 1978

'The way we write songs is so easy. Someone will just bash out something and everybody will fall in and I'll babble over it, which is great – because, I mean, there's so much to yell about. My number one target has always been hypocrisy.'
Sounds, July 1978

'We've no image at all. We do not present any image at all, and I will fight for that utterly and totally. I refuse to be put in any bag ever again...'
Melody Maker, October 1978

'There was no reason for the Pistols to bust up. No reason at all... except McLaren... Malcolm would tell me we were banned from playing everywhere. And I believed him. It took six months to discover he was lying.'
Record Mirror, November 1978

'I do interviews because I don't want to fade into oblivion and never be heard of again. All forms of communication are important. People know you exist.'
Record Mirror, July 1979

'I'm afraid I don't live in history books. We're trying to write the next chapter not look back pages.'

'It's always been that toe-rags like us could never do what we're doing. It's always been for the university boys. You know what I mean? They don't like the yobbos to take over. They don't like that at all.'
Zigzag, December 1979

'All I can say is that Public Image is everything The Sex Pistols were meant to be – a valid threat to rock 'n' roll. In the end, the Pistols weren't any more threatening than re-treaded Chuck Berry.'
Rolling Stone, 1980

'We didn't wanna make another *Metal Box*... now it's up to the imitators to continue it, as they are doing. Reaping the praise for their efforts!'

'All the rest are electric teapots. Spandau Ballet! Have you heard their album? Worse than Bay City Rollers could ever hope to be! Amateur Hour!'
Zigzag, 1981

'I'm not the angry young man any more. I used to be angry about my own lack of alternatives, and since nobody bothered to give me any I made them up for myself.'

'Hindsight is what Malcolm suffers from. I did this, that and the other, he'll say after the dust has settled. He did very little. Everybody else did it for him.'

'Once I was scared of reaching 21, let alone 30. But now I feel, so what... I've got at least 40 more years before I call it a day and I mean to use them all up, they're all I got.'
NME, February, 1986

'I've never made any two records that sound even similar. That's the way it should be, I think. I don't run out of ideas. I enjoy myself. I do it to entertain myself and then if Joe Public likes it, fine.'
Zigzag, April 1986

'I find it disturbing that punks these days insist on a regimented approach – they must all look the same. Sad. They just replaced the Teds.'

'I'd rather be drunk and happy than miserable and thin.'
Melody Maker, August 1987

'Leftfield didn't ask me in because they wanted a pop star floating around on top like a fluffy, little cloud... I'm simply into anyone who puts a lot of effort into being themselves, rather than following formats.'

'I am not a walking history book and should just be judged by what I do, as I do it.'
NME, November 1993

'I consider myself working class. We're lazy, good-for-nothing bastards... we like to be told what to do, led like sheep to the slaughter.'
Rotten: No Irish No Blacks No Dogs, 1994

'Absolutely the price was right. Money is obviously a great part in all of this and there ain't nothing wrong with that, because for

once in our poxy lives we're actually going to get paid for doing something.'
Q, before the Filthy Lucre reunion, June 1996

'The cack they turf out of Hollywood, they're desperately in need of someone like me!'
Modern Rock Live, August 1997

'The lyrics to 'God Save The Queen' and 'Anarchy In The UK' meant something, they weren't just done for shock value. They have a point and a purpose. I think it's too damn near the truth... and far too accurate for the establishment to tolerate.'
Top 10 Banned Records, Channel 4, 2001

'If I stopped to think I'd realise I'm an old man and I'm not having that. Fuck that. You're only as young as you feel and I've been feeling quite a lot young lately! A lot of people have got to realise it's my Jubilee too!'

'I've always wanted to get into the Queen's knickers. Let's be honest, we are The Sex Pistols.'
Daily Star, 2002

'I'm no one's lap dog, you can't put me on a leash.'
Filth And The Fury website, 2003

'I'm splendid, I'm super, I'm cute and cuddly. I'm irresistible, that's what I am,'
John in the jungle for *I'm A Celebrity Get Me Out Of Here*, *The Sun*, February 2004

'I have changed the world twice and I'm going to do it for a third time. I'm a survivor.'
Evening Standard, February 2004, after walking out of the jungle

'Certain words are banned but they're only words. It's our right to use them. Fucking cunts. Let's face it, we all know a fucking cunt when we meet one.'
Friday Night With Jonathan Ross, March 2004

'Discordancy and things out of tune with each other create to me brilliant other harmonics'
Fodderstompf website, June 2004

'I like living. Every minute that I live is fine by me, even the bad stuff. Surely our main motivation each day should be to have a good day and not bugger it up?'
Mojo, March 2006

SEX PISTOLS

WOR
EXCL
INTE

PiL

ADMISSION £9.50 ADVANCE

#27, HIGHGATE ROAD
LONDON NW5 1Y

t&c

0032

music and m

ADE HALL

HTER
E DOGS
TED BY R. & B.

TOLS
M McLAREN

RT

LY 1976

.m.

.00

or pay at the door

ANARCHY
IN THE U.K.

SEX PISTOLS

ENVOKE

PiL PiL

UBLIC

SEX PISTOLS

F*CK
forever

JOHN Lydon's

megabug

TOLS

U.S.

olid

wd

pil stewa

PiL

ADMISSION £9.50 ADVANCE

eec PRESENTS

SATURDAY
2ND MAY
AT 7.30 P.M.

TO BE RE TAINED
NO READMISSION

OLYMPIA

PUBLI
IMA
LIMI

DISCOVERY
CHANNEL

t&c

0032

Public Image

Juni 1986 · 21.00 Uhr · Große Freiheit 36

Standa

www.thisislondon.co.uk   Incorporating TH

JOHNNY WALKS OUT
OF THE JUNGLE

TECH ENTS PRESENT

SEX
PISTOLS

JOHNNY THUNDER/HEARTBREAKER
DAMNED   CLASH

DUNDEE CAIRD HALL
WED. DEC. 1ST. 1976
AT 7·30
TICKETS £2. £1·50. £1 AND 50p

LONDON'S MOST NOTORIOUS BAND!

SEX PISTOLS

INAUGURATION DU NOUVEAU

ANARCHY IN THE UK TOUR

SEX PiSTOLS

GOD Save THE QUEEN

SEX Pistols

DAMNED   JOHNNY THUNDERS & THE HEART

With Special Guests

SEX Pi

GOD SAVE THE QUEEN

ANARCHY IN TH

ROCK GROUP START A
4-LETTER
TV STORM

Evening

THE FOUL
MOUTHED
YOBS — by TV's Bill Grundy

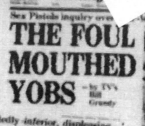

'Worthless, decidedly inferior, displeasing...'
The Punks—
Rotten and
proud of it!

Fury at filthy

en.Foulkersweg 74 Wageningen

UNITAS

Afterword
by Rob Johnstone

It's July 4th 2006. Independence Day passes pretty much un-announced in territories outside of North America. The weather in the UK is as blistering as it was 30 years ago and over coming weeks temperatures will top anything 1976 had to offer. The hose-pipe ban is in force again this year, but now everyone knows why it's so darn hot!

Political discontent today relates more to foreign policy than anything out-of-the-ordinary on the home-front; and while there's still a million people out of work in Britain, the goalposts have moved exponentially over intervening decades and such a level is now considered rather low - bearing in mind during the early 1980s it ran at 3 times this figure. There are two main issues on the agenda right now that cause major concern to much of the population. One is the state of the earth and whether we can reverse the effects of everything we've been doing wrong since the industrial revolution. But with the majority of those who are employed in the affluent world almost addictively spending money they haven't got on things they don't need, the future for subsequent generations looks bleak. The other is the ongoing threat of terrorism, which now seems a thousand times worse than that faced by British mainlanders in the mid-70s, when the Troubles in Ireland had only recently spread to Great Britain.

On this day in 1976, as stated at the beginning of this book, punk was only just kicking off in England, but since the beginning of 2006 every monthly rock music magazine, and the one remaining weekly, have been putting out 'Punk Specials', in commemoration of that oeuvre's Diamond Jubilee, as if their circulations depended on it: by April, unsold copies had been sent back to the publishers. The rather accurate types who edit these periodicals, for once seemed unconcerned with exactitude, instead employing a first-past-the-post regime to signal their credentials in this arena.

While this approach is somewhat understandable and can be seen either as sharp commercial practise or cynical marketing, depending on which side you dress (either way a window still exists for further excursions later in the year), it says more about punk itself than the

309

compilers of these 'collector's items'. What was often considered a necessary but short lived novelty at best, an ugly undignified era of rudeness and loud shouty records at worst – but in any case one that was over in the time of a seasonal sale, a stock clearance and a special offer – has tended to resonate loudly ever since; but never as loudly as it does today.

The nostalgia trend of course greatly contributes to this deluge of ephemera, but last year saw the 50th anniversary of rock'n'roll itself – surely a more significant event in the diary of modern music – but nary a mention in any one of these journals was witnessed – with the exception of Elvis Presley's achievements, acclaimed for far more than his first few records. Likewise, the hippy movement and associated trends have had any number of potential celebrations open to them over recent years, and while there still is plenty of coverage for this era in its various guises, it doesn't come close to the plethora of punk outpourings.

'One of the first things I was ever quoted as saying was "I'd like to see more bands like us". Right? When I said that, I didn't mean exactly like us. Unfortunately that's what happened. Imitations. Billions of them. And I wanted nothing to do with any of them. There were a few originals, but not many.' John Lydon 1977

John Lydon came to hate punk as soon as the multitudes cottoned on. When it existed as an underground movement of true originality and, to a certain degree, an extension of his own persona, his contributions were delivered proudly. Once it became the inevitable rule book of dos and don'ts and it presumed a limited outlook, it was as good as finished as far as he, and, to be fair, others from punk's sharper edge, were concerned.

As Lydon was pivotal to the necessary emergence of punk, he was equally important to its downfall – or more accurately, its evolution. A feebler soul would perhaps have considered the commercial potential of stringing it out a couple more years and shut up about trivial grievances, but Johnny wasn't of that ilk. Of the various factors that contributed to the Sex Pistols' split in early 1978 – which prompted so many others involved to move on, give up or mutate – none was so important as Lydon's feeling that quite what it was he had contributed to punk so eloquently, was no longer appreciated. One of John Lydon's musical inspirations, Neil Young – no fool himself – used Lydon as the subject for his all too good advice, 'It's better to burn out than to fade away' a year later. But Lydon knew that already.

So when he found himself without a band, less than three years after he'd first been elbowed into one, as a non musician, a rather acquired vocalist, and a songwriter who couldn't work alone, he may have found it difficult to envisage many options.

After the Pistols, John was legally forced to revert to the name on his birth certificate – or at least something not ending in Rotten – due to the immediate freezing of any assets associated with Malcolm McLaren and his limited company, Glitterbest – which, it appears, included John Lydon's *nom d'everything* for the past 30 or so months. But that suited him fine; enough is enough after all and the return of the artist formerly (un) known as John Lydon, in the latter half of 1978, was, if anything, embellished by the use of his non-punk associated family name.

The years that followed, in Lydon's new and just as radical collective PiL, are covered expertly and in-depth at the core of this book, but what is interesting about his pioneering role in what has come to be termed post-punk, is that, both in historical terms and in punk-rock itself, there was nothing to suggest it was going to happen. In the wake of rock'n'roll's first wave, which itself 'burnt out' in as short a timespan as punk, came a barrowload of nancy boys with a watered down, limp and soggy rendering of the form. The wild beasts that comprised the cream of rock's awakening were not replicated. With a few notable exceptions, it would take the best part of a decade for a new galaxy of brighter stars, infused with the rock ethic, to come up with something of their own.

But with punk being just as startling and life-changing as rock'n'roll, 20 years before, it had the same sense of an all encompassing movement; an era of its own with little to recommend it beyond its presumed natural cycle. That it merged into any number of valid follow-on movements – New Wave, Ska (and to a lesser extent, Mod) revivals, Power-Pop, New Romanticism, Liverpool's new-Psychedelia and perhaps its most logical descendant, Post-Punk – until recently virtually undocumented but now more fashionable a form to namedrop than anything else from the rock era – is quite astonishing. Each of these media-tagged styles had their share of the good, the bad and the much in-between, but such a generally positive fallout – should anyone during those amphetamine fuelled months have had the capacity to sit down and think about it – was wholly unexpected.

Suggestions that post-punk was actually a far more realised, ambitious and creative form than its forerunner have made for a popular view, which when expressed is often tied to intellectual reasoning and wordy explanation: but such rhetoric misses the target on two counts. While John Lydon and a few others, such as Howard Devoto – out of Buzzcocks and into Magazine when the Sex Pistols were still a viable commodity – and Subway Sect's Vic Goddard – essentially an anti-Rock explorer whose rouse came via punk but who ultimately went in more directions than Spaghetti Junction – had actually planned moves out of the gig they were questioning the validity of and into whatever next took their fancy, for the most part what has come to be labelled post-punk was created by punks, albeit ones who'd either naturally moved on as bands and performers, or were too young for the first wave. The sonic sophistication that put the Banshees debut ahead of The Damned's, was 15 months of record company wrangling. Equally, the essence of the argument that puts the new form in front of its father-figure is based on a twisted logic that somehow suggests post-punk could have existed alone. With all due respect, 'Rip It Up And Start Again' – the title of a recent study of punk's mushroom cloud – isn't quite what happened.[1]

Post-punk is such a 'one size fits all' description for so much that came along after the main event, but which didn't slot into any of the *other* categories mentioned above, it can't be claimed exclusively by any individual or band – and certainly no flamboyant mover or shaker , however visionary, had any involvement in its strictly organic unfolding. But the bit of it that John Lydon and his new partners, Keith Levene and Jah Wobble, pioneered, was certainly a form original to PiL, albeit with nods, nay bows, in the directions of dub-reggae, prog-rock[2] and, god forbid, punk. Further, suggestions that

Lydon wasn't a creative equal in his new assembly are as unfounded as those on the blunt edge of the punk vs. post-punk debate.

But few would argue that most of the music made by John Lydon once the original PiL line up was no more was inferior to what came before. Opinions differ, but even the oft-acclaimed third studio album, *Flowers Of Romance*, produced without the fitting bass lines of Jah Wobble, made PiL sound less compelling, rhythmic, and ultimately listenable. Once Levene split too, Lydon was without a collaborator with whom he could ping-pong ideas, for the first time in his career.

So while there were moments of glory still to come, most notably collaborations with like-minded Time Zone, Bill Laswell – under his Golden Palominos brand – and most notably, Leftfield – with whom John Lydon created one of dance music's most enduring performances on 'Open Up' – and also on occasional delights still under the PiL banner, such as 'Rise', among 1986's best singles, these were few and far between, and were largely overshadowed by what many saw as foolishly impulsive decisions. But if treading the boards with a hotel cabaret act and performing a set that included a cheesy 'Anarchy In The UK' as a finale every night, and with whom he'd, later on the same tour, attempt further forays into the Pistols' back catalogue, was purely a money making exercise or the old punk proving he'd still do anything to wind-up the cognoscenti, doesn't really matter; while it added little to his reputation, Lydon's never been one to worry over such trivialities.

At least he'd later decide to do the old tunes properly, alongside those with whom he'd written them, and this time wouldn't have any hesitation in letting everyone know they were in it for the bread. The 'Filthy Lucre Tour' in 1996, illustrated far better what Johnny Lydon was all about than anything else he'd been involved in since the middle of the 1980s, and when the opening salvo on certain nights began, 'We're reunited for a common cause – your money' the old fellah was back, witty as ever, and, with his fellow Pistols, breathed at least a little new life into the songs that had changed music forever. It was galaxies away from the cutting edge achievements Lydon had been pivotally involved in between 1976 and 1983, but this didn't mean it was not worthy. The ultimate show, performed

313

on Lydon's home turf in Finsbury Park and with support from all manner of other punk credibles, from Iggy Pop to Buzzcocks, was part nostalgia trip, part punk celebration – but a marvellous time was had by most, so what the heck. Another show on the same tour, caught by 1990s visionary maverick, our very own Alan McGee, prompted the great man to take out full page ads in all the music weeklies, at 50 grand a throw, expressing how affected he was by witnessing, after all this time – this was McGee's first experience of the band live – the group and the singer that inspired him to go out and do something for himself. And lest we forget, Alan's a PiL first, Pistols second kind of chap.[3]

The second set of reunion shows in the summer of 2002, punk's own silver jubilee, or more accurately that of 'God Save The Queen' – the subject of which was herself busy celebrating 50 big ones on the throne – passed without the fanfare of the first return. After telling the crowd he hoped they'd missed warm up act The Cure, the antichrist of yore tossed a seemingly quite genuine 'God-bless' to those half filling Crystal Palace sports ground, before the band launched into an all but Xerox copy of Hawkwind's 'Silver Machine' – eventually segueing into 'God Save The Queen.'

Lydon's recent TV appearances, and his more general return as media guru, didn't come as much of a surprise – he wasn't ever going to grow old gracefully. Accusations flew once more from quarters that will never learn. Would this man do anything to keep himself in the public eye and his bank accounts topped up? Well of course he bloody would, it beggars belief anyone still thinks he wouldn't do anything that pleases him. He can hardly 'sell out' from something he'd never bought into.

Johnny Rotten was a stage name, the Sex Pistols were a vehicle, and Public Image, although probably where he felt most at home musically, was just his most focussed outlet. But all that was more than 20 years ago; Johnny still fascinates and bewilders and continues to move in mysterious ways. The character behind all these guises was connected to them by his very soul: John Lydon defines 'punk' far more accurately than 'punk' defines John Lydon. The dictionary definition of the term; 'A young person, especially a member of a rebellious counterculture', goes little further than a most rudimentary, albeit well recognised, description. An online encyclopaedia entry includes, 'For many still has an unpleasant taste': now that's more like it.

John Lydon never did buy into punk; he didn't have to, he exemplified it; it was created in his image. What became the punk-rock movement, the one he came to detest, is a separate issue. But he has remained a punk in its wider context – a context he was responsible for widening – throughout. He is not just the focal point for the music, theatrics, and cultural legacy, he is the epitome of its spirit.

In 2002, The Ramones were invited to attend their inauguration into America's Rock'n'Roll Hall Of Fame, an institution that celebrates all those the judging committee consider have contributed sufficiently to that genre of music. With Joey already passed away the previous year (Dee Dee died 2 months after this event and Johnny two years later), the others attended, received their award, and, in uniform leather jackets and ripped jeans, mingled with dickie bowed music industry types and other artists receiving the same accolade that evening. Pearl Jam's Eddie Vedder was their presenter. This is not to be criticised. The band has surely paid its dues. They've gone through hell and back, made some great records, played more shows that The Grateful Dead – without all the hoo-ha – and remain an inspiration to many – they deserve a little backslapping once in a while.

The Sex Pistols were offered a table at the 2006 event; whether they liked it or not they were being sucked into the fold. They were expected to show up around 4pm, drinks and dinner would follow. From here, after perhaps a small but not unexpected incident when Steve Jones, always the joker, lobs a bread roll in the direction of an earlier inductee, and follows it up with a bawdy, unsophisticated comment to an attractive female record company employee wearing a low-cut evening dress, the band hear themselves described in terms of achievement and influence, and are then expected to cheerily, if a little sardonically, approach the stage. Shaking the hands of those introducing them – perhaps a bear hug is appropriate if any of them has previously been introduced to the presenter – they move towards the microphone with traditional belligerence. The audience love them for it. When aired on television, the odd bleep to cover something Johnny was shouting at the back, would signal to viewers these boys have lost none of their old cred, as one by one they give a monosyllabic 'cheers' before returning back to their table, good-naturedly mock-wrestling one another for whatever fine statuette is deemed appropriate to welcome this 'sensational' group into the academy. Further hugs, kisses, and back slapping would be expected from loved ones and others sharing the night's festivities with the group. Somehow it makes it all feel worthwhile.

Cook, Jones, and Matlock would probably have gone if Johnny had agreed. They may have attempted to persuade him; the costs were on the high side but, hey, everyone else shows up; The Ramones aren't rolling in it either. If they *had* all attended, Lydon would have an explanation as to why, and it'd likely be a good one. But the letter opposite, in his very hand, proves – without slight on those from other bands, or indeed his own – that John Lydon's dignity is in place.

John Lydon is easy to criticise and there's plenty of material to choose from. Not a man of clemency or tolerance, he can be unkind, without empathy or courtesy and, often, a royal pain in the arse. But his downside is generally limited to spoken criticism usually delivered with some sense of amusement. And for every tongue lashing there's a Johnny style compliment; for every condemnation of others there's one directed inwards. He can come across as an egomaniac in print, but his autobiography often reveals a man of unassuming character, absolute loyalty, and self-mockery. He never wanted to change the world but if he made a few people think in a different way some of his ambition has been realised. John Lydon is impossible to categorise, but that seems to be the way he likes it; he's the ultimate punk only because there's no other word fit to describe him.

Rob Johnstone, July 2006

Next to the SEX - PISTOLS
rock and roll . and that hall of fame
is a piss stain . Your museum . Urine
in wine . Were not coming . Were
not your monkeys ond So what? Fame
at $25,000 if we paid for a table,
or $15000 to squeak up in the gallery,
goes to a non-profit organisation
selling us a load of old famous.
Congradulations . If you voted for us,
hope you noted your reasons . Your
anonymous as judges, but your still music
industry people . Were not coming .
Your not paying attention . Outside
the shit-stem . is a real SEX
         PISTOL

Notes:

1. The opening line in the first proper study of post-punk and its 'New Pop and New Rock' cousins, Simon Reynolds' Rip It Up And Start Again: post punk 1978 – 1984 (Faber & Faber, 2005), *is 'Punk bypassed me almost completely.' The author explains that this was due to his tender years when the first wave exploded.*

2. Despite having been involved in punk - as this book has already confirmed he was an early member of The Clash – Keith Levene's major musical inspiration was, in addition to the same style of reggae as Lydon and Wobble, the music of the much derided Yes, and particularly their guitarist Steve Howe, whose lines he would practise along to as his contemporaries did to those on The Ramones' debut. And let's not forget Lydon's own admiration for all things Van Der Graaf Generator, part of Prog's second, if less self-obsessed, league.

3. Alan McGee's second independent record label, Poptones, is of course named after a track from Metal Box. *His first, Creation, after the band the Sex Pistols were introduced to by Malcolm McLaren, and whose 'Through My Eyes' they would occasionally perform live.*